FROM SWAMPOODLE TO MELLON BANK CEO

An Irish-American's Journey, the Autobiography
of Martin G. McGuinn, Jr.

MARTIN G. MCGUINN, JR.

LYONS
PRESS

Essex, Connecticut

An imprint of Globe Pequot, the trade division of
The Rowman & Littlefield Publishing Group, Inc.
4501 Forbes Blvd., Ste. 200
Lanham, MD 20706
www.rowman.com

Distributed by NATIONAL BOOK NETWORK

British Library Cataloguing in Publication Information available

Library of Congress Cataloging-in-Publication Data:
Names: McGuinn, Martin G., Jr., 1942- author.
Title: From Swampoodle to Mellon Bank CEO : an Irish-American's journey,
   the autobiography of Martin G. McGuinn / Martin G. McGuinn, Jr.
Description: Guilford, Connecticut : Lyons Press, [2022]
Identifiers: LCCN 2022000108 (print) | LCCN 2022000109 (ebook) | ISBN
   9781493069071 (cloth) | ISBN 9781493068517 (epub)
Subjects: LCSH: McGuinn, Martin G., Jr., 1942- | Chief executive officers—
   United States—Biography.
Classification: LCC HC102.5.M348 A3 2022 (print) | LCC HC102.5.M348
   (ebook) | DDC 338.092 [B]—dc23/eng/20220302
LC record available at https://lccn.loc.gov/2022000108
LC ebook record available at https://lccn.loc.gov/2022000109

∞™ The paper used in this publication meets the minimum requirements of
American National Standard for Information Sciences—Permanence of Paper
for Printed Library Materials, ANSI/NISO Z39.48-1992.

This book is dedicated to my wife, Susan, and my sons, Patrick and Christopher

INTRODUCTION

I ORIGINALLY INTENDED TO WRITE THIS AUTOBIOGRAPHY FOR MY FAMILY and friends. I wanted my family to know about their heritage and my life, and I wanted my family and friends to understand the good fortune that I have been blessed with, as well as how my Irish Catholic heritage has been an important part of me. As the book developed, I realized that my story might have a broader appeal. An important, but secondary, part of my story is to recount my twenty-five years at Mellon Bank, especially my seven-plus years as chairman and CEO, and to set the record straight about how it ended.

I began this project in late fall of 2020 by being interviewed over a period of several months. The tapes were then transcribed, and the manuscripts went through many drafts and edits. I decided early in the process that I wanted to include many photos and documents either within the book itself or in the appendix. In order to ensure accuracy and completeness I asked five former Mellon colleagues to review and comment on a later draft, which they did enthusiastically. My wife, Susan, also read several drafts and, in addition to her general encouragement, gave me many helpful comments.

I have been a very fortunate person. I grew up as part of a solid family, have had a good education (and continue to learn), have been generally healthy all my life (so far), have my own family, which includes two terrific sons, five granddaughters, and a stepdaughter, and am married to the love of my life. I have many friends, several for more than fifty years. My career has been full and satisfying in large part.

Writing the book has been a journey down memory lane, and in many ways satisfying and cathartic. In looking back on my life, there are lots of things I would do differently, especially with the benefit of hindsight. But there have been many more things which have turned out well. So, all in all, I have been a very fortunate person. I hope readers will enjoy going on the journey with me and maybe take away some thoughts about how my life has been lived and what can be learned from that.

Martin G. McGuinn, Jr.
November, 2021

1

CHILDHOOD

I WAS BORN ON SEPTEMBER 9, 1942, AT ABINGTON MEMORIAL HOSPITAL outside of Philadelphia. My mother was Rita Horgan McGuinn. My father was Martin Gregory McGuinn. And I was named Martin Gregory McGuinn, Jr. (I stopped using "Junior" after my father died.)

My family was Irish on both sides. My grandparents on my mother's side were the Horgans, Eugene and Frances. My grandmother's maiden name was Bonner. The Horgans emigrated to the United States in the mid-1800s from the County Cork area in Ireland and ended up in Mahanoy City, Pennsylvania, near Scranton. At least some of them had been in the coal-mining business. My mother was born in 1925. She was the oldest of two. Her brother Jack died very young.

My grandparents, the Horgans, lived in Narberth, Pennsylvania, which is on the Main Line of Philadelphia. The Main Line was where the Pennsylvania Railroad started on its way to Chicago, and every mile and a

Eugene and Frances Horgan

1

half, you arrive in a different town. There are a lot of colleges there, too—Haverford, Bryn Mawr, Rosemont, Villanova. And it's just beautiful. Villanova is one of the most attractive residential areas in the United States.

Grandpop Horgan worked in a Ford factory and had been a foreman or supervisor for a construction company. He later worked for the post office. He had not gone to college. He was a jolly person, and loved to party. Grandmom Horgan was more serious. They lived in a nice middle-class house.

My grandfather Horgan kind of knew everybody. He was very gregarious, and he wouldn't hesitate to ask someone to take care of his grandson. And he did take good care of me, getting me some very good summer jobs. I loved him.

I was very blessed to know both sets of grandparents well and to be able to visit with them, at least until my early twenties.

The McGuinns were teachers and farmers. I know more about their history because I researched them in order to become an Irish

McGuinn family (grandparents and children). Seated (L-R): Patrick, Katherine. Standing (L-R): James, Martin, Rosemary, Francis, John

citizen, which I was able to do twenty years ago by proving that my grandparents were born in Ireland. My father's parents were from a small, rural village in the west of Ireland, near Charlestown in County Mayo, about an hour and a half northeast of Galway. Charlestown was the subject of a book by John Healy, *No One Shouted Stop* (formerly *Death of an Irish Town*), describing the difficulties its residents experienced during the Great Depression years of the 1930s.

When I received an award from the American Ireland Fund, they did some further genealogical work on my family. There were about twenty-five of us upstairs at the magnificent Trinity College Library in Dublin, and the student who did the genealogy started to giggle as she said, "Well, your great-great-grandfather was a lunatic!" They all thought it was hilarious.

I didn't think it was particularly funny, and when I got back to the United States, I called one of my uncles—my father was dead by that time—and he said, "No, no, no. He was head of the teachers' union. And the British locked him up for a while on the charge that he was a lunatic, because he was standing up to the British in order to obtain better working conditions."

The Great Famine (many Irish call it the Great Hunger) was in 1845, and Ireland went from about nine million people to about five million. Only about a million emigrated. The rest of them died. This was the great migration from Ireland to the United States and elsewhere.

My McGuinn grandparents emigrated to the United States in about 1900, to build a better life. They had lived in the same village and they knew each other. They were in their mid- to late twenties when they came over on the boat together, but they didn't marry until they got here. They came to an area of Philadelphia where many Irish immigrants settled. Known as "Swampoodle," it was located near 23rd and Somerset Streets.

My grandmother was Katherine Kilbride McGuinn, and she was a housewife. A classic grandmother, I remember she made Irish soda bread.

My grandfather Patrick J. McGuinn worked as a trolley car operator in Philadelphia, and occasionally I would ride along with him. I once said he was the conductor and one of my uncles corrected me. There was a big difference between being the conductor and the operator; the conductor took tickets, but the operator drove the trolley. My grandfather spoke with a true Irish brogue, and I could just sit there on the floor of his living room and listen to him talk forever. He always wore a three-piece suit with a vest. He really was a handsome gentleman.

The part of Philadelphia where my father's parents lived was a real Irish immigrant area, famous for its row houses. My grandparents lived in one of those row houses, next door to actor Dennis Day's parents. It was a nice part of town. The church (St. Columbia's Catholic Church) was at the end of the street, and Shibe Park, later known as Connie Mack Stadium, was three blocks away. That was the original park where the Philadelphia Athletics played baseball, and two or three times a year, I'd walk over to A's games. I'd go over when the game was midway through so I could walk into the game without paying admission. New Jersey and Delaware were right across the river, and Philadelphia was then the third-largest city in the country.

My father was born in 1915. He had one sister and three brothers, and another brother who died at birth. My uncle Jack stayed in Philadelphia until he died. My uncle Frank moved to New Jersey and then to Minneapolis. My uncle Jim moved to Richmond, Virginia. And that's when the family closeness really changed. Frank was with 3M; Jim was in sales; and Jack was a manager for the Philadelphia Electric Company. Their sister, Rosemary Gavaghan, stayed in the Philadelphia area and raised a family.

Before World War II, my father went into the St. Charles Seminary in Philadelphia to become a priest. That obviously didn't happen, but he was there for a few years and received some college education in the seminary. I think he also took some night school classes at the University of Pennsylvania. My father went into sales, generally an area where everyone can compete, regardless of your schooling. It depends on your willingness to work with people, and to work hard.

My parents were both living in Philadelphia before they met through friends, probably down at the shore at Ocean City, a fun place where Philadelphians went. They were married in the late 1930s. During World War II, my father was in the Coast Guard; whatever he did with the Coast Guard, I don't think it was too exciting.

I was born in 1942, and we lived in Philadelphia until I was three. We then moved to Hershey, Pennsylvania, where my father worked in sales for a steel company. Hershey was a small town, and the chocolate factory, from my recollection, was on the edge of a residential area. Our house was only a block and a half away, and you could smell chocolate all the time; the aroma was stronger or weaker, depending on the wind. On Saturdays they gave out free chocolate, so we'd all line up there every Saturday. It was a pleasant experience, growing up and smelling chocolate. I went to nursery school and maybe kindergarten there. Walking to school and the smell of chocolate are my only memories of Hershey.

Martin and Rita McGuinn

After a couple of years in Hershey, we moved back to Philadelphia, to a suburb called Drexel Hill. I went to

5

Marty at age 3

St. Dorothy's grammar school, which was a new school at the time, with a church next door. We lived in Drexel Hill until I finished fifth grade. My father worked for Acme Steel, which became Interlake Steel. He got a promotion to become manager of national accounts, and since most of his accounts were in New York City, we moved to Princeton, New Jersey, equidistant between Philadelphia and New York City. He made the long commute—about an hour—as a lot of people did.

I consider Princeton my hometown. We moved there when I was just beginning the sixth grade. Definitely middle class, Princeton was a small but bustling town; because of the university, there was always plenty of activity. It had both a borough and a township. The borough was the center, where the university and the town were located, and the township was the residential area around it. The university is on one side of Nassau Street, the main street, and the town is on the other. There were always town–gown issues, but they were managed pretty well. It was mainly a white area, but there was a black part of town, not large, but very middle-class and in a nice part of town, near the high school. The governor's mansion was at one end of town. The state capital was in Trenton, twenty-five miles away, but the governor's mansion, a historic colonial house, was in Princeton.

We lived in the township, one house away from Lake Carnegie. That's where the crew races were held, and where we ice-skated in the winter. I could ride my bicycle into town, which I did frequently. It was two miles, maybe, and I'd bike in to go to school, to the playgrounds, to play sports, or to attend other activities.

We had a nice home in a new development that had been a farm, so there were no trees. I remember that we planted all the trees on our property. I came back years later and saw these monstrous trees, where once there were none at all. My parents lived there until they died.

I went to St. Paul's Grammar School. It was a typical, small Catholic school with about twenty-five kids in a class. I was a fairly good student. Learning was new, engaging, and pretty interesting, and there weren't many distractions. I basically studied and read. We didn't have a lot of sports at St. Paul's, but I played basketball and was captain of the team. I was tall as a kid—I ended up being six-foot-two—and coordinated, so I played center. Upon graduation, I received the American Legion Award for student athlete. I was also president of the eighth-grade class.

I had been an altar boy at St. Dorothy's in Philadelphia, starting in second grade and continuing through the fifth grade, and until the eighth grade at St. Paul's, where I was the master of ceremonies when the bishop came. I was also in the Boy Scouts, which was great. I quit at the Life Scout level. I should have held on for another six months and become an Eagle Scout.

I would make two points here. First, to have priests or scoutmasters abuse you, or attempt to abuse you? I never heard of any of that stuff. The second point stems from this: Life was great then. It was simple, good, and clean. You went to church. You went to camp. You played sports. You were always out of the house. It was an idyllic time—a great place and time to grow up.

My parents were terrific, and I had a happy home life. For holidays, we alternated between both sets of grandparents in Philadelphia. But Christmas was always in Philadelphia with my father's parents. Christmas Eve was the big day in our family. We'd have our Christmases down in the basement, where there was a coal chute. All of my father's siblings and my cousins were there, and that went on until I was in college. Since I was the oldest grandchild, I would play Santa Claus, and we'd sing Irish songs. "Christmas in Killarney" comes to mind. Great memories. I was the oldest grandchild on both sides of the family. And now, of course, my grandparents, parents, and their siblings have all died. I'm the oldest in the family, period. It was fun growing up. The world was great, and I had a really nice childhood.

2

THE WORLD OPENS UP:
HIGH SCHOOL AND BEYOND

I GRADUATED FROM ST. PAUL'S GRAMMAR SCHOOL IN 1956. I FELT PRETTY well prepared for high school in Latin, reading, writing, and arithmetic. There wasn't a Catholic high school in Princeton—the nearest was in Trenton—so I went to Princeton High School, which was so good that everybody in town went there. At that time Princeton High School was rated seventh or eighth in the country.

Marty's graduation picture from St. Paul's Grammar School

Princeton High was a regional public high school, which meant students came not only from the town itself, but also from schools in the outlying agrarian areas. Academically, it was divided: If you were going to go to college, you took college preparatory classes; if you were going to go back to the farm, you took shop and general education classes. I'm sure there was a way around that, but even then, the better students were in college prep and the not-so-good students were in general ed.

The academic environment was really great. The teachers all had PhDs. Not only was Princeton home to Princeton University, but it was also home to the Institute for Advanced Study where Albert Einstein did his research. So we had the sons and daughters of these faculty members in class with us—a lot of really impressive students. There were several geniuses at our school. The son of Robert Oppenheimer, one of the fathers of the atomic bomb, was there. I thought it was terrific. I was obviously a little overwhelmed by them, but I thought it was really great, going to school with them.

One classmate and good friend was Peter Kann, who became the publisher of the *Wall Street Journal*. Many years later, after I became CEO of Mellon Bank, the *Journal* asked me to come in and meet with the editorial board, and Peter Kann and Paul Steiger, a grade school classmate and friend, were both there. Paul was the managing editor, and I hadn't seen him in a long time. He opened the meeting by recalling a favorite memory: "Picture this—you and I are in the car. You're driving. Neither of us had a license, and the question was: Will Joanne [my sister] tell on us?"

We had around 350 students per grade, and about 1,400 total, so high school was a totally new world for me. I knew some of the kids from the neighborhood, but not many others. It was a chance for me to meet lots of new people and make new friends. There were more athletics, more activities, and more academic courses.

In eighth grade, I had been keen on a girl from St. Paul's, and at our fiftieth high school reunion, she said to me, "Why didn't you date me in high school?" First of all, I was taken aback by the question. But my answer, which I think was honest, was, "There were so many new people and new girls. There was a whole new world to see." That's how I felt about high school. It was a whole new world. And I made friends who are very close even to this day.

Paul Perry was in my class and lived up the street. We went together to many parties. He went to Rutgers and Georgetown Medical School and became a psychiatrist, practicing in New York City. We see each other about once a year even now. Peter Kann sometimes joins us. Tom Brophy and Tom Borger were in the class ahead of me, but we hung out a lot together, playing poker and basketball. "Broph" died in 2019. Tom Borger went to Lehigh, and then worked for Goldman Sachs before leaving to start his own investment firm. He married Marcia Mondavi, from the wine family. We get together frequently in Manhattan, because they live there (as I did for about twelve years), and in the Hamptons, where they have a house and my family has spent summers for many years. And the Borgers and McGuinns have traveled together many times, including to Egypt, South America, France, and Italy.

The Princeton High sports teams were called the Little Tigers, after the Princeton University Tigers, and in the fall of freshman year, I went out for football. I'd never been on a football team before—and no one else had either. It wasn't like Texas, where you start when you're six years old. We were all starting from the same level.

Princeton University dominated the town, and in those days, they were playing the single wing offense. So Princeton High played the single wing. That's where you have a tailback and a wingback, instead of a quarterback and a halfback. The tailback is the equivalent of the quarterback; he takes the snap directly from the center. So I became the tailback. I was actually pretty fast.

The very first game, and the very first play, the center hiked the ball over my head. I ran back and fell on it, and about five of the opposing team jumped on me, breaking my elbow. My father had come to see the game and was a little late. "Well, where's Marty?" he said. Someone replied, "He's at the hospital." That was the end of my football career. I was out for the season, and I decided there were other things to do. Basketball season wasn't that far off, and that was my favorite sport. Football was a big deal, though. All my friends played, and in our senior year, the team was Central New Jersey champions.

I loved basketball, and I practiced a lot. We played in the neighborhood, and I spent a lot of time in the gym. I had played three years at St. Paul's and was a starter and captain of the team. I played in the Catholic Youth Organization league. I used to practice dribbling with both hands in the garage, and I became quite skilled at dribbling with my left hand. But I was never a guard. I mainly played forward and sometimes center, which shows you how small we were.

After a while I had a fair move to the left, but I could never shoot with my left hand. I might drive left and then go up with a jump shot or bank it in. I had a pretty good jump shot. Those were the days when you'd play on the playground and someone would say "Foul" if you barely touched him. Now, of course, they hack the hell out of each other, and they travel all over the place. You don't have three seconds in the paint. To travel now, you have to take about ten steps.

At Princeton High, I made first team on the freshman team. As freshmen, we played ten games with other schools and we scrimmaged a lot. I played all four years and scored in the teens a lot. We didn't have a very good coach, which makes you appreciate the positive impact a good coach can have, for a lot of reasons.

In the spring I went out for track. Princeton High had a wonderful track coach and track teams. The coach wanted me to run the hurdles; he said I had high hips. I tried the hurdles a couple of times, and didn't like them at all. I didn't like catching my foot on them and falling head-first into the cinders. So then he said, "Maybe the half-mile." Well, that was too long, so I ran the quarter-mile. That was between a sprint and a long-distance run in those days.

The key to the quarter-mile was you had to go out fast to try and get position—ideally, the lead. The first quarter you sprint, the next two quarters, you coast or float along until the back stretch, stretching your legs out. And then for the last quarter, you sprint. You had to have the energy left at the end, because that's where it was won or lost. If you went out too fast or pushed too hard, you wouldn't have anything left at the end. I think I got down to 54.5 seconds—not bad in those days.

We went to the Penn Relays each year, and the mile relay was the famous event. As a sophomore, I ran the second leg, and as a junior, I ran the third leg. The Penn Relays was big stuff. Runners came from all over—from high schools and colleges—and in the stands there were more competitors than fans. I did the quarter-mile freshman and sophomore years; by junior year, I wasn't in as fit, so I moved down to the 100- and 220-yard dashes. I couldn't keep it up for that quarter-mile, but I still did the mile relay.

When I was a junior, I ran in the Central Jersey championships down at Asbury Park. At that time, there was a guy named Frank Budd, who was later known as the World's Fastest Human. He was there. He later went on to Villanova and won the Olympics and played in the NFL. When I was a junior, he was a senior, so I ran in the same heat with him, and I watched him run the whole race. I think my best time in the 100 was 10.7. He was breaking 10 seconds, and later was timed at 9.2.

My senior year I went out for baseball instead of track for two reasons.

First, I'd always played baseball in the summer, and I liked it a lot; plus, I was getting tired of track. I had previously played first base or outfield. I loved the outfield—and center field, particularly—because you covered most of the territory. I had good speed and a pretty good arm too. I was a right-handed hitter, albeit, a little weak. But with my speed, if I got on base, I was a good base stealer. The second reason was that the team was good, and would be competing for the state title.

The baseball team had been playing together for several years, and all of a sudden the catcher broke his hand (or arm), so I had to catch. I had never caught in my life, but that moved me up to first string, so I got to play. The hardest part of playing catcher was when the guy was swinging the bat and missing, and making sure you caught the ball and didn't take it in the . . .

We had a great team—we won the state championship in 1960— and we had a great pitcher, Jack Lackey. Jack was a lefty, and the

Yankees signed him. I was good enough as a catcher, but I particularly remember the last out of the last game, the state championship. The batter had swung at the last pitch and had struck out. But I dropped the ball. So I had to pick up the ball and step out to the right, because the batter was running down the first base line toward first. Fortunately, I threw to the first baseman and threw him out. If I had screwed that up, I would have really been in trouble. That's why I remember it.

Academically, I took all the basics freshman year. I wasn't really working that hard and was spending a lot of time chasing girls. It was like being a kid in a candy store. I was playing three sports and socializing a lot. I was probably a B student in high school.

I loved English and history. Math and science, I didn't like at all. I also took Spanish. Latin was very helpful, not just in terms of learning other languages, but also in terms of learning the derivation of English words. The *Aeneid* is probably one of my favorite books ever. The opening words are *Arma virumque cano*—"Of arms and the man I sing."

In my junior year, I went out for the chorus. We had a very special choir. The director later went on to the University of Michigan. We didn't do songs like "Oh Shenandoah"; we did Bach's Mass in B Minor and other really wonderful classical works, and we traveled to other towns and conferences to perform. I joined because I was dating a girl in the class ahead of me who was the soprano soloist. I became close to a bunch of the guys. I had always loved to sing. (In fact, in the eighth grade I'd been asked to take on a lead in a musical, which I stupidly turned down—a decision I later regretted.)

I think I had a fairly good voice—I was a bass—but I didn't know how to read music. So the director properly said, "If you really want to do this, you have to come to summer school and learn to read music, and also, how to breathe correctly." I was a lifeguard and swimming instructor in the summer, so he had me come in before I started work for the day. He gave me classes all summer, so in my junior and senior years, I was in the choir, becoming president of the choir in senior year.

The 1950s were really the golden years in the United States, and the world, and musically, this was also the case. Elvis was big, and the doo-wops were coming—Little Anthony and the Imperials, and all those really good groups. A couple of the groups were from Princeton, and in Philadelphia, there was a nationally televised music performance and dance show called *American Bandstand*. It was on every day, hosted by Bob Horn, and later, by Dick Clark—big stars in those days. You watched it every afternoon during the week if you could.

I don't have the faintest idea how I got involved with American Bandstand. We used to have canteens on Saturday nights where we'd go to community centers and there would be a record player playing 45s. We did a lot of dancing, which was a lot of fun. I think somehow somebody said, "I wrote to *Bandstand* and we've got ten tickets. Would you like to be one of the dancers?" So, freshman year and then again sophomore year, I went on *Bandstand*.

We took a bus down from Princeton to Philadelphia, a group of us. It was a dance floor in a television studio. You were hoping you'd be on camera. That was the whole point. You basically got out and danced. They did slow dances and jitterbugs. I'm going to say there were twenty-five couples, an even number of girls and boys. If you got into the spotlight dance, you knew you'd be on camera. The spotlight dance was where they'd spotlight one or two couples, and if you were in the spotlight dance, you knew it. You were picked and you could feel the spotlight on you. I got into the spotlight dance once, and it turned out it was a war; the regulars on the show, including a well-known couple named Bob and Justine, would try to elbow you out of the spotlight. Being on *Bandstand* is one of my biggest claims to fame.

Dating in high school meant going to the movies or a school dance, or a Saturday-night community dance. I had a ball. You might go have a Coke or something before or after. I lived out in the township, where most of the kids lived. You couldn't drive, so you had to depend on your parents to drop you off and pick you up.

I was very active in student government all the way through high school. I was on student council. And then, in the spring of freshman or sophomore year, I was elected president of the class. In junior year I became vice president of the student council, which was unusual for a junior. I lost the election for president of the student council in my senior year. It was a holy day of obligation, so the Catholic students were absent. I don't think they went to mass, but they sure didn't go to school that morning. I lost by three votes to a guy named Jack Copeland, who ended up being the quarterback on the football team. He went on to Stanford and became a famous transplant surgeon and cardiologist. A hell of a guy. I was later elected president of the senior class.

I always worked during high school. During the school year, after school and on weekends, I worked in a shoe store, selling shoes and fitting them. And then I worked in a clothing store, and at Easter and other holidays, after I got my driver's license, I worked at a flower store, delivering flowers. I always had a job. I don't think it was that typical at the time. There weren't that many jobs. It wasn't that my parents didn't give me money; we were middle class, maybe lower middle class. It's just that I wanted to have money for nice clothes and to take girls out. There was only one way to get the money, and that was to earn it.

My first two summers in high school I worked as a swimming instructor and lifeguard, and as a camp counselor. The third summer, after junior year, I went down to Philadelphia and lived with my Horgan grandparents. My grandfather had gotten me a job in road construction, which paid more than my other jobs. I was sixteen and had just gotten my driver's license in Pennsylvania (versus New Jersey, where you had to be seventeen).

It was 4:30 p.m. on a Friday afternoon in Center City, Philadelphia—heavy traffic—the end of my very first day on the job. They told me to get into one of those huge flatbed trucks with the big cab and the big boom and crane hanging out of the back. Of course, I'd never driven one of those things before. I never found out whether they were pulling my leg. They told me I had to take it from the site back to the yard, which was about two miles away. Two miles of city streets. The thing was probably thirty feet long, it was a stick shift, and I'd just gotten my license. I wasn't going to say, "I can't do it" on the first day of my summer job. I'm sure my grandfather said, "Oh, this kid's got all kinds of experience." I was scared to death, but I made it. And that was my first day—trial by fire.

That summer, we worked on extending the Roosevelt Expressway in North Philadelphia. I had to join the International Union of Operating Engineers, and I would drive this big rig. It was actually a hell of a job, because I would drive it and then park it. We didn't move that much during the day, and we'd leave it at night. I probably made $10 an hour, which was a lot of money in those days.

I came home a week early that summer because in the preceding school year, my junior year, there had been a terrible traffic accident where four students were killed. They were in the senior class and had been speeding; they didn't make a turn and crashed into a telephone pole. There was a national student traffic safety conference in Kansas City in late August, and I was asked by the school to go. I was asked to represent the school because I had co-chaired a committee to find ways to promote safe driving. We had sponsored many lectures and activities to help kids learn how to drive better and to focus on driving safely.

At this national conference they had different people talking about what they were doing in schools to encourage safe driving. They decided to form the National Student Traffic Safety Association, and I was elected the first president. Instead of going back to Princeton, I was taken off to New York City to appear on the *Today* show with Dave Garroway, the founding host and anchor. I was on for two or three minutes, but it was national TV. I met Governor Nelson Rockefeller and had my picture in the papers that existed in New York City in those days. I visited the New York City Police Department, and when I came back to Princeton, they made a big fuss. The nuns from St. Paul's were so excited.

I actually spent part of my senior year going to Washington, DC, with this association, participating in events related to traffic safety. The idea was to do whatever we could to promote safe driving. We did all kinds of things in different schools around the country and shared best practices. In Princeton, we presented lectures and had lots of projects; we even had equipment brought in to test your peripheral vision and your driving skills, things that were actually kind of fun but also made you aware of the level of your skills. It was an appropriate response to this tragic accident.

Marty's Princeton High School graduation picture

3

MY PARENTS AND SIBLINGS

LATER, AFTER I WENT TO HIGH SCHOOL AND COLLEGE, THE COUNTRY changed. Popular entertainment certainly changed; it was no longer as clean or as natural. The Vietnam War came along. People became disillusioned with their governments. There were protests. Drugs. But when I was growing up in Princeton, it was post–World War II America. The country was strong and vibrant and growing. What a time and place to grow up! Princeton was a small town, but it was close to Philadelphia and New York, so although rural in a sense, it was also very cosmopoli-

(L-R): Martin, Rita, Joanne, Marty, Joe, Greg

tan. As a kid, I didn't go to New York City very often. I went a little bit more in high school, but I went to Philadelphia a lot to see relatives, at least four or five times a year.

I was the oldest of my parents' four children, and there were wide differences in age. My sister Joanne was two years younger. We weren't close. She was kind of loud and not a very good student. I'm sure some analysis could reveal the real reasons, but we just weren't very close. We grew up together but were sufficiently different in age that we were in different social groups.

Joanne married a guy from Princeton, John Dallepezze, who went to Princeton and then MIT, where he got an MBA. He went to work for Corning, and later they moved to Houston, where he worked for a company that makes oil-drilling equipment. It was the classic story, where they thought they couldn't have children, so they adopted two, and then they had one of their own. Joanne got cancer and died fifteen years ago. She was in her late fifties. Their adopted daughter went to Villanova and then got interested in art. We didn't see them very much. But we got to see their daughter, and then she died of cancer, too. John got married again to a wonderful woman, and I've seen him a couple of times at family events.

My brother Joe was twelve years younger than I. He was five years old when I was a high school senior, and he'd come to the basketball games and yell my name, which made folks in the stands laugh. Everyone knew Joe. In the summer I played junior league baseball. I'd be pitching, and the guys would let Joe sit in the dugout. They'd give him a can of beer and send him out to the mound. I was very close to Joe, despite our age difference, and of course, I was his big brother. He was a great kid.

By the time Joe went to first grade, I was off to college. He was both a good athlete and a good student. When I was home during the summers, I'd go and watch his games. He was very good in Little League. Joe went to Princeton High School, where he was the quarterback on the football team. He played basketball and baseball, and he was all-

(L-R): Greg (brother), Chris (son), Marty, Patrick (son), Joe (brother)

state in lacrosse. He was a little stockier than I was, and maybe an inch shorter. (Our father was also six feet tall.)

Joe went to Ohio University for his first year, followed by the University of New Hampshire and then Rutgers. He played lacrosse in college. Unfortunately Joe became an alcoholic. I supported him a lot. Joe didn't marry until late in life, and he never had children. But he married a wonderful lady named Kathy, a nurse who had graduated from Georgetown. Joe worked in sales and was doing well, but then he lost his job because of downsizing. He later committed suicide, at the age of fifty-five. It was very sad.

My youngest brother Greg is twenty years younger than I am. I remember coming home from college my junior year and my mother told me she was pregnant. I was so embarrassed. So, it was like two families. I was more like a parent to him. I still am.

My father became an alcoholic later in life, when Greg was in eighth grade. Those are formative years, and this was very tough on Greg. In essence, Greg grew up in a totally different family. Greg, now

(L-R): Martin, Rita, Joe, Greg, Marty

divorced, lives in Atlanta. A recovering alcoholic, he's been sober for more than thirty years. He has two daughters (I was able to help with their education).

My sister was an alcoholic, too. It runs in the family. It's terrible, and way too common. I hate to think it may be more common among the Irish, but that might be the case. I've often wondered about it. I've been a pretty fortunate person for the most part. I must have been, with the genes for alcoholism all around me. I love to drink wine—my doctor tells me to drink less—but I think I'm okay in terms of overall health. My personal feeling is, a lot of it depends on psychology. There's often a trigger. In my brother Joe's case, he was a salesperson. He was a manager, with his own team, and he lost his job unfairly. They just cut a whole layer of management. I could see it happening.

That happened to my father, too. He was getting close to retirement, and he didn't want to retire. He felt that other people had been promoted ahead of him and that he wasn't being treated fairly. My mother did the best she could with it. My father lost his driver's license, and being in sales, my mother had to drive him around. He was always trying to better himself, and I think he never felt he was sufficiently recognized for that. I think it made him bitter, and I think that's what led to his alcoholism. That's my amateur psychoanalysis.

Kathy and Joe at their wedding

Both of my parents died young. My father had his first heart attack when he was in his early to mid-forties, and then he died when he was around sixty-five. He was coming back on the train from New York City when he slumped over. They got him out and into a taxi and brought him home. They weren't sure what was wrong at first. He died that night, from another massive heart attack.

I was thirty-eight then, and living in New York City. My mother called me and I came right home to Princeton, but my father was dead by the time I got there. It was kind of the first family death, and it hurt. My father was the oldest in his family, and his siblings were all still alive. They all came to the funeral. My father's father had also died of a heart attack, while shoveling snow. He was at least in his late seventies. Because of this family history, I have always worried about having a heart condition.

My mother had breast cancer in her late fifties and had a mastectomy. The cancer spread, and she died in her late sixties. She had been sick that whole time. She'd had a swollen arm after the mastectomy, and it was very visible. During the last couple of years of her life, she lived with my sister in Houston, where she went to the MD Anderson Cancer Clinic for treatment. I was around forty-five when my mother died.

I think I take after both of my parents, but probably more so after my father. He was fairly intelligent and had a very curious mind. He loved to read, so I'm sure I got my love of reading from him. He was successful in sales, not only in the sense of making the sales, but also in knowing the business and the product, and knowing what the customers' needs were.

I'd like to think I'm like my mother in the sense of being empathetic. From a very early age, I definitely liked people, and I want people to like me. I think that probably came from my mother. I don't think my father gave a damn. Actually, he probably did, but it certainly didn't show. My mother was a more sympathetic person. She was more of a people person. It wasn't that she was outgoing or gregarious. If anything, she may have been a little shy.

Physically, I'm more like the McGuinn line, except, of course, the male pattern baldness, which comes from my maternal grandfather. My mother's father was very gregarious and outgoing, so I probably get some of my outgoing nature from him. But overall, I'm probably more like my father and the McGuinn family.

4

OFF TO COLLEGE

I GRADUATED FROM HIGH SCHOOL IN 1960. I HAD ALWAYS ASSUMED I'D GO to college, although for about six months, back in the sixth grade, I'd wanted to be a Jesuit priest. I was in Catholic school, and Jesuits were the great teachers. I sort of liked teaching, I thought. And in typical Irish tradition, the oldest child was supposed to go into the church—not that there was any pressure on me to do that.

Beyond that, though, I wanted to be a lawyer, mainly because I wanted to go into politics. I'd always been a student leader—I was president of the class in the eighth grade, as well as in my sophomore and senior years in high school. I really had a notion that you could be constructive and do good things, and I thought going to law school was the best means to achieve that end. And that's where I was headed.

I didn't really start thinking about where to go to college until senior year in high school. I wanted to go to Princeton, so I applied, but didn't get in. I would have needed a scholarship to go there, as well. I also applied to Colgate and Villanova. I went up to Hamilton, New York, to visit Colgate with my father on Easter break during senior year. The students were all on break and nobody was on campus. And it snowed.

We stayed at the Colgate Inn. I had a drink with my father and I said, "Geez, if I come to this school, I'm going to become an alcoholic." I mean, what else would you do? Now obviously, it was a combination of bad timing and circumstance. It was a great school and I actually liked it a lot.

When I went to visit Villanova, it was a beautiful day. The kids were out throwing Frisbees and picnicking. I thought, "This is heaven." Today it's a hot school academically, but in those days it was more of a local school. There were students from all over the Eastern Seaboard, but mainly from New York, Maryland, New Jersey, and Pennsylvania. In those days it had around six thousand students, and its reputation was good, not great. It was very much a Catholic school, and to me, going to a Catholic university was a positive factor. I was offered scholarships to both Colgate and Villanova, but Villanova wasn't as expensive. I had a good friend, Dan Buckley, who was at Villanova, and it was a socially attractive school. It was all men, except that it had a nursing school, so there were maybe 40 nurses out of a class of 1,500. But there were many girls' colleges all around. At that point, pretty much only the big state schools were coed.

Playing sports was not a factor in my decision to go to Villanova. I doubted I was good enough to play basketball. Even then, they played in the Big Five and were big-time in basketball. But I did decide to go out for the freshman team.

In those days, freshmen didn't play varsity. About forty of us went out for the freshman team. They already had four or five guys who had scholarships and were guaranteed spots on the team. That included the backcourt of George Leftwich and Wali Jones. Jones was from Overbrook in Philadelphia, the same high school that Wilt Chamberlain came from. He went on to play pro with the Philadelphia 76ers. Leftwich was one of the best players ever to come out of Washington, DC. He was later drafted by the Detroit Pistons, but he got into an automobile accident, which was a shame. Both of those guys started as sophomores at Villanova. Leftwich and Jones were both about six-foot-one—not like the guards today, who might be six-foot-five. But they were both great shooters and ball handlers, and they both ended up as All-Americans. By the time they were seniors, they were the best backcourt in college basketball, leading Villanova to the National Invitation Tournament championship.

The tryout period for freshmen was two or three weeks. There was a lot of scrimmaging. The first cut down to thirty players was pretty fast. Then they cut to twenty, then fifteen, and then to twelve. I was still in, so I called my parents and said, "I made the team! I'm so surprised." I was telling everyone. In the final scrimmage, I guarded Leftwich. I didn't score, but neither did he. I felt pretty good about that. The next day they cut to ten, and I didn't make it.

So I went back to drinking beer.

The campus wasn't that big, so you got to know people pretty quickly. I lived in a freshman dorm. There were a lot of football players, and some of these guys were animals. But it was a nice dorm. It was coat-and-tie, all the time—coat-and-tie for classes and coat-and-tie for meals. Women were allowed on campus, but they weren't allowed in the rooms.

It's a nice campus today—spectacular, really. They've built like crazy, and almost all of the students live on campus. In my day, we had a lot of day students.

I initially went into the business school because they had a pre-law program. I took economics and accounting and certain core courses as well. Princeton High School had prepared me very well, and I made the honor roll. I realized during the second semester that I would be better prepared for law school if I were in liberal arts, so I switched. I ended up without an official major, but with enough credits for a major in English and a minor in history. Some might debate it, but I felt there was a higher-caliber student in the liberal arts program than in the business school. Since then, the business school has become extremely good and is highly ranked, but in those days it didn't have the same reputation.

During the spring semester of freshman year we held elections, and I formed what I called the "Right" Party. It sounded good. I ran for president of the sophomore class. We didn't have e-mail in those days; you had to go around and ask people for their votes. I printed up lots of mimeographed flyers that I put in the classrooms, dorms, and various other places. I ended up being a great candidate but a lousy party chairman: I won, but everybody else in my party lost. So I was president of the sophomore class, which didn't entail much. It meant a seat on student council, and you had to chair one event, as I recall.

That's also how I got my nickname—Slim. I had a terrible memory for names, so when I was campaigning, I'd call everyone "Slim." By the time I graduated as a senior, my nickname was Slim. It had nothing to do with my physique. In fact, some of my best friends—my three roommates from junior year—still call me Slim. We're still very close, and they're very accomplished guys. Jim O'Connor became president of Ford Motor. Dick McDonough held the world record in the 100-yard butterfly, was co-captain of the swim team, and was a Rhodes Scholar candidate. He became assistant general counsel for IBM, and general counsel for IBM for Europe and Africa. And Jack Geoghegan was co-captain of the swim team, went on to Fordham Law School, and became president of the Westchester County Bar Association. Both Dick and Jack were All-Americans. They're all really good guys—my three closest friends from college. I'm godfather to one of Dick's kids.

Marty, Jim O'Connor, Dick McDonough, Jack Geoghegan

Jim O'Connor, Jack Geoghegan, Father George Riley, Marty, Dick McDonough, Father Peter Donahue, President of Villanova, at our 50th Villanove reunion

We still e-mail and talk and get together a couple times a year. Sadly, Dick died in April of 2021 following a painful brain aneurysm.

In my senior year I lived off-campus with five classmates in a rented house in the nearby town of Ardmore. It was a six-bedroom house, so it was quite comfortable. I had bought a TR3 sports car with my summer earnings, so I was living high.

Among my roommates were Rich Connors, Chuck Damico, Jim Dwyer, and Mike Loia, who have been lifelong friends. Rich went on to Columbia Law School and practices in his hometown of New Haven, Connecticut.

The summer after my freshman year, my grandfather Horgan got me another job: digging ditches out in New Jersey. We were digging ditches for a pipeline, and it was good money. They had some machines, but you had to do a lot of manual work, hitting hard clay and rock with picks and digging it out. During the summer, I was in pretty good shape. We'd start at about 7:30 a.m. and work until 4:30. I had to join the union, but that wasn't a tough decision. The guys I worked with were all laborers—no other college guys.

At first, I was the kid, and I had to learn the ropes. I was really digging fast to show everybody I could do it, and then I figured it out when one of the guys said, "You're making us look bad. And you're going to wear yourself out." They were in their twenties and thirties—all decent people. They probably figured, "Here's a kid out trying to make some money and willing to work hard." One of the guys, a foreman, was my fourth cousin.

During summers after my sophomore and junior years in college—in 1962 and 1963—I went down to Quantico, Virginia, because I had enlisted in the Platoon Leaders Course (PLC) summer program of the US Marine Corps. I enlisted for a couple reasons: One, I still wanted to be a lawyer and, ultimately, become involved in politics. And two, I had a patriotic feeling. I thought serving your country was a good thing to do.

The Vietnam War was just beginning then (we may have still been advisers at that time). I wanted to go to law school, but was afraid I might not be able to if I got drafted and had to go into the military. Part of the attraction of this PLC summer program was that they guaranteed you would be commissioned when you graduated, after which you would get deferred for three years to go to law school. When you finished law school, then you could go into an active-duty position as a lawyer.

This was exactly what I did.

With the PLC, you had to go six weeks a summer. Because it was voluntary, a lot of people dropped out. It involved a lot of typical marine programs. There was a lot of physical conditioning, but there were a lot of classes, too, learning about military warfare and military history, how to assemble and shoot rifles, and so forth.

In the Marine Corps, every man's a fighting man from the commandant on down. So everybody has to go through the same training, whether you're a lawyer or whatever. You had to be qualified as a fighter—as a marine. The physical part was tough. Remember: I was a beer-drinking college student, and I wasn't in the best of shape. I went down that first summer, and I think I weighed 195. I came back six weeks later at 170. And I lost it the hard way. I just wasn't in shape. We probably had three hours of conditioning a day—it was all sort of interwoven.

When I went to the program between junior and senior years, I tried to get in better shape beforehand. That was the summer they brought up the drill instructors from Parris Island for these "college boys." That made it extra "fun." They were mean bastards. There was none of this political correctness. You were maggots, scumbags, and assholes, like the guy in the movie *Full Metal Jacket.*

When I came back from Quantico, I only had four weeks left of summer, so I worked for a moving van company in Princeton.

For my senior year, I was president of the student council. That meant I was also student body president. In November 1963, I was on my way down to Philadelphia, where we had sponsored a jazz festival. I had a meeting with the radio people. I'll never forget that. We were in the car on our way to Philadelphia when we heard the news that President Kennedy had been killed. We just turned around and went back to campus. My family members were probably Democrats when I was growing up, but we never really talked politics. We all certainly loved Kennedy. That was really devastating—just the fact that the president was assassinated, and that it was Kennedy. And the way it happened. It was a shock.

Later, near the end of senior year, the administration had put all of its eggs in one basket and invited President Lyndon Johnson to be our graduation speaker. Not surprisingly, two weeks before, he canceled, for some good reason, I'm sure. So they got some auxiliary bishop from the nearby town of Norristown to replace him.

The students were just livid. One, they were getting an auxiliary bishop. And two, they hadn't consulted us. There wasn't a committee, and the faculty hadn't been consulted.

There was a demonstration, and as student body president, I got in front of it, along with the president of the class. In those days, the student body was almost all men, and everyone wore coats and ties. We marched on the administration building, about 250, maybe 300 strong. This was 1964. I respectfully handed the president of the university our petition to try and get somebody else, and in the future, to have some process that would involve the students. One of the reasons I got in front of the march was to try and keep it peaceful and orderly—which it was.

Well, one of the kids called the press, and the headline the next day was "Catholic Students Revolt Against Bishop." Can you imagine? Supposedly this news made it all the way to the pope. This was really terrible.

Then girlfriend, Carole McDermott, pinning my second lieutenant bars on me upon being commissioned an officer in the USMC immediately after college graduation

The class president and I were asked to go and call upon the auxiliary bishop, which we did. When we got there, the bishop looked at me and said, "Are you related to Ock McGuinn?"

I said, "He's my father." Ock was my father's nickname.

And he said, "We were in the seminary together."

So the bishop ultimately spoke, and he was a delightful man. He made a joke about it and said, "Sorry to disappoint you all, but now I'm one of the graduating class."

When I graduated from college, I got my diploma in my marine dress whites with my sword, and I was commissioned a second lieutenant in the US Marine Corps. I was immediately deferred to go to law school.

Later, by the time I'd graduated from law school, things had changed. There was a draft, and kids in law school were getting drafted. There was no longer a deferment. And in basic training, there were guys who had graduated from law school who had enlisted and didn't get legal assignments. Instead, they were designated infantry platoon leaders (O3), which had a high mortality rate.

So, going through those two summers in advance had been a very fortunate move on my part.

5

LAW SCHOOL

I HAD APPLIED TO HARVARD LAW SCHOOL, WHICH WAS A STRETCH, BECAUSE my grades weren't really that good. I had fooled around too much in college. I have no regrets about that, because I've been pretty fortunate.

I had a room-and-board scholarship to Villanova Law School, in return for which I was expected to be a dorm counselor. That summer between college and law school, I was working as a bartender and waiter on Fire Island, the barrier island off the southern coast of Long Island. I was on the west end of the island, which was very much residential. Harper Lee of *To Kill a Mockingbird* fame had a cottage there. You would see her sitting on the porch.

That summer, I got a letter from my father saying, "A letter came to the house from Villanova, and we opened it. They're taking away your scholarship because they don't think you're the type of student who should be a counselor resident in an undergraduate dormitory."

This was all because of the march; they didn't want me to be near college students because I was a radical in their eyes. My dad said, "You'd better start looking for something else," adding, "They'll allow you to keep it for the first year, and you don't have to be a dorm counselor." This was because it was now August, and the first year of law school was only weeks away. Even they weren't that nasty.

Well, I worked really hard in law school and did very well, so the dean gave me a tuition scholarship. And the summer after my first year of law school I got married, so I didn't need a room-and-board scholarship.

Essentially I went to law school for three years, paying for just one year of tuition, which was terrific.

I also met Pat O'Connor at the very beginning of law school. He had graduated from King's College in Wilkes-Barre as a top student. He was smart with a good sense of humor, and we became good friends. Pat went on to become the head of his own law firm, Cozen O'Connor, which is based in Philadelphia and today has about 650 lawyers in offices around the United States and abroad. Even today Pat is my closest friend, and serves as trustee for my sons' trusts. Pat roomed with Ed Murphy, who had graduated from Princeton, and both were dorm counselors. Ed became a trial lawyer in Philadelphia, and also became a good friend.

Law school was a grind, but I loved it because there wasn't any math or science. I wanted to be a lawyer, and I knew I had to work hard. We had what were called study groups, which were very common, and I hooked up with a couple people who were very smart and very disciplined. It made me disciplined, too. There were about 125 in our class,

Pat O'Connor, Pennsylvania Governor Tom Corbett, Marty in May, 2013 when Governor Corbett was commencement speaker and Pat and Marty received honorary degrees from Villanova University

including one woman, and I finished fifteenth in the first semester and twelfth for the year. I really loved it. I was very engaged. Intellectually it was very appealing. I was willing to work hard. Plus I didn't have the distractions of being president of the class and stuff like that.

Between my first and second years in law school, I married Carole McDermott, who had gone to Rosemont, a Catholic girls' school, like a sister school of Villanova, which was located literally down the street.

Carole was from Plandome, on the north shore of Long Island. We dated during my junior and senior years of college. She was two years younger, and she dropped out of Rosemont after one year to go to Katharine Gibbs, a secretarial school in what was then the Pan Am Building in Manhattan. They had to wear gloves and little hats.

We continued to date in my first year of law school, but she was in Long Island and Manhattan, and I was in Villanova, working hard in law school. She came down maybe once a month. In order to be together, we decided to get married.

Carole McDemott

I knew that I wanted to be married and start a family, but of course I realized I had to finish law school and then go into the marines for three years. It really wasn't an opportune time to start a family. We worried about our unsuitability as a couple before the wedding—I guess I was aware of it more than she was—but we went through with it all the same.

Carole was very sweet and attractive, a lovely person. I was twenty-two and she was twenty when we got married. We took a little apartment in Narberth, which was only five miles away from Villanova. I got a job taking out the trash and replacing lightbulbs in the apartment building, so that helped pay some of the rent, and she got a job as a secretary.

I worked hard the second year of law school—the year they decide who will be selected for law review, probably the biggest thing in law school. At that point they took the top 10 percent of the class, so if you said you were on the law review, everyone knew you'd made it into that top group.

In the first semester, I finished second in the class, which brought me up to eighth overall. This meant I was selected for the law review. The next semester, I was chosen as editor in chief of the law review. Often that would go to the person who was number one in the class, but the number one had a weird personality. And since I was number two for a semester, even though I was eighth overall, I think they felt they could justify it. This was very fortunate for me.

Villanova was then only in its tenth year as a law school, but it was the first Catholic law school to get Order of the Coif, which is an honor society. Notre Dame and Georgetown law schools got it subsequently. Our dean had come from Yale, and he really built a hell of a law school. We always felt that the top of the class could compete with anybody, and in some ways, we couldn't wait to go out and prove it. This was a very critical factor in our success; we wanted to prove we were as good as any other law school. We really felt we received a good education, because it was a teaching law school, as opposed to professors who were being driven to publish. It was a big investment on Villanova's part to build this law school, and it really helped to elevate the status of the whole university.

For the third year in law school, as editor in chief I really spent a lot of time working on the law review. In the second year, which is your first year on the law review, you spend a lot of time writing. Every law review has at least two parts, sometimes three.

First, they have articles written by professionals—usually law school faculty, but they could be written by judges or practicing lawyers, too. You solicit those, and obviously Harvard gets the best. Law review articles are cited by the courts, from the Supreme Court on down. And when there are good articles and they have a point of view, which is supported by good research, you'll frequently have a citation in a judicial opinion that will cite the law review articles.

The second part is student articles. These can be case notes, which are short articles about recent cases that analyze them, sometimes even going so far as to say whether the writer thinks the decision in the case is right or wrong. Then there are longer articles, called comments, maybe twenty pages written on an area of the law, not just a single case.

The third part might include things like book reviews, for example.

Professionally, law review is very important. And in terms of the education of the students, it's crucial, because legal writing is such an essential part of being a lawyer. It gives you great training.

We had a whole board of editors, but I was the editor in chief, which was a great experience for me. I liked writing, and I took to editing pretty well. I got a copy of *The Elements of Style* by Strunk and White. There was a law version of that reference book, and we tried to conform to judicial writing style.

Law school was a wonderful experience for me. There was an old saying: The first year, they scare you to death; the second year, they work you to death; and the third year, they bore you to death.

The first year, you're definitely running scared, like in that movie (and later, TV show) *The Paper Chase*, with Professor Kingsfield. The professor would call on you and use the Socratic method, and you had to explain your answer to the question. The courses were very interesting. You did the basic courses—contracts, torts, real estate—your first year. I made many friends in law school, and we found time to socialize. I introduced Pat O'Connor to his future wife, Marie Mahoney. And we all went to football games and parties together. Sometimes Pat and I would buy steaks and cook a special dinner and drink a bottle of wine and speculate about what a good life we would live someday.

I had decided at that point that I really didn't want to be a politician. I considered that it was one thing to get elected, but it was something else if you wanted to be effective. In other words, you had to promise one thing in order to be elected but actually do something different in order to be a good legislator or leader. I couldn't reconcile the two. It also meant raising money the whole time. For Congress, they're running for election every two years—constantly fund-raising and campaigning.

So I gave up on politics and decided I wanted to be a corporate lawyer. In my second and third years, I took a lot of elective courses in corporate law and international law.

I graduated from law school in June of 1967, and then I took the bar exam. I thought I had a record high on the bar—I thought I'd killed it. Pat O'Connor and I were always teasing each other. We studied together and went down to the Penn campus where the bar exam was given. We both thought we did great.

We got the results in late November or December. I didn't want to tell him how I did, and he didn't want to tell me how he did. Finally we both learned that each of us had earned a 70, which was just a passing grade. Nonetheless, we were pleased to have the bar exam behind us. We were now licensed attorneys!

Because I knew I couldn't go on active duty until January, after the bar results had come in, I had applied for a job at Ballard, Spahr, Andrews and Ingersoll, a top Philadelphia law firm. I got the job! I was the first Villanova law student to be hired by the firm, and I started work there after taking the bar exam in July.

At the end of the year, Carole and I took an apartment in Quantico, Virginia, where I would have six months of basic training with the marines, starting on January 1, 1968.

6

OFF TO WAR

WHEN MY WIFE AND I WENT DOWN TO QUANTICO, VIRGINIA, AT THE BEGIN-
ning of January 1968 for basic training, those who were assembled there
were all brand-new officers who had either gone through OCS (Officer
Candidate School) or PLC (Platoon Leaders Course) to become an
officer. But before they got an assignment—before they'd be sent off to
war—they had to receive additional training.

I got put in with all these guys who'd been down there already for
six months, having just finished their OCS class. Major "Sweat Socks"
was the commanding officer. He was head of physical training for all
of Quantico. I'd been a civilian for three years, sitting on my rear end
in law school. The major started training the first day, saying, "Since
all you guys have been doing all this training and physical conditioning, we're going to step it up because I've got to keep you sharp." And
I'm thinking, "Holy smokes!" I had been working out a little bit for a
month, but I was not prepared, and it was miserable for me. The major
looked like a real jarhead. He was big, wide, and bulky—like a fullback
on a football team.

There was a lot of physical training but also a lot of classroom
training: leadership, military history, advanced warfare, guerrilla
warfare. And since we were in the middle of the Vietnam War, basic
training was condensed from the usual six months down to five months.
In those days there were only two kinds of marines: those who were
coming back from Vietnam, and those who were going over.

If you had enlisted in the navy as a lawyer, they sent you away for one week to learn how to put the uniform on and salute, and that was it. In the Marine Corps, you had the same training as every other officer before you got your assignment. And a lot of lawyers didn't get a legal assignment; instead, they were sent out into the field to lead platoons of forty-five men into battle. These were the second lieutenants, whose death rates in Vietnam were literally 40 percent. It was pretty awful.

This was my rank, too, but I would be a lawyer, not a platoon leader. And because I'd technically been a second lieutenant for three years, I was close to being a first lieutenant, and then a captain. They wouldn't promote me, however, because the head of the training class platoon was a captain, and I couldn't be of equal rank. So, the day I graduated, they made me a captain. Unfortunately, because the navy, air force, and army were making all lawyers captains, the Marine Corps had to go along with it, so every other marine lawyer got the rank of captain, too. Thus, what I'd thought would be an advantage disappeared.

After basic training was finished, I got my legal assignment, which I'd been guaranteed by going through the PLC law program in college. I was assigned to go to the Twentynine Palms base in California, a pretty big marine base south of Los Angeles, near Camp Pendleton.

But first, I was sent off to Newport, Rhode Island, for Naval Justice School, because technically, even though most marines don't like to admit it, the US Marine Corps is part of the US Navy. We didn't have our own justice school, so we had to go to the navy's.

They'd warn you when you went on a naval base, "Look, they're not going to salute you." We called them squids, and we didn't pay any attention to them. Fortunately, Naval Justice School was interesting and not too demanding. I took sailing lessons in the afternoons. It was only maybe six weeks. I was there when my grandfather Patrick McGuinn died, and his funeral was the day of the final exam, so I could not attend.

By that point, my wife Carole and I had separated. She wasn't with me in Newport. While I was there, I called up marine headquarters and said, "Instead of going to Twentynine Palms, I'd like to go to Vietnam now." And they said, "Well, we don't get many requests like that," adding, "Sure."

My reasoning was very simple: I knew I was going to have to go, and I didn't want to be coming back from Vietnam at the end of my three years, shortly before I was going to get released. When I came back, I wanted to be able to look for a job and get ready to go back into civilian life. Added to this was the fact that my marriage was on the rocks.

So, in September of 1968, I was off to Vietnam.

We flew on civilian planes from San Francisco to Okinawa. I was on Okinawa for about a week, getting ready to transition in. While I was there, there was a cyclone. I was in a room that had maybe four bunks in it, but I was by myself and I couldn't even go out. There was no electricity for a day and a half. It was a huge storm. I'd never seen anything like it.

I arrived in Vietnam, to the First Marine Division headquarters, outside of Da Nang, where I spent the next thirteen months. Da Nang was the second-largest city in Vietnam. It was beautiful, and featured a horseshoe harbor. We were up on a hill probably ten miles outside the city—Hill 327. At the top, you could kind of see the city.

The base looked like a camp. It had these Quonset huts with plywood floors and walls and corrugated aluminum roofs. These buildings housed the offices, and also what we called the hooches—where we slept. There might have been three hundred guys in the camp, which was made up of a bunch of these simple buildings. Our office was small, and contained just a group of desks and a few chairs.

We lived in one of these Quonset huts, built into Hill 327. We were practicing what was called reverse slope defense, which means if the enemy's on the other side and they sent the mortar shells over, they'd go over your head, because you're on the reverse slope. As long as that holds true and the enemy remains on the other side, that theory works. I was in a headquarters area, where there were a lot of guys like me.

But there were also a lot of guys who'd been out in the field—the bush, as they called it.

I got there in mid-September of 1968 and left in October of '69. Guys were coming in and out all the time. Typically, the guys who were going out to combat wouldn't come through headquarters. They would go right to the field. When I arrived, it was hot, and then you had the monsoon season, where I had an electric blanket sent from home so I could put my clothes under it to dry them out.

We wore the Marine Corps uniform—green khaki utilities, green blouse, and green trousers, which you tucked into your boots, and a cap. We had a general in charge of the division, and a colonel who was head of the legal team. We had a lieutenant colonel, too. Usually we worked from eight a.m. to six p.m., so we had evenings free. We worked every day, although we usually had Sunday afternoons off. During the free time I read a lot, and played a lot of bridge and poker.

Marty in Da Nang,
Republic of Vietnam, in 1969

I had to go out on guard duty now and then. In the Marine Corps, everyone had to do guard duty on the perimeter—even the lawyers—since we were in a war zone. One day I was walking up to chow and the mortars started flying in, because the enemy had gotten over to the other side. "Incoming! Incoming!" someone yelled, and we all dove for cover. Mortars had a distinctive whistling sound that definitely got your attention.

Da Nang is on the South China Sea, and the USS *New Jer-*

sey was there at that time, with 16-inch guns. They would fire over our heads and it sounded like a train. It was unbelievable. They also had a couple of hospital ships out there.

In Da Nang itself, there was a big air force base and air force headquarters, along with a navy headquarters. Every now and then on a Saturday or Sunday night, we'd try to get a jeep and then we would drive into the naval area. They had an officers' club, and we'd get a steak and some wine. It was like heaven. The naval operations were a little bigger, and they were more civilized, too—the difference between the US Navy and the US Marine Corps. We were limited as to where we could go. There were always a couple clowns who tried to go find prostitutes, and some of them got killed. But our base was generally secure.

My worst memory of Vietnam was of—I hate to use the word—the "shitters." We had to use a little outhouse on the side of the hill with three 55-gallon drums filled with kerosene, and a wood top with holes cut in it. You had to go in and sit next to two other guys and do your business. You could see them burning these off every now and then. They'd take them out and light the kerosene; that was their plumbing. This was a very basic camp.

As a lawyer, I was assigned to prosecution, to be part of a team trying court-martial cases. We had to go out into the field a lot of times to do the investigation, riding out, if it wasn't too far, in a jeep.

In the field, you didn't know who the enemy was. There was the North Vietnamese Army, but there were also the Viet Cong, who during the day were probably South Vietnamese farmers, but during the night, would come out to fight. For their part, they were fighting because they were caught in the middle. They would do whatever they had to do to stay alive.

Most of the time when we went farther out in the field, we rode in medevac helicopters. You knew what was in the back when you were returning to the base. The reality of war was all too evident.

I did try one first-degree murder case as assistant counsel.

I'd been out of law school for just a year, and there I was, trying a first-degree murder case. The defendant was Private Alvarez—I'll never forget his name—and he had fragged his superior officer. That's when they threw grenades into the bunks of their commanding officers if they didn't like how they were being treated. There were a lot of drugs, and racism was a big issue. The blacks would tend to gather together and then complain that they weren't being treated fairly. *Matterhorn*, a novel by Karl Marlantes, covers this side of the war. Although I think this book overstates the problem, it was a significant issue.

Alvarez was found guilty. I presented what was called the case in chief, which proved that he was guilty. Military trials are bifurcated: The first part is held to determine guilt or innocence, and the second part deals with sentencing. It's a pretty good system, keeping them separate. You can later bring in character references for the second part: they don't have any bearing on guilt or innocence but might have an impact on the sentencing.

The guy who was senior to me was arguing the sentencing phase, and Alvarez was sentenced to life in prison. The judge did not instruct on the possibility of insanity to the jury, because no evidence of insanity had been presented. Two years later, the court of criminal appeals reversed the case on the theory that the accused's own testimony sufficiently raised the issue of insanity, even if no expert testimony was presented. I thought it was a questionable decision. He was later retried, but I don't know what happened.

In every other military service, you were in Vietnam for twelve months. In the marines, you went for thirteen months—an extra pound of flesh.

After several months, I became chief trial counsel, which meant I assigned the cases and made decisions among the fifteen lawyers for the First Marine Division, one of two marine divisions over there. Cases were anything from a marijuana drug case to an unauthorized absence, from desertion to assault to homicide. I also defended a few cases, because we took turns doing that.

About nine months through my thirteen months, Congress passed the Uniform Code of Military Justice Amendments, and they created the position of military judge for special courts-martial. I was appointed a military judge; people were rotating in and out all the time, and after nine months, I'd been there a relatively long time. Because the four of us at the headquarters who were made judges were in Vietnam, and because of our time zone, we were among the first judges appointed anywhere in the whole military, which was kind of cool. (When it was Monday in Vietnam, it was still Sunday back in the States.)

I was a judge for special courts-martial, which was the middle of the three kinds of courts-martial in terms of seriousness. Summary courts-martial were for the least serious infractions, and were generally handled by commanding officers. Special courts-martial were limited in both the crimes they could consider and the sentences they could give. Special courts-martial were for crimes with up to six months in jail as the maximum sentence. General courts-martial were for everything up to murder, with possible sentences of life imprisonment all the way up to execution.

I spent four months being a military judge in Vietnam, which was very interesting.

Chuck Robb, President Johnson's son-in-law, was a marine in Vietnam at that time. He had met the president's elder daughter, Lynda Bird Johnson, at the White House when he was on duty guarding the White House. He was a real gung-ho marine, so he later went out in the field. Of course, the enemy would have loved to have gotten the president's son-in-law. So they brought him back to headquarters after a shorter time than usual. Chuck was a captain and a company commander, and he got assigned to my hooch—the plywood structure we slept in. My hooch had four bunk beds on one side and half a divider and then four bunk beds on the other side. Everyone in the hooch was a captain.

Chuck came in and was on my side of the hooch, and we got to be pretty good friends. He was later promoted to major, but he stayed in the hooch because we were all comfortable.

This was in 1968 and '69, and at that time, there were three ways you communicated with your family. One was letters; mail call was a huge thing. (Pat O'Connor was good at writing letters to me. He postured himself as Justice Holmes and we exchanged letters as two prominent jurists.) Second was to make a tape, put it in an envelope, and send it. And the third was by radio. On Tuesdays and Saturdays, you could go up to the top of the hill where they had a radio station, and they would radio in to Providence, Rhode Island. You'd get in contact with ham radio operators, and then they would patch you in by phone to your home.

Now the problem was, you had to stand in line at the top of this hill; they could only do one at a time. And if there were too many clouds or there were other kinds of bad weather, they couldn't do it. So you could wait in line for a couple hours and never get through. And when you did get on the phone, you'd be on for, like, two minutes. Still, it was great to hear your family's voices. (Of course, they could send back tapes, too.)

One night we were in the hooch and the phone rang. Now, you have to understand how basic everything was. There was something that looked like a phone, but it was more like a tin can tied onto a string. Chuck's wife, Lynda Bird Robb, had just had a baby. So the White House had called Okinawa; Okinawa had called Da Nang; Da Nang had called Division Headquarters, and they got on this little tin can down to the hooch.

I answered the phone and heard, "Is Major Robb there?" It was the White House calling to tell him his wife had had a baby. We couldn't get over it!

After Chuck left, he got out of the Marine Corps and went to the University of Virginia Law School. He became governor of Virginia and then US senator from Virginia. He was one of the most moderate Democrats at the time, and was on a presidential path. But he got caught having a massage—and apparently, it was only a massage—and it really destroyed his career. He was a hell of a nice guy and very capable and smart.

My father used to send me the Sunday *New York Times* "Week in Review" section. I'd get it a week later, and I used to say, "All the enemy had to do was subscribe to the *New York Times* to find out what we were planning. And what was working, what wasn't working."

Tet is a big religious holiday, and the first Tet Offensive had been in February of 1968. I was there in February of '69, which was post-Tet. So post-Tet, the North Vietnamese had tried this major offensive, but it was beaten back. The media made it seem that because they were able to attack, it meant that we weren't in control. Well, the enemy can attack at any time. It's like anyone can sue you. The media coverage of the Vietnam War, at least from the perspective of those of us who were there, was not very accurate.

You never were sure how things were going overall because you only saw a piece of it. We believed we were superior. I don't mean ethnically, but in terms of firepower and forces. But we were really unable to fight effectively sometimes in this kind of warfare because you didn't know who the enemy was and where they were. It's very hard to win that kind of war. I always felt it was the wrong war. If you look at what the French had done in Vietnam before us and what the Russians had done in Afghanistan, we don't seem to learn.

But I was in the military and I'd been given orders. There may have been occasions where something would happen and you'd say, "Geez, why did we do that?" But in general, we didn't sit around debating the rightness of the war.

We called the situation in the United States "Guns and Butter." There were so many people in the United States who really didn't know there was a war going on, except when they turned on the TV or read that section of the newspaper. That's because they had all the butter they wanted. It wasn't like World War II, where you had rationing and the women were working in the factories. A lot of people had been deferred from service because they were in graduate school or because they were married, so there was a lot of resentment about that.

The saying was, when you came home from serving in World War II, they had parades for you. When you came home from the Korean War, they bought you beers. When you came home from the Vietnam War, they looked the other way. And that's the way most of the military felt, which was a very damning psychological disadvantage, really-to be in a war when you don't think you're being appreciated or supported.

We did a lot of field investigations, and really did get out to the country and the villages. Sometimes, we'd get there by hitchhiking with units that were going back and forth, trucks and convoys. In the marines, they didn't treat me any differently as a lawyer because they knew we'd gone through the same training. But the guys out in the field, even though I was am officer, they knew I was a lawyer, and they probably did't think of me quite the same.

I remember post-Tet, I went up to Hue, which was a big old historic city with a lot of temples. It had been a beautiful city and was pretty much destroyed by the North Vietnamese. The Americans and the South Vietnamese had taken a lot of casualties.

I didn't feel physically in danger often—not at headquarters. But we actually had trials out at some of the units, where we camped out in the jungle. I remember we were in the middle of a trial one time, and someone yelled "Incoming!" Nobody cared about the defendant. Everybody just ran for cover, including the defendant. We had to regroup afterwards and were glad that he hadn't run away.

Officers used to carry only .45s, but when you traveled, you'd take an M16. When you went on these trips you were on alert the whole time. You'd probably get one or two enlisted men to go with you—hopefully guys who'd spent some time out in the bush. Jungle warfare was very tough, and we were fighting with our hands tied behind our backs, because we had a policy of no pursuit. So, the North Vietnamese would come down and then go into Cambodia and Laos, and you couldn't pursue them. It was politically driven, because we would be violating the sovereign rights of other countries. That's why we stopped the bombing. Another lesson: If you're going to fight a war, fight it to win.

To me, the My Lai massacre proved two things. One, Lieutenant Calley, a second lieutenant, was young and probably didn't have the right training. There were nineteen-year-olds leading seventeen-year-olds in combat situations for which they weren't prepared, especially psychologically. And two, you could go through a village and they'd wave at you. Or they'd say, "Yay, yay, US," or something like that. Well, all of a sudden there'd be a three-year-old little kid who'd throw a grenade at you. So, the military people got very antsy and trigger-happy, because if you saw a three-year-old raise an arm or something like that, you'd turn quickly, and you only had a second to decide whether to shoot or not.

We lost fifty thousand people in Vietnam. You never knew where a bomb or a mortar or even a bullet was going to come from. And you couldn't just hide in your foxhole forever, so you became fatalistic. You obviously tried to avoid danger, but you can't do that completely when you're fighting a war. People like me back in the rear in the headquarters area certainly had it better than those out in the bush who frequently engaged with the enemy.

Being Catholic probably reinforced that fatalism. That notion of predestination—God knows what's going to happen—which has always been theologically problematic to me. You have a free will, yet God knows what's going to happen. How do you reconcile those two? I never figured it out. But I thought about it a great deal.

The marines felt they had it worse than the other branches—thirteen months versus twelve months for the others. But it was the kind of thing marines thrive on. It's a badge of honor. I'm absolutely imbued with that same feeling. Even in basic training, we'd banter: "Well, who had it worse? Major Sweat Socks? Oh, you guys had it easy. We ran ten miles today. You guys only did eight?" So, we were proud, and we would argue about who had it worse for bragging rights.

I support the Marine Corps Scholarship Foundation. When they gave me an award three or four years ago, I gave a speech about what the Marine Corps means to me. Semper Fi—Semper fidelis—Always faithful. It's very meaningful to me, because I think first of all, the Marine Corps is probably one of the most elite—and I mean that in the best sense of that word—organizations in the world. Because of the culture, the discipline, the training, the education, the esprit de corps— all those things are just incredible, and they're lifelong values that you learn. And so—always faithful—when a marine greets another marine or signs a letter to him, he signs it Semper Fi. It means you never leave another marine behind. It means you take care of each other. It means you're always faithful to God, country, and the Corps. It's powerful.

The marines have many mottos and traditions. You can argue that some of it may be silly, but it's extremely powerful. And every marine believes it. Some examples: Every man's a fighting man from the commandant on down. Once a marine, always a marine. There are no ex-marines, only former marines. A marine leads from the front, not from the rear. Officers are the last ones to eat; they never go to the head of the line.

There are these traditions. And when you're in combat, it's second nature—you don't think about it. The marines always say, "Follow me." You get into a battle; you don't think about it—where you're going to be or what you're going to do. I think it's a little different from the other branches, in essence.

Now, are there brave army and navy people? Absolutely. But I don't think that they have the same traditions or that they are as pervasive.

Except for two periods—World War II and Vietnam—the marines have always been a voluntary force. You had to qualify to get in. I think that's part of it. There are always jokes about how a judge has sentenced someone to go into the Marine Corps to straighten him out. But they have to get through the training. So, there's a real winnowing-out process. For me, I spent three years on active duty and training prior to that. It was a very critical part of my life.

As I was coming to the end of my thirteen months in Vietnam, the Marine Corps was getting very liberal. They said, "Well, where would you like to go next?" So, I said, "I would like to go to Washington, DC, and work on the Military Court of Appeals." And they wrote back and said, "Extend a year." And I wrote back and said, "What else do you have?"

So, of all things, they decided to send me to New York City, to be on the staff of the Commandant, Third Naval District, and to be the military judge for the New York region. My wife was then living in New York. We had met for R&R in Hawaii for seven days and ended up reconciling. It was wonderful—idyllic after being in Vietnam.

When you didn't have much time left in Vietnam, they called you a "short-timer." A lot of guys got calendars out and marked off the date; you got an assigned day of departure and a certain flight, because there were only so many flights, all through Okinawa.

Oh my God, I was so happy to be getting out of there. I couldn't wait. We flew out and landed in Saigon. Although I'd never been there, we didn't get off the plane. Then we went to Okinawa, where I got dysentery—I don't have the faintest idea how, or when.

We had to wait three or four days until we got assigned a flight to San Francisco. I was in pain, as sick as I could be, with extreme gastrointestinal distress. They wanted to take me to the other end of Okinawa where there was an army hospital. They got an ambulance for me, and I said, "I'm going to be better. I don't want to miss my flight." They got me to this army hospital anyway, and there was an Indian doctor who looked me over. He said, "Yeah, you've got amoebic dysentery, but I'm from India. I've seen a lot worse cases. You'll live."

And I said, "That's fine. Don't cancel my flight."

So, I got on my scheduled flight. And I did feel better!

7

TRANSITIONS

I LANDED AT AN AIR FORCE BASE NORTH OF SAN FRANCISCO, AND THEN I got a flight to Newark to meet my family. I was back in the States, and it was great to be back. What a moment it was to see my parents and my wife again for the first time in thirteen months. Carole and I had corresponded while I was in Vietnam and had met in Hawaii for my R&R, where we'd agreed to try and revive our marriage.

I joined Carole in an apartment she had rented in Manhattan and was assigned to the Commandant, Third Naval District, a unit in Manhattan two blocks from the World Trade Center. I was also assigned to the Brooklyn Navy Yard, so I spent time in both Manhattan and Brooklyn. As the military judge for the US Navy and Marine Corps for the whole New York metropolitan area, I also traveled out to parts of Long Island and New Jersey.

This was the fall of 1969, and there are a couple of things I remember most. One is that this was the time of the Black Pan-

Carole McGuinn

thers. William Kunstler was a well-known criminal defense lawyer and civil rights activist who defended the Chicago Seven, a group of radical antiwar protesters. He was an older, gravelly-voiced guy with long hair and glasses that he wore on the top of his head. He had several cases where he appeared in front of me. In many of the courts-martial, judges wore a robe. But in the Marine Corps, we wore our uniform. And since I'd just come back from Vietnam, I had several ribbons, which always put the defendants on high alert.

Kunstler was trying to do two things when he appeared in these cases. First was to acquit his clients, who were frequently accused of desertion or unauthorized absences or some other crime. But second, he had a political agenda. On one case, I was assigned as co–defense counsel with him. Kunstler didn't care about this defendant. He actually wanted the military to find the client guilty, so he could appeal it and argue that the war was illegal. His agenda was so clear.

This case was held in Garden City, Long Island, before a jury of three marine officers. The defendant was charged with desertion. I made the closing argument, where I said, "I really do believe the defendant is not guilty for the reasons I stated" (because he intended to return at some point). It was questionable, but I said, "Don't fall into this trap that's being created for you." In other words, it was clear to me that Kunstler wanted our client to be found guilty, and I was suggesting to the court that they not fall for that.

The client was indeed found not guilty, and I was proud of that.

Kunstler did not share my feelings. He thought I was the biggest jerk in the world because I wasted his time, and his grandiose plan had been thwarted.

The other guy I remember was Gerald Lefcourt. He was of the same ilk, a criminal defense lawyer and a Black Panther. Like Kunstler, he was white, but he was more involved specifically with the Black Panthers, where Kunstler had a wider portfolio. Both Kunstler and Lefcourt had several cases before me. I disagreed with them both intellectually and emotionally, but I didn't let my emotions get in the way. I tried to be objective, and I think I was.

I was due to get out of the Marine Corps in another year, so I wasn't a lifer. We non-lifers used to joke among ourselves that the only way the Marine Corps could hurt us was by rolling up our personnel report, throwing it at us, and hitting us squarely in the eye. Otherwise it really didn't matter. I didn't have to worry about playing politics, or future promotions, or the repercussions of decisions, whereas a lifer arguably might have those concerns. This was good, because it meant I could truly be objective.

One very memorable case involved a navy sailor who had a low IQ—like, in the 80s—and his low IQ was part of his defense. I don't remember whether he enlisted or was drafted, but he was on a ship, and he was outwardly mentally impaired. Apparently he was ridiculed, teased, and harassed, and this all came out as evidence in the trial. He was accused of desertion, which in the military could be punishable by death. Because of extenuating circumstances, they were just charging him with unauthorized absence. But he was gone for maybe a year—a long time—which is more evidence of desertion than going UA (unauthorized absence) for the weekend and coming back.

He had a right to a jury, but for special courts-martial, most defendants waived a jury trial and asked to be tried by the judge alone. They do this presumably because they believe the judge will be objective and fair, and they'll have a better chance without the military jury.

I found him guilty, because I thought he was. But I ruled no punishment, because I thought he had already been punished enough, both from having to hide while he was absent, but also by the way he was treated when he was on the ship. I felt really good about that. I thought justice had truly been served. I got more than a little criticism from others in the office for it, but I felt it was the right decision. The defendant and his counsel were surprised and delighted; he thought he was going to jail.

Although we'd reconciled, I still worried that Carole and I really weren't suited for each other. For example, she wouldn't fly on a plane and wouldn't go out socially very often. I really wanted to grow and travel and do things, whereas she was happy to be a homebody.

Carole had been living in Manhattan, so when I came back, we lived together on the Upper East Side. I don't think I'd ever been on a subway before, and to get to work, I had to go all the way to 90 Church Street, down at the bottom of Manhattan.

On my first day of work, when the first couple of trains came in, everybody rushed forward, and I stepped back. I thought, "I'll just wait for the next one." Of course, I realized after a while that each train was crowded, and you had to push your way on. I was also in uniform, and I'd been warned that not everybody liked people in uniform. Just because you'd recently returned from Vietnam, you couldn't think you were ready to take on the world. A lot of these people on the subway trains carried knives and guns and didn't care about a fair fight.

I was twenty-seven, and I still hadn't had a real job in my chosen field. I thought I was so far behind all my peers because they had had a head start. People from my law school class were now in their third year of practice. After I left the marines, I didn't have any money in the bank. We got paid, but it was a pittance.

While I was in New York, as my time with the marines was nearing its end, my old firm offered me a job to come back to Philadelphia. But I was enjoying New York, so I took the New York bar exam. Unlike when I took the Pennsylvania bar and believed I had the highest score in the world—and then found out I'd just passed—I thought for sure I had failed the New York bar exam. I'd been out of law school for three years and did not go to a bar study program.

Unlike Pennsylvania's bar exam, which was mostly essays, New York's was multiple choice and true and false, which I thought was dumb. One question was, "How long do you have to file an appeal after a case is decided?" The choices were ten days, twelve days, fourteen days, or sixteen days. I thought, any lawyer who wouldn't research that and look it up should be accused of malpractice. You don't do things like that by memory. But that's the kind of test it was. It must have been graded on a curve, because I passed.

It was the end of 1970, and I was starting to look at firms in New York. I met somebody from Sullivan & Cromwell, which was a very well-established firm, an old, white-shoe Wall Street law firm. I interviewed, and they hired me. I think I was the first guy from Villanova Law School to go to a major Wall Street law firm. At that point the school was just fifteen years old. Sullivan & Cromwell was a corporate firm, and still one of the top firms in the country. I went there and started to practice, and I enjoyed it very much.

Most people would start at nine or nine-thirty in the morning. I would start at eight, and I'd work until maybe seven p.m. A couple of nights I'd have to stay really late, until ten p.m. or so, to get something done by a deadline or filing date. I used to go in at least one day per weekend. Since I lived in Manhattan, it wasn't as if I had a long commute.

During these early years with the firm, Carole and I separated two or three more times, but kept trying to make our marriage work. I remember she called one day and said, "We have to meet." And when we did, she said, "I'm pregnant." So, we got back together once again, and on June 25, 1971, our son Patrick was born in New York. With the McGuinn men, the names Martin and Patrick alternate. My father was Martin and his father was Patrick, and Patrick's father was Martin. I continued that tradition, naming my first son Patrick. Patrick has always been a fabulous kid.

Carole and I separated a few more times. I was working pretty hard in those days, and a large part of the problem in our marriage was me. Carole had worked as a secretary until she gave birth, and then she stayed home afterward. I would spend time with Patrick on weekends, as I was able. I'm sure it wasn't unusual, but it was tough.

Ultimately, though, the marriage didn't work, and we got divorced. We got an annulment from the Catholic Church because of our immaturity when we were married.

Carole had a sister in Washington, DC, and she thought Washington would be much better for a single mother than New York. So in 1976, when Patrick was about five, she moved with him to Washington, DC. That's really where he was brought up.

When she moved, it was a big deal, because I'd been seeing Patrick at least once a week, on Sundays. It used to be a joke—you'd go to Central Park and see all these fathers with their kids. A lot of them probably were still married, but it was sort of the fathers' day.

When Patrick went to Washington, we worked out an arrangement where Patrick would fly to New York at least once a month, for the weekend. In those days, if one parent delivered the child to the plane and the other parent met the flight on the other end, they would allow children to fly by themselves. It was actually kind of exciting for the kids.

So, Patrick would come up to New York at least once a month, and I would go down to Washington frequently, as well. Until he graduated from prep school, whenever I went down to Washington on business, I always carved out time to go see him. We'd throw a baseball or football around, or I'd actually sit in on his class, much to his embarrassment. I also saw him on holidays and vacations, and we took trips together. We maintained pretty good contact through the years.

Carole was one of the nicest and sweetest people in the world. She never remarried, and died about fifteen years ago of cancer. In the early years after our divorce our relationship was very strained, but in later years we became much closer. This was because once there had been real love between us, but mostly because we shared a wonderful son.

In some ways, I got into what would become the focus of my career somewhat by accident. At Sullivan & Cromwell, I didn't want to do tax, litigation, or estates. That left me with corporate law, which among the four categories was really what I wanted to do. So, I started doing corporate work, a lot of securities work, and acquisitions work. And then I started doing a lot of bank financing and mergers.

Like a lot of things in life, you may do your first transaction quite by accident. But then, with your second and third, you become, if not an expert, at least more informed or knowledgeable. And then if you get to the fifth or sixth, maybe you're close to being an expert. That's how I got into banking law. I had initially wanted to be a corporate lawyer, not necessarily a banking lawyer. I didn't object to it; I just followed the coincidences.

I worked at Sullivan & Cromwell for six and a half years and enjoyed it tremendously. In those days bank mergers were not that permissible; they were very limited. You had to get regulatory approval, and you could only do mergers in the next county, or nearby. There was no such thing as interstate banking yet. In a lot of these mergers that I worked on, ironically, I represented the Bank of New York, which was one of Sullivan & Cromwell's major clients. I would do these small mergers for them, up in the Adirondacks or in Queens. Because they were relatively small, I would end up handling the whole merger. I would present it to the regulators, and at the end of the day when the merger was done, I knew more about the bank that was getting acquired than anybody at the acquirer knew.

I would send a bill out and go on to the next case, always wondering what happened after the merger. How was it going? Were the promises we made to the regulators and to the communities being fulfilled? I started thinking more and more that I'd like to work inside a corporation or bank. It was more interesting to me. I didn't want to be just a transactional lawyer, sending a bill and moving on. There was no continuity, no implementation of what you said was going to happen. You just handed it over to somebody else—someone who wasn't nearly as knowledgeable as you were. Not that they couldn't become qualified, but I was already there, having put the whole transaction together.

One of my talents, I'd like to think, is that I do like to plan ahead and build teams, bringing people together to achieve an objective. I think in that sense, over the years, I've had a lot of experience and have become pretty good at it. I wanted to work in such a way that I could achieve some continuity, where I could measure success over time and see tangible results.

Concurrently, I was told that although I was doing fine and still had a chance of becoming partner, there were others at the firm who had a better chance than I of becoming partner. It was 1977, and I'd been there about six years. How long it took to become a partner varied at different firms, but at Sullivan & Cromwell, it was seven or eight years.

I had enjoyed working there, but I wasn't achieving my long-term goal. That's when I started to do research and put my name in for certain openings elsewhere. I got a couple of offers through headhunters and through jobs I'd applied for in the area. These were inside counsel jobs. I turned down two of them, but finally, the Singer Company offered me a position as the number two in a legal department they were building. Singer is associated with sewing machines, but they did a lot more. It was a real conglomerate, and in 1977, I took the job.

8

ALL AT ONCE

THEY USED TO SAY THERE ARE THREE THINGS YOU'RE NOT SUPPOSED TO DO all at once—get married, get a new job, and buy a new house. I did two of them in September of 1977 (and bought a new house months later, in Ridgefield, Connecticut).

I used to joke that I met Ann Muldoon at the Metropolitan Museum, but we actually met at this bar called the Red Blazer on Second Avenue, at 82nd Street. The Red Blazer actually became sort of our club—not just Ann's and mine, but my buddies' too. They had these great steak sandwiches, and we knew the bartender, Mickey. You'd go there and you'd know half the people in the place. It was fun.

Ann Muldoon, Marty

It was also in the neighborhood. I was in an apartment by myself at 77th and Second. When I'd gotten divorced in 1975, I literally got nothing. I think I had a couch and a table and a bed, and that was it. I got this apartment and it was underground—one of those classic places you had to walk down the steps to get into.

Ann was working in the fashion industry and living on East End Avenue, around 83rd Street. She's from Brooklyn, and she's an identical twin. We started to date, and she and her sister Margaret, who also worked in the fashion industry, would give me things like toasters and other kitchen items. They'd say they'd gotten them at the bank as leftover promotional items (one of them had worked at a bank for a while). I found out years later that this wasn't true. They were buying me this stuff, and didn't want me to think I was just getting handouts. That's how poor I was.

Ann also had two older brothers. Neither she nor her sister Margaret had gone to college, and the reason was their father had left them about five years before they graduated from high school. And then he died. He had never gotten a divorce, and had left a huge tax bill behind that he had never paid. Ann's mother was a teacher in the New York school system, and to her credit, somehow she paid it off. There had been enough money to send the two boys to college, but not the two girls, especially being twins. So they went to Fashion Institute of Technology (FIT), which was more for fashion degrees than it was academic, but it served them both very well.

It turned out to be very helpful that Carole and I had received the annulment from the Church, because Ann was Catholic, and her mother was very Catholic. So Ann and I got married in September of 1977.

Concurrently, at the Singer Company, my finances were finally looking up. When I had first started as a lawyer in Philadelphia the prevailing annual salary was $8,000. At that time, they paid $9,000 in New York City because of the higher cost of living. But while I was in Vietnam, a lot of the firms went to $15,000. At Singer, I started at $75,000, which was a lot.

I heard from Sullivan & Cromwell that I'd gotten the highest starting salary of anybody who'd ever left the firm. Of course, partners in those days never left the firm. Only associates left, so the salary was within the associates' category. If I'd stayed and become a partner, financially it would have been among the best for practicing law anywhere. In those days, the idea that you would make more money as inside counsel for a corporation was questionable. Since then, it's been proven, but it was a slow evolution in terms of whether you could leave as a partner in a great firm and make more money as a general counsel in a corporation. Now it's more common, but it wasn't then.

Singer was at 30 Rockefeller Plaza, one of the most iconic office buildings in the world. The location was in the center of Manhattan; I used to call it the center of the universe. We had about six or seven floors just below the top floor, the Rainbow Room. That was the next floor up, the Top of the Rock. It didn't happen right away, but I ended up getting a corner office overlooking the Empire State Building. I remember having my father come visit, and I said, "Look, I'm on top of the world!"

After about a year and a half, Singer was able to sublease the space for something like $50 a square foot. They had been there for years and years, paying something like $15 a square foot. They moved to Stamford, Connecticut, and built a brand-new headquarters just out of the money they were making on the sublease. This meant that I had a reverse commute out of Manhattan, which I wasn't crazy about. But I did it for another year and a half. I only stayed at Singer for three years, but they were memorable.

Singer was one of the great brand names of the world, originating in the late 1800s with Singer Sewing Machine. They tested the Singer name against the biggest brand names, including Coca-Cola and IBM, and Singer was fourth or fifth globally. Part of that was because in Africa and Asia, they were what was called a white goods distributor.

They used the Singer brand name, but they distributed washers and dryers and refrigerators manufactured by others, which meant the brand was truly global. It was a real conglomerate in the era of conglomerates. The question ultimately became whether you could effectively manage companies with all of these different businesses.

Singer still had the sewing machine business, but it was rapidly declining because, as with a lot of things after World War II, we had invested in Japan to help them modernize. So they had the latest sewing machine manufacturing in the world to compete against us. This was true in many industries. By comparison, we had a plant in Newark, which was built around 1900, and we were still manufacturing sewing machines there.

Singer also had an aerospace division and made simulators for pilots. It was fascinating. Joe Flavin was the CEO, and he had just been named "CEO of the Year" before I arrived. They had brought in Bartow Farr from IBM as the general counsel, and he was building a legal department that would include me. There's an old firm in New York called Willkie Farr & Gallagher—that was Bartow's father. Bartow had been at IBM for years as one of their top associate general counsels, and he really wanted to build a top in-house firm, and Singer gave him the money to do it.

There weren't many inside counsels in those days. Companies just didn't have big in-house legal operations, and lawyers who worked in them were often looked down upon, as only those who couldn't make partner in a firm. For me, leaving Sullivan & Cromwell was a decision based not on money but on interest. And I really enjoyed Singer. I was made managing counsel of the consumer products division, which made Craftsman handheld power tools for Sears. We made all of them. We made wooden furniture, called "case goods," for Sears—all of it. In those days Sears had about 500,000 employees and was about 2 percent of GDP. The bad news was, they were our only customer for those things, so they had a lot of leverage. This would become a problem in later years.

Among Singer's different businesses was the American Meter Company, which made gas meters. As counsel for the consumer products division, I went to Yugoslavia about ten times because they were "gasifying" their country from coal, and we sold them all the gas meters. I had to go and negotiate all the contracts, which was fascinating. Even then I really had an interest in the business part, not just the legal aspect. So I asked and was granted the ability to spend a day a week in the strategic planning department. In a lot of businesses, the regulations are such an important part of the business that being a lawyer can be a big help. So while my job was to be general counsel for consumer products, within my domain there were these very different businesses: furniture, handheld power tools, gas meters, and auto parts.

My second week on the job, I went to visit the American Meter Company division for the first time. I went with the vice chairman of the company, who was responsible for consumer products. He took me there to meet the president of American Meter at the headquarters outside of Philadelphia. We were walking toward the president's office at the end of the hall when some guy stuck his head out along the way and made a, Psst—psst!, sound and motioned us in. The vice chairman said, "You go talk to him, and I'll go down and talk with the president. Just come down when you're finished."

So I went into the office and the guy said, "I hear you're the new counsel. I gotta tell you something. I've got some real worries. It's just not right, and I don't want to be part of it." There were only three gas meter manufacturers at that time, and he said, "We'll go in, and these are mostly bid contracts. We go in to a meeting and talk about the bid, and then the president of the company would say, 'Okay, I'll think about it, and I'll let you know.' And then he'd come back and we'd get this bid price, and we had no idea how he got it. And that was what we'd bid."

At that time, price fixing was a big problem. I went down and said to the vice chairman, "I have to tell you what I've just heard." He didn't believe it. I said, "We've got to investigate this. Let me do the questioning. We can privilege it if we have to. I'm not going to go in and just attack him."

So I went in and said to the president, "I'm the new guy. Tell me how you establish your pricing." I didn't lead with that, but we got to that point fairly quickly. I don't remember exactly what I said, but something to the effect of, "There've been rumors about . . ."

Ultimately he broke down crying and admitted it. It was like, "Oh my God!" This was my second week on the job!

So we went back to Stamford headquarters and talked to Bartow Farr. Based on our advice, the company agreed to self-report to the government that we'd discovered a crime. There was a certain amount of self-interest involved here, because we thought we'd get better treatment if we self-reported. Either way, we had to deal with this. If it had become public that we'd known about this and done nothing, the penalties would have been multiples of what they would have been otherwise. We couldn't take that chance.

So of course, after we reported, the plaintiffs' lawyers came out of the woodwork. The plaintiffs were all the utility companies that had bought gas meters. The lead lawyer was one of the most famous plaintiffs' lawyers in Philadelphia, Harold Kohn (coincidentally, we were both on the Villanova Law School Board of Consultors). We got into this litigation and they sued us for price fixing and triple damages. We went back and forth, trying to negotiate with these people. Kohn, the dean of the plaintiffs' lawyers, finally called me and said, "Marty, here's my final offer." He said it was going to go up $1 million per day. I was thinking, "Oh shit!"

I went back to Farr and the CEO and said, "I think we ought to accept the offer. We're guilty. The only thing we've got going for us is we're good corporate citizens. It wasn't something we pressured them from headquarters to do, and we self-reported. This guy was a lone ranger, off on his own." I said that while we had a lot of circumstances that were mitigating or extenuating, or both, we were still guilty. "We don't have a defense on the merits," I said, "and then we're just dependent on the emotion of the government or the jurors. And corporations aren't that lovable. So we may not get much on the emotional side."

I advised them that we take it. That was the second or third day after the offer of settlement, so it had gone up $2 or $3 million by then. But we did settle the case. This was part of my introduction to being a corporate lawyer!

The upshot was that the president of American Meter was fired. I don't remember if he went to jail. He had developed the scheme with the CEOs of two other companies, and of course they were all in trouble. Unfortunately, there's a lot of history of price fixing in the US corporate world. Sometimes it's more subtle, but it's still a problem.

As corporate counsel for Singer, I'd go out and lecture: "If you go to trade conferences, have a lawyer present. And do these kinds of preventive things so people can't accuse you of price fixing. You might end up with the same price, because you all buy the same materials and have similar costs, but it will be coincidence, and we can defend that." This was an important type of preventive law often practiced by inside counsel.

Among the utilities were some really big companies, one of which was Consolidated, the big coal and gas company in Pittsburgh. They bought a lot of meters from us. Bartow and I went around together to these utilities and tried to negotiate settlements with each of the plaintiffs. We did a lot of research, and I think we made fair offers to compensate them for their losses. We were very apologetic, saying that we'd discovered and reported the problem, and so on. We were not able to get individual settlements because Kohn convinced the utilities to sue us as a class, saying that as their counsel he would get them a better outcome as a group. That's what they did, and why we had to settle with Kohn.

I remember we came to Pittsburgh in the spring. Consolidated was located down at the Point, in Gateway Towers. It was one of those days where the sun was shining, and people were out sitting all around on the grass. I said, "Wow, Pittsburgh is beautiful." We had come in through the tunnels and the first thing I saw was the Point. That was my first impression of Pittsburgh.

At the end of 1979, I went to China, which had not been open to commerce previously. It was just being opened, and I stayed at the Peace Hotel, along the Bund in Shanghai, which looked very European. The people were all wearing Mao suits, with the black tunic and black slacks. I'd walk out along the Bund, and although I'm just slightly tall, I was taller than most of the Chinese. They'd walk up and gather around me. They were all on bicycles; there were no cars.

We spent two weeks there. After World War II, China had nationalized all the Singer Sewing Machine plants, and in the late 1970s, they were interested in getting all the latest technology and business practices. We were interested in getting them to manufacture and drop-ship through Hong Kong so we could compete with the Japanese and their lower-cost sewing machines.

So we went from Shanghai to other provinces to negotiate with local governments. Then we visited Xian, where they have the Terracotta Army. People were living in caves. China was just unbelievable in those days. After that, I went to China once a year, and it was amazing to see how fast the country developed. Every year I'd go, and there would be a new airport and a new super highway to connect it. There were new trains. One side of the Bund in Shanghai then was all swamp, called the Pudong. It now has three of the tallest skyscrapers in the world. What the Chinese have done and are doing is incredible; in my opinion they're the next superpower, for sure. And Shanghai is the next New York City—the next world capital. It was fascinating to see how fast they were evolving.

On this trip, we were negotiating with different provinces, as you had to deal on the provincial level and obtain individual contracts. The day after we left, we got notice that the central government had abrogated all of the contracts we'd negotiated because they didn't want to be obligated to pay dollars, and they wanted to maintain central control. So while it was a hell of an experience, it turned out to be an unsuccessful business trip.

After I'd been at Singer for two and a half years, Bartow Farr got into an argument with the CEO, Joe Flavin, and was fired. Singer brought in the senior lawyer from the law firm that represented them and made him general counsel. I thought Bartow was going to be there a little longer, and then I thought I would at least be considered for his job after he left. I was thirty-eight at that point, so I began thinking of going elsewhere.

Flavin, incidentally, was the guy who directed the strategy of turning Singer into a conglomerate, and he ended up dying unexpectedly in 1987, at the age of fifty-eight. The conglomerate business model never really succeeded. General Electric probably came the closest to succeeding, but even today, they're finally unwinding. Singer finally went bankrupt, unfortunately, in 1999.

Though I was beginning to think of making a change, I had loved the transition to the corporate world. I was doing a lot of business strategy work—I didn't just negotiate contracts—and then I was involved with the implementation. It was everything I wanted.

My request to be involved in strategic planning was very unusual. Most corporate lawyers like to be just lawyers. That would be a big decision for me, later in life, when I decided to go into business, leaving behind my legal training and experience. I was confident that I could do it, but I was taking a risk, for sure.

Risk is a fascinating and essential issue. I gave the commencement address at Villanova Law School once, and my topic was the willingness to take risk. As a speaker, you don't want to be too pompous or try to be some kind of teacher or adviser, but hopefully you can leave them with some good advice. I decided that risk was the one issue I wanted to discuss with them in a relatively short address. My point was, how do you choose your job? Even once you're in a job, you have to make choices along the way. Regardless, it's important to take risks because otherwise you'll just atrophy. You'll stay in the same place. So you need to take risks, but you need to take them in an informed and reasonable way.

I used my own experience to give examples: when I didn't go back to Philadelphia where I already had a job and stayed in New York; when I took on banking and continued to build on that, because I felt comfortable with it; and then when I got a new job and tried to get business experience. The willingness to take risks and knowing how to do it can be a key part of your life, no matter what you do.

Of course, there's no question that some people aren't quite as cut out for taking risks as others; they are resistant. We all have different characteristics. Before taking a risk, it's important to be informed and test the proposition as reasonably as you can, doing your thinking and being prepared—even if it's a stretch.

When Singer started to consider moving its headquarters to Stamford, Ann and I bought a little country house in Ridgefield, Connecticut, but kept our apartment in Manhattan. I'd been making pretty good money, and this place was great, out in the woods on three acres. Patrick came up once a month and we'd go out there for the weekend. We really enjoyed it.

But I was coming up on three years with Singer, and since I hadn't gotten the general counsel job, I started looking for other possibilities. I'd had several interviews, but it came down to two. One was an offer to go out to Los Angeles and be general counsel for a company called Norton Simon. And then I got a call from Rodgin Cohen at Sullivan & Cromwell, which represented the Mellon family, saying Mellon Bank was looking for a general counsel. So I went out to Pittsburgh and interviewed there at the end of 1980.

We'd been out to Los Angeles several times and looked at housing, which even in those days was expensive. Interest rates were around 20 percent. LA was kind of appealing, but we felt the housing market was too inflated and was going to crash. Of course, it just kept going up.

We drove up to one of the canyons to look at a brand-new house, thinking it was going to be cool. We walked out into the backyard—

except there wasn't one. Instead, we found a 1,000-foot drop. And they said they had snakes. Well, that was the end of it for Ann, being from Brooklyn. And I was going to be doing a lot of international travel, so she would often be alone.

Ann has always done well financially. When we first got married, I was paying alimony to Carole, so Ann had more money than I did. And she continued to rise. She had several very good jobs and got a lot of promotions. She was the buyer in charge of the menswear line for a company. She would go to Hong Kong and get clothes made. She had just gotten this big job offer to be director of marketing at Diners Club Credit Card. It was a very good job, and we were trying to figure that out in connection with the move.

I had been to Pittsburgh a couple of times—to visit, and to have the interviews with Mellon. They offered me the job. So I had two job offers: Norton Simon in LA and Mellon in Pittsburgh.

To figure it out, Ann and I went off to Ridgefield to think about all the components going into making the decision. My job, her job, my family, her family. All the relevant factors. Then we went into separate corners and added them up.

I think I came up with 101 for Pittsburgh versus 99 for Los Angeles, and she came up with 100 for Pittsburgh and 98 for Los Angeles.

So we decided to come to Pittsburgh.

9

BUILDING A CAPTIVE LAW FIRM

MELLON IN THE EARLY 1980s WAS CALLED THE J. P. MORGAN OF THE WEST. It was a wholesale bank because it dealt with so many large corporations. J. P. Morgan was the wholesale bank with the biggest corporations, but Mellon banked a lot of the same Fortune 500 companies, because these companies needed more than one bank. Some have called Mellon Bank the first venture capital bank, as it funded many, many companies, including, most notably in the early days, Alcoa and Gulf Oil. That's what they did in those days, when banking was different, before the Glass-Steagall Act in the 1930s. They were almost like investment banks, famously taking stock in all of these corporations.

Mellon also had a retail branch network in Pittsburgh. Until the mid-1980s, there was no interstate banking. Until then, Mellon could only branch into contiguous counties, so it had some branches in Westmoreland County and maybe one or two in Butler County, but that was about it. We had a very good trust department, partially because we represented the Mellon family. But basically we dealt with corporations. Mellon had a great family name and reputation, going back to 1869, when Judge Thomas Mellon founded it. It wasn't the First National Bank of Nowhere. It was Mellon Bank.

The bank had been run by family members for almost seventy years, from Thomas Mellon to Andrew Mellon, later the longest-serving US Treasury secretary, to Richard B. Mellon and then Richard King Mellon, who, along with Mayor David Lawrence, was responsible for the famous Pittsburgh renaissance after World War II. The family owned the bank exclusively until the middle of the twentieth century. The first non–Mellon family CEO was Frank Denton in 1946, followed by John Mayer in 1963, Jim Higgins in 1974, and David Barnes in 1981.

In Pittsburgh, Mellon was dominant, much to the chagrin of Pittsburgh National Bank, which later, through expansions, became Pittsburgh National Corporation (PNC). When I arrived, Pittsburgh National was very envious of Mellon's business and its reputation. Many executives at Pittsburgh National, including former CEO Tom O'Brien, had gotten their training at Mellon. So there was a real rivalry, although not on Mellon's part in those days. It's ironic, of course, the way things turned out, with Mellon being sold and PNC ultimately remaining independent and becoming one of the nation's biggest banks.

At that point, Pittsburgh National was more of a local bank, and Mellon was more of a national bank. It had been that way for years. For example, PNC probably did not lend to a company such as General Motors, either because they didn't have the expertise or because General Motors wouldn't let them into the group. No one bank could handle the needs of a company such as General Motors, so they had what they called syndicates. J. P. Morgan might be the manager of the syndicate, but it would bring together maybe ten banks around the country. There wasn't enough capital in one bank to handle General Motors's needs, nor would you want to have that much tied up with one customer. So it was risk dispersion on both sides.

But PNC started to make a lot of acquisitions, too, and increased its size. Then it started taking on bigger loans and becoming more competitive in that space. We at Mellon also were interested in buying other retail banks, because the consumer was considered to be a reliable source of funding with the deposits. Over the years when the Federal Reserve (the Fed) evaluates a bank, they give you higher ratings for having consumer deposits as opposed to corporate deposits. You could raise money in lots of ways, but they weren't considered to be as reliable or stable as having consumer deposits. If you had more reliable sources of capital, you were considered to be much more stable, and that gave you more freedom, to lend more and to acquire more. The move in later years to interstate banking with increasing acquisitions and the evolving regulatory environment required considerably more legal support.

My job was to be the general counsel. Because of my previous experience, I believed that corporations should have what I called their own "captive law firm." I wanted to get away from using the pejorative term "legal department" or "in-house counsel." So I had the support, at least verbally, of building such a captive law firm at Mellon. That was the main priority of what I wanted to accomplish. It was the only way that Mellon could get the best legal support and also get it at the lowest price. It meant getting the quality, the right quantity, the efficiency, and the lowest cost. Of course, a lot of times when push came to shove and you were asking for the money to actually implement things, it could be a little different.

The other part of the job, depending on your relationship, was that I was also consigliere to the CEO, advising him on various matters. The CEO is the general counsel's primary client, although in my case, I was also secretary of the board of directors, so I spent a lot of time working with them, as well.

Jim Higgins was CEO just before I arrived. He was a tall, heavyset guy. Huge mind and brilliant. Very formal and very intellectual. He was a deep thinker, a great visionary, and a great policymaker. He was well known in the industry for his views—for instance, that we should have interstate banking. Those kinds of things are discussed years before they come to pass through legislation. He was also a very effective leader, but I don't think he was a hands-on manager or a real people person. He was more professorial.

To pick his successor, the board created a beauty contest in which three people—Dave Barnes, George Farrell, and Sy Keane—were asked to run the bank, as I recall, for just a month each. It could have been a quarter. And then they were observed. I arrived just after this, but I heard about it. I'm not sure it was the best decision-making process, but what I was sure of—because I saw it—was that it was very divisive and disruptive in the bank. Lots of people lined up behind their candidates. They were trying to support their person, and when their person lost, those feelings of resentment lingered in terms of relationships with the others.

Ultimately, Dave Barnes was chosen. Educated at Harvard Law School, he never practiced law. He was a corporate banker, and had called on businesses in the southwestern United States. He was on the board of an energy company based in Dallas. He was in the Jim Higgins mold, in that he was not a people person. He tended to delegate to others, and, at least in hindsight, he was not an effective manager.

Both Higgins and Barnes had been with the bank their whole careers. The culture was very corporate. Retail banking was important, but largely just involved the day-to-day business of cashing checks and taking deposits. The people responsible for dealing with the branches and with those customers only needed a certain level of expertise or sophistication, whereas if you were trying to lend money to General Motors Company, where they all went to top business schools and were at the top of the corporate world, you had to have a pretty high degree of sophistication. So people in the corporate banking world—at Mellon and at Morgan—were of that ilk. Higgins and Barnes fit that mold.

I used to joke that they both denied hiring me. Higgins hired me, but Barnes was already selected to take over in April, so there was that interregnum after I arrived in January of 1981. I had a good relationship with Barnes. I respected him in many ways. We spent a lot of time looking at possible acquisitions. We must have looked at five banks for every one we acquired—a time-consuming but important part of the process. With my background in mergers and acquisitions, and with some of the people I hired, we brought some very good experience to the table. This was very helpful in terms of building credibility and a relationship with management in general, and with Barnes in particular.

Building a captive law firm was my total goal—my objective. I wasn't a pioneer in it, but we were pretty early in the game. When I arrived, Mellon only had two or three lawyers in a small legal department, and they weren't the people I would have hired. I had to decide first in what area I wanted to build expertise. Regulatory was obvious. We had to deal with the Fed, the Office of the Comptroller of the Currency (OCC), and the state superintendent every day. I expected that interstate banking was around the corner, which would really change things. So I started hiring, and found Mike Bleier, who was then serving as assistant general counsel at the Fed. I wanted somebody who was strong in regulatory matters, and coming from the Fed, he had credibility. Mike turned out to be a fabulous hire. He later became general counsel and a senior leader at Mellon and in the banking industry as a whole.

Michael Bleier

I started adding other lawyers, including Jim Gockley, Len Heinz, and Joe Camp, and there were other lawyers spread around in the corporation, especially in the trust department. They had their own lawyers and wanted it to stay that way; they had their own little fiefdoms. I finally said, "I have to give opinions for the corporation. I can't make exceptions for certain businesses that are part of the company." Besides, this notion of more centralized services was more economical than having all these separate legal areas having their own support services. I thought it was a better way to run a corporation.

This was always controversial, because any business manager wants control over everything, whether it's human resources, finance, legal, or technology, i.e.—"I don't want to fight bureaucracy. I want control and I want loyalty." These are all natural tendencies. However, you have to balance and offset this against the desire not just for efficiency, but for corporate control. Today it's not much of a controversy, but in those days it was a big issue. Changing it meant going against tradition and the status quo.

At that point, we were spreading our legal business all around the world. That was because, for better or worse, Mellon had a pretty big international business. I also wanted to control which law firms we used. This was another huge battle, because the head of the trust department might have had his brother-in-law at the Reed Smith law firm or his best friend at another firm, and they took him out to dinner once a week. I was upsetting things that had been that way for decades. That's the way every place was. But Pittsburgh, being a big city/small town, was definitely that way.

Ultimately, though, you don't just tell people what you want them to do. You've got to convince them that it's in their best interests. At the age of thirty-eight, I was the youngest senior vice president in Mellon history, and ultimately, I went to each business area and built relationships with them. What I said to each one of them was, "If I can't get you at least the same quality legal service at a lesser price, then you can go outside. You'll have to go to a firm that I approve, and I'll approve more than one to make sure they meet our standards, and so we can negotiate special fees."

If we couldn't provide the expertise, they could go outside. We didn't have expertise in every area, and I never wanted to develop it in some areas—litigation, for example. The volume of litigation is always shifting. You can have big cases where you need specialized expertise and a certain number of lawyers. The same is true with acquisitions. If you've got a big merger, you're going to have to bring in experts such as Sullivan & Cromwell—firms that do it every day. Most business leaders were very leery and skeptical and wanted to maintain their own positions and control, but I ultimately convinced them. Over time—several years—this model worked out.

An example of a hire for the needs of a specific business was Otto Chu, who was responsible for the cash management business. Here's a guy who went to Yale and Harvard and had worked for a large law firm. We were getting top-quality people, all from good firms with good experience. We wouldn't hire out of law school. Somebody else had to train them.

The way it worked was Otto was assigned a client, and he had to become an expert at cash management, and he had to build a relationship with that client. Similarly, Joe Camp handled litigation; Jim Gockley did all of the securities work and was involved in acquisitions; and Len Heinz handled the retail business. Jim Gockley later became deputy general counsel for BNY Mellon and general counsel for BNY Mellon Asset Management.

Jim Gockley

I made it clear that all of the lawyers reported to me on a straight line, but to their client on a dotted line. "Straight line" means that that's where the primary relationship is, and where the ultimate decider is. The "dotted line" means there's input and participation. This meant that I would control the final decision on salary adjustments, promotions, and things like that for the lawyer. But if the client said the lawyer was slow or not responsive, or they didn't think they were getting the support they needed, that would go into my appraisal of that lawyer. I wanted to make sure that ultimately, it was one lawyer appraising another. If a client said to me, "I didn't like their advice," it still may have been the right advice.

I felt it was very important for professionals to supervise professionals. That was another one of the reasons for having a captive law firm. Without it, you had a business person—for example, a trust officer—evaluating the lawyers in his department. The head of the trust department would evaluate the lawyer—at least in part, maybe subconsciously—based on whether he liked the advice or not, and how the advice impacted his business, which a lot of times is not black or white.

As general counsel, I had to be more lawyer than executive, at least in the beginning. However, I had to be an executive, because I was the senior lawyer, and I had to run the department and hire, fire, promote, and evaluate. In addition, I was out building business for our captive law firm. So I was probably 51 percent lawyer and 49 percent executive. It was pretty fascinating.

I had the commitment to build this captive legal department with everyone being employees, and I kept building over the years until at some point, we had over 120 lawyers. I remember seeing former CEO John Mayer out at the Rolling Rock Club on the practice tee. I hadn't met him before, and someone introduced me. "McGuinn," he said. "I hear you have more lawyers than Reed Smith."

10

CRISIS AND CEO TRANSITION

DAVID BARNES TOOK OVER AS CEO IN APRIL 1981 AT THE MELLON annual meeting. Statewide banking was approved and went into effect in March of 1982. There was a lot of attention on expanding statewide, and the most obvious first target for us was Philadelphia, one of the largest cities in the country, and much bigger than Pittsburgh. There were some good, large bank candidates in Philadelphia.

It really was helpful to me as general counsel to have Mike Bleier as my first hire. As assistant general counsel of the Federal Reserve, he had reviewed merger applications that had to be approved by the regulators, not just the shareholders. With Mike on board, we were immediately able to be of help to the CEO and also to the senior management in the mergers and acquisitions area.

Our first major acquisition in 1983 was Girard Bank, one of the oldest and largest banks in Philadelphia. As inside lawyers we hired outside firms—Sullivan & Cromwell and Reed Smith—to assist us, but we played a major role in the negotiations and the regulatory application process. We acquired several others in central and northeast Pennsylvania and Erie over the next couple of years.

Then, in late 1985, the Saudis caused a dramatic collapse in oil prices, and a global economic crisis ensued. Mellon had a lot of loans to South American countries, which were struggling economically. We also had a lot of loans in the southwestern part of the United States, some to energy-related companies and others to real estate developers. While seemingly unrelated, the risk managers failed to realize that the energy and real estate loans were very much connected. If one was going to go bad, the other was going to go bad. That's the problem with risk management tools and what you learn from so many of these crises. You would see many of the trees, but sometimes not the whole forest.

As it turned out, we had more bad loans than anybody realized. In the first quarter of 1987, the regulators—the Fed and the Comptroller of the Currency—were reviewing our loan portfolio, as they regularly did. They did continuous reviews and made recommendations. You could negotiate and try to reason with them, but in the end, whatever they decided was the final decision.

We had just finished a meeting one day, which I had attended, and they were making these recommendations about how much we were going to have to write down in loans—"writing down" is an accounting term, meaning you reduce the value of the loan on your books. This would mean we'd take a big hit to our capital reserves and to our earnings. It was ominous.

So I called Dave Barnes, who was at a Federal Reserve Board meeting in Cleveland, and I said, "Dave, you better come back here. We've got some real problems with the regulators."

So he came back and we had a special meeting with the regulators the next day, at which he was present.

They made the presentation all over again to him, and he kind of dismissed them and basically said that they didn't know what they were talking about. Things were fine. The outcome was that the regulators insisted that we had to write down these loans. So for the first quarter— just one quarter—we reported a loss of $60 million. I think that was the first loss in Mellon history during a reportable period. There could have been monthly losses, but they didn't get reported.

The board wanted to know what was going on, so the regulators came in and reported to them. It was rare that they reported to the full board, but this was important enough that they did it. Barnes was chairing the meeting and tried to explain his position. I think the board was persuaded that either he didn't sufficiently understand the depth of the problem, or he hadn't taken it seriously. Either way would have meant the same thing. The board decided to fire Barnes.

Nate Pearson was designated as the senior director of the board to meet with Barnes, and they asked me to join Pearson for the meeting, which I did. It was very uncomfortable and unpleasant. Nate explained to Barnes that the board had lost confidence in him and felt it was time for a change, because things were, if not out of control, in real trouble.

After Nate left, I sat there with Barnes. I'll never forget it. It was a dark room. This was in the original Mellon boardroom at the top of Three Mellon Bank Center, off of William Penn Way, the joint US Steel/Mellon headquarters built in the 1950s. I was sitting with Barnes in the dark and he said, "What happened?"

He was in shock; I guess that's the best way to describe it.

So I immediately said, "Dave, I can't help you, but you need help. As general counsel to the corporation, my ethical obligation is to the corporation and its shareholders. But you need counsel. I suggest we call Chuck Queenan at Kirkpatrick and Lockhart and see if he'll help, or at least, what he would recommend."

I got through to Queenan and connected him with Dave, and then I left. And that was it. The details of Dave Barnes's termination were negotiated, and they made an announcement in the next couple of days. He was gone.

Nate Pearson was designated as interim chair, which was kind of funny, because he was well into his seventies. He represented Paul Mellon on the board. Nate was a wonderful, smart gentleman, but he had no real experience in banking, so he asked me to be his informal chief of staff. He knew some people in the bank, but he probably knew me best because I was secretary of the board.

So in April of 1987, Nate Pearson was running the bank, with the behind-the-scenes but very active participation of Drew Mathieson. Nate had a sharp intellect and high integrity, and he had the support of the board and shareholders, but he wasn't involved with the day-to-day operations. Fortunately, we had a lot of strong managers. I was practically following Nate around all day long. He was asking, "Who's this?" "Who do I call?" Some of it was mundane. Some of it involved corporate governance and process. I remember explaining that the proper role of the board was to oversee, not to manage. That's the management's job.

Nate was a pleasure to work with, and as a result of our working together, I had this sort of informal and unofficial role, which not only enabled me but also required me to be almost the conduit between the board and management. As a practical matter, some of the support functions—human resources, marketing, government affairs, community development, strategic planning—were almost literally reporting to me at that point. This gave me a more active role in the organization.

A search for the new CEO began right away, and they soon found Frank Cahouet.

Cahouet had been at Crocker National Bank in San Francisco, which was wholly owned by Midland Bank, a British institution. They sold it out on him when he was CEO, and he was understandably furious. They could do that because they were the sole shareholder. So Cahouet moved to Fannie Mae as the president, but not as the CEO, and he had only been there a few months when he was recruited.

It happened pretty fast. Cahouet saw Mellon as a wonderful opportunity, and started in June of 1987. He was an experienced banker and the first Mellon CEO hired from the outside. The board needed someone objective who could come in and really see things clearly. Someone from the inside might not have had the ability, the confidence, or the objectivity to move fast and make difficult decisions. Cahouet was able to do just that.

Cahouet fired almost 4,000 people out of Mellon's overall employment of about 18,000 at that time, from the top down. While he had to cut expenses to match the decrease in revenues, he also felt that the bank was fat and could use some leanness. Cahouet had never lived in Pittsburgh. Who could he rely on and trust? His own people—so he brought in some of them, which was natural enough. The interesting thing was that many of the new people had the attitude that employees already at Mellon were suspect: "You guys are part of the problem, not the solution. Because you were here."

There was a lot of consternation, and it was a very difficult time. Cahouet would have meetings on Saturday mornings and expect reports to be ready. I remember some guys were complaining, saying things like, "He's telling us we have to submit a new budget by next week that shows a 20 percent reduction—I can't do that." I said, "Guys, you have to do it. I don't think this is a question of 'give me your best shot.' I think this is going to work out very quickly that either you're on the new team or you're not."

A lot of guys resisted or decided this was not the way they wanted to work. So it was pretty clear who was who. Some self-identified. Some quit. Some were fired. But it was pretty clear they were fired because they weren't on board.

The first time I met Frank Cahouet was in July of 1987 at a welcome reception for him. I was there as secretary of the board. (Coincidentally, the next year I was elected to a one-year term to serve as chairman of the American Society of Corporate Secretaries, which was another opportunity to learn about the corporate governance process.) I was also the only current manager there with all the directors.

Even though Cahouet might not have been sure he could trust me right away, he understandably looked to me—as secretary of the board, and the guy who had been guiding Nate Pearson—for assistance. I was in an impactful position. He was going to have to decide whether he wanted to keep me or not, but from day one, he had someone who had the confidence of the board. He needed some help, and he couldn't hire fast enough.

Cahouet said to me almost immediately, "Okay, you're running all these administrative things. I want you to keep doing that. I don't know them, and it's not my priority." So I started out working pretty closely with him. He was about ten years older than I, and a pretty difficult and demanding person, to say the least. That was a first and lasting impression.

Among my responsibilities were community affairs and marketing and PR. Cahouet wouldn't hesitate to call anyone at any time of the day or night, on weekends or holidays—it didn't matter. And it could be over the silliest things. He called me at eight o'clock one night and said, "I just had my picture taken today, and I didn't realize my slacks didn't match my jacket. Can you get those people back and get a different photo?"

He didn't care if people didn't like him; he expected they wouldn't. Understandably. He was firing a lot of people and changing things. He was an outsider.

We needed the change. It had to happen. The regulators were telling us our financial situation was really bad. The real fear was that the $60 million quarterly loss was just the tip of the iceberg. As we came to realize over the next several months, Mellon was probably close to bankruptcy. Because again, if the loans, instead of being worth 90 cents, were only worth 60 cents or 50 cents on the dollar, and you don't have enough capital to cover it, you're technically bankrupt.

The share price obviously got hit when the $60 million loss was reported. The definition of "share price" is the expectation of future earnings. So the worst part of it was that people were trying to guess how bad it was. If you're reporting $60 million in losses and the rumor mill says that number may be higher, the price has got to come down. This was a stock that people and institutions had counted on. It had paid a dividend every quarter for years and years. What was more reliable than Mellon Bank?

Cahouet was intelligent, but he didn't trust people in general. After a while he trusted certain people, but in a limited way. He micromanaged everything. His background was finance, so he was very expense-oriented. He realized the biggest problem he had to deal with was the loan portfolio. So in the fall of 1987, he hired Drexel Burnham, an investment bank, which had a questionable reputation at the time but which was very imaginative and aggressive, and also Lionel Pincus and John Vogelstein from the boutique private equity firm, Warburg Pincus. The theory was that Mellon had to raise capital to fill this hole in the balance sheet from the loan write-downs. And how were we going to do it? If we tried to raise money as Mellon Bank without divesting more bad loans, nobody would give us money because they didn't know how bad the problem was.

The team included Drexel Burnham, Warburg Pincus, our legal department (including Mike Bleier and me), as well as Sullivan & Cromwell and Reed Smith (which supported us with a large team of lawyers led by Tom Todd). We came up with the idea of a good bank/bad bank. The theory was that you'd identify all of the problem loans: If you found any weakness in a loan, you'd call it a problem loan, because you weren't going to get a chance to do this a second time. So we had to be very aggressive. I'm going to say we identified $1 billion worth of problem loans out of several billion.

We would create this bad bank where all of the problem loans would be transferred. We would then sell shares in the bad bank, and the income for the investors would come from the money we recouped collecting a portion of these bad loans. We'd transfer people to the bad bank to collect the loans, and they would be solely focused on collecting them. Part of the theory, which was very perceptive, was that, even though we had a bad loan department at Mellon, they were still part of the bank and we still wanted to keep the client. This is because after they worked out the bad loan, you might decide to do more business with them. But with the bad bank we were solely focused on collecting, and we didn't care about any other relationship with that client. They were done. We had to collect as much money as possible to pay off the debt investors in this new, bad bank.

We named this bad bank Grant Street National Bank. I remember going down and explaining to the regulators what we were doing, because this was a novel, unique concept and needed their approval.

Not many people could raise the capital to cover the transfer of the bad loans from Mellon to Grant Street National Bank. That was the key that a lot of people missed. When you transferred the bad loans out—off of Mellon's balance sheet—they hadn't been completely written off. So you had to write the rest of the loans down, creating a big hole in Mellon's balance sheet.

New capital had to be raised to fill that hole. We did that by offering more stock in the good bank—Mellon Bank. According to our theory, Mellon was the good bank. All the bad loans were gone. All the people who remained at Mellon were focused on new business and taking care of client relationships. The idea was that it was a new beginning for Mellon. And it worked!

The announcement of the Grant Street National Bank plan was in July of 1988. Cahouet had been at Mellon since June of 1987, and in December of that year, he wrote off all sorts of things, which anyone would do. He was essentially saying, "That's gone. That's not my fault." He really got aggressive in writing down assets. So we took an additional loss of $844 million. That's how you know we were close to bankruptcy. That was his new base. Everything that came before was not his fault, and everything that came after, he would get credit for.

The write-offs were accurate, but to an extreme. And again, the impetus—and the correct decision—was to get it done then, because we were not going to be able to go back and do it again. If there was any question about an asset's value, it was written down. There was some judgment to all this. Was it worth 20 cents on the dollar or 25 cents on the dollar? Go for 20. And this wasn't just loans. It could be any other assets—buildings, anything.

That fall also saw the October 1987 market crash, which was scary. It happened when we were in a board meeting. That probably helped in some of the write-downs too. It was a big crash—the Dow fell 22 percent in a day—but it was short-lived. It showed how fragile and precarious the markets were, and that we had to get control of our destiny and dig ourselves out of this hole.

We ended up raising a lot of money for Grant Street National Bank. We sold a lot of bond securities for it; that was the key. What happened over the next year and a half to two years was that Grant Street succeeded in getting rid of all those loans and was able to recover more than what the assets had been written down to. So the securities of Grant Street National Bank appreciated a great deal and investors made a ton of money. The values of those loans turned out to be higher than the bottom prices we thought they could have been.

In turn, Mellon was able to grow and focus, and its stock price went up. So it really worked. It later became a case study at Harvard Business School, and McKinsey and others published major reviews of it. Cahouet drove this effort, and through his constant management of the process, made it happen. It saved Mellon Bank, and he deserves credit for that.

11

SINKING ROOTS
AND MOVING AHEAD

WHEN I STARTED AT MELLON IN JANUARY OF 1981, ANN HAD GOTTEN THE job as head of marketing for Diners Club about six months earlier. She didn't want to just leave them, so she stayed in New York for about the first six months I was in Pittsburgh, which was fine. We didn't have a house yet, and I was taking on a new job in a new city, so I was really working hard.

When Ann got to Pittsburgh we started looking for houses. We looked at different areas around town—Sewickley, Mt. Lebanon, Fox Chapel, and Shadyside—and we started to learn about the city. For example, on a Sunday when the Steelers were playing, people didn't want to be distracted, and they wouldn't let us in to see their house that they wanted to sell. We finally decided on a house on Amberson Avenue in the Shadyside neighborhood. It was a big old house, so we had to stretch our budget a bit. Mellon picked up our house back in Connecticut, which helped, and I got a mortgage at an interest rate of 20 percent.

Ann was also looking for a job. She met Joe Calihan, who ran a company that provided secretarial services downtown. He hired Ann as head of placement, and she got to work trying to place these secretarial graduates in all the local corporations. She was meeting everybody around town. She'd go to EQT Corporation or PNC and ask if they needed secretarial services and then she'd match them up. Ann had been in sales and marketing and was very outgoing and experienced.

Ann and Marty

Tom Todd and Marty

And Pittsburgh, being both a big city and a small town, was very welcoming.

By moving into the middle of the East End of Pittsburgh, we got to know a lot of people very quickly. Tom Todd (a partner at Reed Smith) had been acting general counsel at Mellon prior to my arrival, so he was introducing me around town. I was going to be hiring all these law firms, so of course they were eager to meet me. It was an attractive way to come into Pittsburgh. Tom and his wife Jamee were also helping us get involved socially. They became and continue to be good friends. (Tom went on to manage the Mellon account for Reed Smith, so he and I continued to work together often during my years at Mellon.) We were introduced to the Pittsburgh Golf Club and became members there; later, we also became members at Fox Chapel Golf Club and the Rolling Rock Club in Ligonier, which was started by the Mellons.

This was a very tumultuous era in Pittsburgh. In the early 1980s, Pittsburgh's steel mills were closing, and in 1983, local unemployment reached a staggering 18 percent. Ultimately, the area lost 150,000 manufacturing jobs, as well as ancillary downstream jobs—a regional economic collapse unmatched in American history. Radical labor groups arose in reaction, and the politicians were running on platforms of opening the mills again, which was awful—just pandering to the people and making promises there was no way they could keep.

For Ann and me, though, it was an exciting place to be. We were getting to know a lot of people. My son Patrick would come up and visit. He had gone to Maret School, a private school in Washington, DC, and as I was getting settled in Pittsburgh, Patrick was in college at Franklin & Marshall. He would spend his junior year at the London School of Economics. And on May 15, 1984, our son Christopher was born. Ann and I were very happy in the community.

It was also in the 1980s that the Mellon family started getting out of the bank's stock. Until the troubles the bank had in 1987, a lot of people and organizations kept much of their money in Mellon stock. Having all your eggs in one basket is a cardinal sin of investing. Many of these institutions had seen their endowments go down, and this was the money that supported them. Some were threatening to sue, so I had to go visit a lot of them. I think that was the time that the Mellons started to reduce their holdings, too. By the time I took over, years later, the Mellons had relatively little stock left, which was a shame. They obviously thought there were better investments in the world than Mellon Bank.

Two of the Mellons were on, or represented on, our board— Prosser Mellon and Nate Pearson (representing Paul Mellon)—so they still owned some stock. Paul had worked at Mellon Bank briefly after he got out of Yale, but he moved away from Pittsburgh and seldom returned. He came back when he published his book, *Reflections in a Silver Spoon*. I was with him, along with Frank Cahouet, and we took him around to see his old house near Chatham University. We had lunch with him. He was a classic gentleman, very polite. He carried himself and spoke like a patrician.

I worked with the Mellon family a lot because the Richard King Mellon Foundation was very involved in Pittsburgh. It was the wealthiest of Pittsburgh's many well-endowed foundations, with Drew Mathieson as the senior staff member. Drew was an amazing person, and he was really my mentor and godfather. He became a good friend, and I owe a lot to him. He was also on the board of Mellon Bank, representing the R. K. Mellon Foundation.

Drew called me one day and asked, "Could you come up to Ligonier? We have a meeting of the Foundation board, and I want you to meet a guy named David McCullough."

So I went up by myself and listened to the historian David McCullough, who is so eloquent—the sound of his voice, as well as the words he uses. He told the story of how Pittsburgh is historically one of the greatest places in the world. Pittsburgh was the cradle of American history—from Lewis and Clark through World War II, being the arsenal of democracy. He said it was a shame there wasn't a museum that reflects this history. It's worse than a shame, he said; it was a mortal sin. Something had to be done about it.

It could be that they had asked Frank Cahouet to come up, but he couldn't, so they asked me. I don't really remember. I was, of course, overwhelmed by McCullough, and the story he told was very compelling. The Mellon family and foundation were going to support this idea, so the stars were aligned. To his credit, Cahouet got involved, and many of us at Mellon went out and raised money to build a new museum, which we did. That was the beginning of my long involvement with what ultimately became the Senator John Heinz History Center.

I got to work doing the initial fund-raising. They had a museum in an old building in the Oakland section of Pittsburgh, dating to 1890, but it was really more of a library. The whole theory was that Pittsburgh needed a real museum, something new and closer to downtown. Initially it was just going to be called the History Center Museum. After we'd raised enough money, we actually took over an old icehouse and renovated it.

Later, they asked me to be chair of the board, so I took that on. The first thing we had to do was recruit a new director. They had one, but he was more suited to be the director of a library than a new museum. We recruited Andy Masich. Some were reluctant to hire him because he didn't have a PhD in history. We had several history PhDs on the board, and to some degree, they were looking backward rather than forward to the new center.

We hired Andy (who later earned a history PhD from Carnegie Mellon University), and we got the Heinz family to support the museum. We named it the Senator John Heinz History Center after he was killed in a helicopter accident. The Heinz Endowments has been a terrific supporter, as has the foundation community, including the Mellon family.

Andy has turned out to be an energetic and very successful president of the History Center, which has continued to grow. He has also become a leader in the community and the museum world. I have supported the History Center for years, and the McGuinn Family Gallery there is used for major exhibitions. I stayed on as chair through this inaugural period, which was four or five years. I spent a lot of time on this project, which was important, given that it was a formative period, and I enjoyed it.

Prior to Cahouet's arrival, I'd been on the Carnegie Museums Board, and I also served on the West Penn Hospital Board. I had been chairing the audit committee at West Penn, but after Cahouet's arrival, I started holding meetings at seven a.m., and they weren't real happy about that. (I chose this early time slot so I could get to Cahouet's meetings on time.) Given that Mellon was going through an intense period, I decided I couldn't do West Penn anymore; there was too much happening at the bank.

In 1988, we went through the good bank/bad bank episode, which even today is kind of a famous thing. We had a big team, and I was working harder than I'd ever worked before. As I said earlier, Cahouet led this process and drove it, and he deserves credit for saving the bank.

By 1989, Cahouet and I had a close working relationship, and he depended on me a lot. At that point, as general counsel, I was the equivalent of an executive vice president. There were about ten executive vice presidents, including the heads of the big business departments. I was then formally called the chief administrative officer. I had kept all the duties of marketing, strategic planning, government affairs, and community development, which was fine. I enjoyed it, and I knew the people, knew the government, and knew the community. I wanted more responsibility, and these areas were easy for me to handle as natural extensions of being general counsel—plus, I'd been doing them since I'd worked with Nate Pearson.

In 1989, I was named a vice chairman. At that point Cahouet was CEO and chairman of the board, and there were six vice chairmen. At the same time, Cahouet gave me my first business responsibility.

There was an economic cycle where real estate collapsed. We had a real estate lending department, and it had a lot of bad loans. The theory was that, with my legal background and my desire to take on more responsibility, and Cahouet's willingness to give me more responsibility, this was a good transition. It required a lot of legal knowledge to go into these companies that owed us money and that were having problems. How were we going to work them out? Were we going to restructure the loans or take over some of the collateral?

I was also giving Mike Bleier more responsibility. Until I took over real estate, I was spending about 75 percent of my time directly as general counsel. After taking on real estate, that dropped to 50 percent on general counsel duties, because real estate was a real crisis situation.

Then in 1992, Cahouet gave me responsibility for our mortgage servicing business, which was a huge business at the time—an $80 billion servicing portfolio based in Houston. He also gave me responsibility for cash management, another huge business. Cash management is literally processing cash needs. Corporations are dealing with tons of cash. Berkshire Hathaway, for instance, had something like $250 billion in cash. They invest it, even overnight, because they don't want to leave it sitting there. And with interest rates still high, it was making money. We'd collect their cash for them, invest it, and then draw it down as they made disbursements. We also processed payments, including tax payments and individual tax filings. We gave the IRS immediate credit for the payments, and then we processed the return and got them the return, which they handled. But we handled the cash part.

While the average person on the street wouldn't know what these things were about, they were actually pretty exciting. It was a huge business that involved a very large number of people, which is why we built the new client service center in Downtown Pittsburgh.

The real estate development wasn't that big a business, but it had significant risk and problems. We had to go through everything case by case to see if we could fix the loans or get rid of them. But mortgage servicing and cash management were big businesses [see appendix 1].

With those new responsibilities, I gave up being general counsel in 1991, but I still kind of kept my hand in. Mike Bleier took over, but he still reported to me. Typically if a general counsel didn't report directly to the CEO, he'd probably quit, but that's the way Cahouet wanted it. He trusted me. So I said, "Mike, this is the way it's got to be." If Cahouet had a problem, he'd come to me and then I'd go to Mike.

Having Mike report to me was not totally illogical, but it also showed Cahouet's management style. He found it difficult to trust people, and he rarely embraced them. So I still kind of watched over the legal department, which by then was over 120 lawyers—the captive law firm I'd always wanted to build.

12

TAKING OVER RETAIL BANKING

In 1993, Cahouet gave me responsibility for our retail banking business, which by then was a pretty big business. Starting with our purchase of Girard Bank in 1983, and then with the advent of Interstate Banking in 1985, you could buy banks anywhere.

Most companies grew by buying into big markets or buying incrementally. You didn't want to suddenly buy a bank in San Francisco. What did we know about San Francisco? But why not go in and buy the market leader in New Jersey? Or even down in Maryland? This is what PNC was doing, too, and they were doing it more aggressively because they didn't have these other businesses we had. Their trust department was not nearly as big as ours. At that point, Tom O'Brien was CEO of PNC, and I knew him well.

Investment bankers would come in every day saying, "We represent so-and-so bank. Their chairman is sixty-five and ready to retire. I don't think they have a successor. They're worried about some new bank coming in to compete. They think now is the time to sell." And we'd look at five deals for every one that we did. We would do the due diligence to see if it was a strategic fit or not.

The guy who had been running our retail bank was a good guy and I liked him. But he hated Cahouet, and he didn't hesitate to share that with others, so Cahouet finally fired him.

When I took over the retail bank, I was overseeing probably a third of Mellon employees and about a third of our income. It was a big responsibility, and I loved it. Retail was a huge part of the corporation, and there was nothing wrong with it. It seemed ripe for growth. It had a huge credit card business as well. I thought it was a tremendous opportunity.

What to do with retail branches was a big issue then, and still is today.

One of my college roommates, Jim O'Connor, was president of Ford Motor Company, and they called their dealerships "stores." So I started thinking. I hired McKinsey, the consulting firm. We hired a retail store consultant, too. We went over to Ohio and went to a mall and walked around. Everybody had their doors open except the banks. They were all closed. I asked, "Why is that?" I was the new guy, so I could ask those questions. It didn't make everybody happy, but I loved it. I was having a ball.

So we began to think more like other retailers, keeping our doors open, longer hours, having loan sales, and so forth. I brought together a team of like-minded people who really wanted to make a change and were willing to do it, so we could improve the business. It was intellectually satisfying, challenging, and fun.

John Buckley acted in many ways as a key chief of staff for me; he was smart and creative, energetic, and willing to speak to me honestly.

John Buckley

John continued to work closely with me during my time at Mellon, especially in changing the culture, defining strategy, and in e-commerce.

We started to do a lot of things. We used our technology and developed more marketing expertise, creating numerous measures of customer and store profitability. We redesigned the branches and made them more like stores. We also closed many. We wanted to make the remaining stores more welcoming and change the whole atmosphere. We wanted to get more business—loans, savings accounts, checking accounts. We made a deal with the Giant Eagle supermarket chain to put small branches in their stores that would be open seven days a week, with Saturday and Sunday hours. We really tried to think like a retailer, developing a concept of ourselves as "the retailer of choice."

Next, we started to develop online banking. We knew that younger people didn't go into branches, but older customers still did. One of the big challenges of any business is, when you're trying to manage change, you can't get too far ahead of it or you'll lose the business you already have. By the same token, you can't get too far behind it, or you'll lose new business to other competitors. We really had to try to manage that process.

In addition to developing online products, we also offered postage stamps in our ATM machines. *The Pittsburgh Post-Gazette* criticized us for selling them for more than face value. This was the kind of thing that used to drive me crazy. I said, "It's like a convenience store. Our customers love it." The post office was only open at certain hours, and it may not have been next door. You've got ATMs all over the place, open 24/7. I forget exactly what we charged, but it was something like if the stamps were 25 cents, we charged 2 cents more. We had to cover our costs of buying the machines and servicing them.

Dick Kovacevich at Norwest Bank was doing similar things, and I learned a lot from him. He went on to lead Wells Fargo. We were especially trying to learn from actual retailers, not just from banks, about hours and keeping your doors open, and about training employees.

This was a departure for Mellon, for which the retail branches were a nice—but not a main—part of the business. That's why it was a great opportunity. And Cahouet didn't bother me. He didn't know retail banking and he really did not focus on it. But he supported me, which was very good.

We started doing a lot of things with employees, including special training. I started to make each one of the retail senior management committee members go in and work a day a month in a branch to find out what it was like on the front lines. We had a big telephone bank that we started, and managers had to listen in on calls. I called in, to find out what it was really like to be a customer. As a result, we learned a lot of things.

There were a lot of resisters. We'd been doing it the old way for a long time, and a lot of people thought, "We're fine. We're the biggest bank in town." So I'd say, "You may be now, but you're not going to last unless you change with the times." I thought it was a very innovative approach. I built a very good team who was making it work.

It was running a big business, and it wasn't complicated. I'm a customer, and as a customer, I feel like we all know a bit about marketing. We're marketed all the time, so we have our reactions to people who are marketing to us. Our instincts may not have been right all of the time, and we needed statistics and data to increase our knowledge, but we could hire that support. We were innovating on the most basic part— the customer experience. And this included credit cards and ATMs.

We hired new marketers to change our approach, working on the "retailer of choice" concept. We put signs in the windows—"Loans for sale." It was so obvious, but nobody had ever done it before. "What do you mean, put signs in the windows?" some asked. Well, there was nothing else in the windows anyway, so why not do it?

There used to be lots of jokes about bankers' hours, and branch doors practically being locked for fear someone was going to rob the bank. "Why do banks have ten teller windows and only three tellers on duty?" was a question that was frequently asked. So it was fun to change that, and fortunately, it went pretty well. It was a business that wasn't broken, so we were building on success, which was a nice opportunity.

You judged the success by profits. The name of the game in any business is how do you keep growing and getting bigger? That's why the comparison is always same store sales versus last year's figures, and profits versus the same period last year. Using new technology we at last were able to measure these things.

These retail changes really worked. Mellon had a tradition of investing in technology, and we were able to benefit from any technological advances. I think we got a little ahead, in terms of changing some of the branches and closing some. We also got a little too far ahead in online banking, in terms of profits versus expenses. It was very expensive to set up because of the technology investment. But that's okay; it's easy to slow down. All of this was just starting in 1992 and 1993. I still have a little billboard we had at the time: "Banking 24 hours a day, 7 days a week."

All in all, taking over retail banking was probably the biggest opportunity for me, and the biggest part of my business experience before becoming CEO.

13

MAJOR ACQUISITIONS/ SLOWDOWN OF MOMENTUM

THE EARLY 1990S WAS A TIME OF RECOVERY AND SOME EXPANSION FOR Mellon. In 1991, we bought United Penn Bank of Wilkes-Barre, and in 1992, we purchased the fifty-four branch offices of the Philadelphia Savings Fund Society, the first savings bank in the United States, founded in 1819. To Cahouet's credit, in 1993, we bought the Boston Company from American Express and AFCO Credit from the Continental Corporation. That set the stage the following year for the most high-profile acquisition during Cahouet's tenure: Dreyfus, the mutual fund company.

Dreyfus was a major transaction in the financial services industry. Mutual funds were becoming an increasingly attractive investment alternative from the consumer's point of view, but banks couldn't offer mutual funds, so we were losing a lot of our traditional deposit customers. Things were changing. The idea was to give our customers an alternative to a savings account, to give them choices. Of course, investment securities could go up, but they could also go down, whereas deposits were guaranteed by the FDIC to a certain amount, even if the bank went bankrupt.

Dreyfus was a great brand name, which we never fully developed. We thought we needed mutual funds in order to keep our customers. Dreyfus was a pioneer in the development of money market mutual funds. There was a question, however, about how banks could sell these new financial products if they weren't FDIC-insured. How do you distinguish between insured bank deposits and uninsured mutual funds, and how are customers not going to get confused?

The legislators were skeptical. We were looking to sell securities through the retail branches. But commercial and investment banking had been separated in the 1930s by the Glass-Steagall Act, and legislators were worried that this was going to bring the two back together, complicating things and causing all the same problems that had occurred during the Depression years. Cahouet wanted me to do the presentation, so I had to go down to Washington and testify before the House Banking Committee. It worked out, and the sale went through.

Cahouet did a great job turning Mellon around, as well as with a couple of acquisitions. He was highly intelligent. And in terms of strategy, there was no shortage of ideas being presented. Investment bankers were calling on us almost every day. New ideas and trends were in the *Wall Street Journal* just about every day, so you had to manage the process. The biggest issue in my view was the ability to execute on the ideas. And as an executor—an implementer—Cahouet really was very good, whether as a turnaround artist or getting a couple of the big acquisitions done. He'd work long hours and expect everyone else to do the same. He would say: "You will do it." And he got things done.

But his nature was not that of an organic builder, and as the 1990s progressed, in his last four or five years, we didn't have the turnaround or big acquisitions, so we lost momentum. Even so, Cahouet didn't relent on cost-cutting. He was eventually so disliked in Mellon because of how he treated people and what he did to them. Word of that got out, and he developed a well-known reputation in the industry that greatly reduced his effectiveness. Other banks didn't want to do deals with him. They didn't want to be purchased by Mellon and run by Cahouet.

The Bank of Boston was one. There was an agreement in place, but the CEO there had worked for Cahouet once before, and there was no way in the world he was going to do that again. We were sitting up in Hartford, Connecticut, waiting for their board to approve the deal so we could go in and sign all the documents. The Bank of Boston people literally ran out and sold to somebody else, just because of Cahouet—a very unusual development.

And then in 1997, we put in an almost hostile takeover attempt on the Philadelphia National Bank, and there was no way they were going to be part of an operation run by Cahouet. This is not merely an interpretation by me or by others; it was verbally expressed by the banks in question.

A few examples will illustrate the issue.

When I was running our real estate business, one of the heads of the business had a son graduating as valedictorian from Brown. We were having a management meeting that weekend, and Cahouet said, "I heard that so-and-so isn't coming to the meeting." I said, "Yes, his son's graduating from college." He said, "Well, you should tell him he can't go." I said, "Well, why would I do that?" He said, "Let him know who's boss." I'm quoting him. I'll never forget this. I said, "He knows who's boss. I can't do that. That's just not right." Cahouet held this decision against me for the longest time.

He also reviewed all the salaries of our approximately 7,000 officers. He would spend a couple weekends doing this. He would just go through and reduce their salaries. Some he knew. Some he didn't. I'd say, for my department, "Well, why'd you do that?" And he'd say, "Well, I think that person has had too many raises in the last couple of years." And I'd say, "Well, he or she is the star in that department." I had a budget and we had guidelines (you couldn't give raises of more than 5 percent, etc.), and I'd say, "I'm within all the guidelines." He'd reply, "Yeah, well, that's just the way it is."

This kind of thing got out. It was all about control, and not trusting people. There may have been some cases where it was personal, but it was broader than that.

Cahouet fired the head of our technology department over improper expense reports—ultimately, for buying pizza for his staff. Cahouet was forcing them to work on Saturdays, so this guy was buying pizzas for his people so they would have an incentive to come in and work extra hours. (They weren't getting paid overtime.) Cahouet found out about it because the department head put in an expense reimbursement form for the pizzas, saying it was for lunches with a customer, or something like that. The department head was wrong to do that, but there was room for some kind of human understanding there. And it was pizza—the cost was something like $100.

I could go on and on.

In some cases, it hurt business. When Cahouet had first arrived, we had had all these bad loans. One of them was to Arnold Palmer's automobile businesses on Route 30 in Latrobe. He had several. Auto lending is a very complicated business because you're lending to the dealer, and you take the cars as collateral. The complication is that some cars are going out of collateral because they've been sold and other cars are coming into collateral because the dealer is replenishing inventory. So recordkeeping is very important.

I'm oversimplifying, but apparently what happened was they had a guy running it—Arnold Palmer had nothing to do with it other than his name—and they lost control of the records. It was sloppy bookkeeping at least. We weren't sure what the actual collateral was. It was a bad loan, and we weren't sure if it was going to get repaid.

Because of Palmer's fame, the situation made its way up to Cahouet. He didn't trust anybody from Pittsburgh to handle it, because he thought, "How could anybody deal with Palmer, this god?" He was concerned that no one from Pittsburgh would be an effective negotiator—that no one would be aggressive enough in collecting. So he brought in a guy from California who was a very difficult guy, to say the least, and put him in charge of collecting this loan.

Well, not only did he aggressively pursue the loan, he also annoyed everybody. There's one way of negotiating, where you do it in a diplomatic, constructive way. There's another where you just slam hammers down on people. It's the question of whether you get more with sugar than vinegar. This guy was all vinegar and turned everybody off.

Whether we got paid in full or not, I don't remember. But in the process, we lost Palmer, who went to PNC. He became their spokesperson for the next twenty years. It just broke my heart every time I saw the advertisements on TV, with Arnold Palmer saying, "Bank with PNC— they're my bank."

Cahouet didn't trust people to handle things, and he wanted to do it all his way.

I've given these tangible examples because I don't want it to sound like it's just a subjective opinion. It was very objective, and very widespread. Because he had built up such a negative reputation, things weren't happening during Cahouet's last four or five years. Ultimately, it was weighing on our share price.

When Cahouet took over at Mellon, the stock had a good run because it was so depressed during the crisis. This was followed by the Grant Street Bank transaction and a great bull market. But in the last five years of his tenure, the bank just really wasn't growing. Our growth was questioned because of our inability to make some of the acquisitions.

We were steady, which is good for a public company, but in terms of stock prices, we were flattening. During Cahouet's entire tenure, our stock had a great run, but its price appreciation turned out to be number four of the four trust companies—State Street, Bank of New York, Northern Trust, and Mellon. They were called the trust companies because they had huge trust businesses—wealth management, asset management, and asset servicing. With the stock price being based on the expectation of future profits, it was perceived that we were not going to grow.

I was beginning to wonder, and worry a little. Had we run out of runway on the approach we were taking? It wasn't keeping me up at night, but it was a question. A lot of us were concerned about Cahouet, and thought that perhaps we needed a different approach if we were going to continue to grow. He was sixty-six or sixty-seven, and he didn't want to leave.

So there we were: We were still working hard, but growth had stalled. We'd had no major acquisitions, and all of us were dealing with shrinking budgets and poor morale.

The question was, what to do next?

14

SUCCESSION

IN DECEMBER 1997, WE HAD VERY SERIOUS DISCUSSIONS WITH BANK OF New York about a possible merger. Both sides agreed it might be a good fit, but we were very worried about their culture, which turned out to be worth worrying about in later years. They were extremely expense-conscious. As an example, they weren't investing enough in technology, whereas we were; even though Cahouet was expense-motivated, he wasn't that extreme. Plus, they just really weren't a growing company.

The supposed merger deal was orchestrated by Bank of New York, but Cahouet was very supportive of doing it. I was part of the negotiations and discussion. When it came down to the penultimate draft of the merger agreement, it was made clear, based on the leadership situation, that it wasn't going to be a merger at all. Tom Renyi, the Bank of New York CEO, was going to be the CEO of the combined organization. I was going to be president of half of the combined companies, and one of their fellows was going to be president of the other half. It would have allowed Cahouet to extend his tenure, because he would have been chairman.

As we got into the final stages, the BNY intent became evident. We had a clause that if Renyi got hit by a proverbial bus, then the board would decide his successor. But they insisted that his successor had to come from Bank of New York. We said, "Wait a second. If it's going to be a combined board of directors, they have a fiduciary obligation to the shareholders to choose the best possible candidate wherever that person might come from." No, no; they were adamant. And that broke off the deal. It also revealed to me that they really looked on this as a takeover.

One could argue that there was a lot in favor of the two entities coming together. It would have been pretty powerful in terms of size and scale if we could have agreed on a strategy for growth and so forth. At the time I believed I would have an opportunity to influence that, and probably Cahouet would have for a while, too. Frankly, though, he was driving it, and there wasn't much I could do about it.

The headquarters would be in New York. One time, Cahouet was saying it would be called Bank of New York, and I said, "Well, that's not going to go over well in the Monongahela Valley branches." But he was really committed to doing it, in large part, I think, because it would have extended his tenure. He never wanted to retire. It was only a year and a half later that he was forced into a succession process.

By the end of 1997, succession was starting to enter my mind and becoming more of an issue for those of us who thought we were in the running. It was certainly coming up more in the newspapers. There was an article in the *Wall Street Journal,* and Cahouet was starting to get more questions about it. The newspapers mattered a great deal in those days. Sometimes it could be upsetting if you didn't agree with what was being said, or you might think it was inaccurate. In any case, it heightened the spotlight on the issue and made it more visible to everybody concerned.

The organization and the shareholders and the board also were beginning to think more about succession. I'm not sure the board was aware of some of the details regarding Cahouet's reputation, because he would have put a different spin on it, but they were aware of the broad outlines. I have a letter—an anonymous letter to Drew Mathieson, which he gave to me, which raised serious concerns about Cahouet. He said, "I don't want to show this to Frank. But hold it in case we need it." This may have reinforced Drew to believe, "Okay, Frank. It's time."

The board would have discussed succession in executive sessions. And over time, they would have been discussing more and more the specifics of succession; that's part of their job. From a corporate governance point of view, succession is extremely important for a lot of reasons. It brings fresh insights and fresh blood. It also keeps the company vibrant and growing. If people don't see room to grow at the top, they're going to leave.

I know for a fact that Cahouet finally got pushed out. The board was becoming aware that he was highly unpopular and that this was negatively affecting the bank. He had had a good run, but it was more than time for Frank to go.

So during the January 1998 board meeting, the board decided. The key board members included Drew Mathieson and Nate Pearson. Some directors were more outspoken than others, but those were the two directors representing the Mellon family interests (in addition to Prosser Mellon), and that still held sway; it was declining, but still important.

Nobody ever said anything to me about being considered for CEO, including Drew, although two years earlier, he had recommended me for the board of Gen Re—General Reinsurance Company. At one time the Mellons had a big investment in this company, so he'd been on the board for years. It was a great AAA-rated company and a good experience for me. The fact that he put me on the board and said, "It'll be good for you to get board experience in a public company"—that probably meant something.

Drew and I spent a lot of time traveling back and forth to the Gen Re Stamford headquarters for board meetings. He was just one director on the Mellon board, but an influential one. This may sound trite, but he was someone about whom it would be said, "He had good judgment." And he was well respected. He expressed opinions that were balanced and thoughtful, and his personality was such that he was very likable. He was a very influential person on our board, partly because of his position as a representative of the Mellon family—even though this role was rapidly declining as the family sold their shares.

So I wasn't aware of anything being imminent, but I probably thought it could be, or should be, or both. Still, I didn't know for certain, and this went on for at least a year.

It was very much a competition between Kip Condron and me as to who was going to get the job. Kip had joined Mellon when we purchased the Boston Company. He had lived in Pittsburgh for a couple of years, but he was going back and forth a lot between New York and Boston while at Mellon.

We were friends, but it was a real competition. You want to run a little faster. Be a little more apparent. Be more successful. Make sure your business line was performing as well as it could, with profits increasing. Do whatever you could. You're not going to suck up to people—that could be counterproductive. But you wante to perform. And I think the fact that I was living in Pittsburgh and established in the community was definitely a help. I know that Kip thought this. At that time, Mellon had about 20,000 employees, with 12,000 of them in Western Pennsylvania. So Pittsburgh was definitely the headquarters town.

Someone told me they would be discussing the subject at the January 1998 meeting, but I didn't know they were going to make a decision. I was in my office and the assistant corporate secretary came down and said, "The board meeting's ended. They want you to come into the meeting. You're going to like what they tell you."

That was a pretty big moment. I walked in and they applauded. That was pretty thrilling. I don't remember exactly what was said. It was kind of a blur.

I remember coming back out, and Kip was there. Somehow somebody had kind of told him too. He congratulated me, and we talked about working together and so on and so forth.

I was elected as chairman and CEO. Kip, who had been in charge of investment management and Dreyfus, was appointed president. And Steve Elliott was made senior vice chairman. Steve had been CFO and was an extremely solid person, and I can't say enough good things about him. So it was good to have the board recognize him.

The three of us were appointed that day, and our positions would become effective in February of 1998, but I wouldn't become full CEO until January of 1999, providing for a transition. We became very much a three-person team, and I intentionally fostered that.

With Kip, it was a plus and a minus. It was a plus because it kept him at Mellon for a while longer and recognized his position and contributions. It was a minus because it forced the CEO to deal with someone

Steve Elliott

that maybe he might have dealt with differently for the good of the company. A couple of directors told me privately, "You're probably going to lose Kip." That happens if you get passed over. After about two years—maybe a little longer—he got a job as CEO of Equitable in New York, which was a subsidiary of a French insurance company. It was a very good job, and he was very happy about that, and he made a lot of money.

I was fifty-five. I'd been running businesses in the bank for ten years—big businesses. I hadn't been involved in the trust department or corporate banking or international. But as general counsel, I'd been somewhat involved in everything. Did I learn from mistakes? Of course. And there were successes to learn from, too. It was broad experience, and I felt well prepared for the job.

So I spent a year not just as a rumored heir apparent but as the board's designate. But we had a whole year to go, and that created some problems when it came to dealing with Cahouet.

In April of 1998, a phone call came in from the CEO of Bank of New York. It came to me because, of all things, Cahouet was out playing golf. In those days, he didn't have a cell phone or anything. So

Tom Renyi said to me, "We would like to reignite our talks, but this time we'd like to acquire you." And I said, "Well, no, we're not interested."

There was no way to reach Cahouet, who was still chairman and CEO. I wouldn't become CEO until next January. So I issued a press release: "Mellon Not for Sale." Then Renyi announced a hostile takeover attempt, and we had to fight them off. And we did [see appendix 6].

Cahouet did not react to my press release. First of all, it was at least a good negotiating tactic, no matter what we did. But I wanted the public, our shareholders, and particularly our employees to know that this was not going to happen. There had been rumors about prior discussions, but they had never been made public.

In order to fight them off, you have to hold a shareholder vote. Or you·have to convince the hostile acquirer that they're going to lose so they'll withdraw their takeover attempt. Or you go all the way to the vote and they lose. We went around and spoke with institutional shareholders. We had a very active defense campaign; we persuaded these shareholders that this wasn't in their best interests because the stock price would do better with Mellon on its own than with Bank of New York. That was the essence of the argument.

Our defense against Bank of New York probably took less than two months. It was all-out warfare. I really didn't think the proposed acquisition was in the best interest of our shareholders, because we had gotten to know BNY pretty well in the previous negotiations. It wasn't a fit, culturally or otherwise. BNY finally withdrew its hostile offer because they were convinced they could not win the shareholder vote[see appendix 2].

So for all that time, Kip, Steve Elliott, and I really worked together as team. Sometimes we disagreed on things, but I think we worked well together overall. The three of us were a good combination of different personalities. I was diligent and hardworking, so we weren't going to fly by the seat of our pants. I was very process-oriented in terms of proper corporate governance. By process, I mean you've got to do things in a way that's transparent and honest—and for all the right reasons. I don't mean process in terms of being bureaucratic. And I had a desire to keep us all working together. Steve was a financial expert. Kip's background was investment management. That wasn't my background, so we actually were quite complementary. And Kip and I were both strongly people-oriented. When the three of us went into a meeting, we'd come out with a better result than if any one of us had made decisions on our own. I believed that.

Becoming CEO was obviously a big deal for me. The feeling of accomplishment was very exciting, to say the least. But the feeling of humility followed about three seconds behind. Because then it was, "Wow, I've got this responsibility. I have to make it work."

Personal financial success has never been a driver for me. Not that it isn't important. I always thought more subconsciously than consciously that if you work hard, you'll do well. And if you do well, you're going

Steve Elliott, President NYSE, Marty, Kip Condron

to get paid for it. So to me, that always came with it, but that wasn't the goal in and of itself. The goal was to take on more responsibility, get more satisfaction from your work, do better in your job, and then you will be financially successful. And, I was already somewhat financially successful.

The board wanted to have a contract with the three of us. They asked Cahouet to negotiate the contract. Of course my negotiating position with him was, "Just give me your contract."

Kip had previously worked for Ayco, a big consulting firm. They advise people on their financial lives. So he came to me and said, "Well, I've retained Ayco for the negotiation. And whatever you get, I want almost the same thing." It was very bold on his part, and he wasn't embarrassed by that. I said that I wanted to negotiate as a team, because that's what we were going to be—but Cahouet was going to be negotiating with me.

When I told him that I wanted the same package he had, he replied, "Well, I've been CEO for twelve to fifteen years; you're just starting." Which was true, but I wanted the basic structure, even if the money was less. He got really mad and threw me out of his office. He said, "Are you ready to sign the contract?" I said, "Well, no." He said, "What do you mean, no? That's the contract." And I said, "We have some questions and requests."

He couldn't stand that he was now negotiating with me. It was a little scary.

"You don't want the job?" he said. "I'll go back to the board."

And I said, "Frank, now look: We're dealing with Kip and Steve too, and we all want to do something we think is fair." Blah blah blah.

He had a temper, which he would use strategically. He had once confided this to me. He didn't really lose his temper; rather, he used bluster to his advantage.

Of course I knew him like the back of my hand. At least twice he threw me out of the office. I was going back to Kip and Steve and explaining it to them. And they said, "Hang in there—you're representing us." Kip had certain things he was concerned about regarding his image—getting a plane and the office he wanted. I figured I'd just take Cahouet's office—I wasn't worried about any of that stuff.

Drew called me one time and asked how it was going with Frank.

I said, "Well, it's a little nip and tuck."

He said, "Well, hang in there. The board has to approve the contract."

The point was that Frank wasn't the final word. And it all worked out. We all got very good contracts. That was the way it began.

In the organization, the news of the succession was received well. The board decision was made on a Friday afternoon, so the announcement appeared in the Saturday edition of the *Pittsburgh Post-Gazette*. My picture was on the front page [see appendix 1]. The article said there was a new "affable" CEO at Mellon, and this was going to be a change. Even the newspapers were picking up on this notion that moving from Cahouet to McGuinn, things were going to be different. One newspaper said it was going to be a "kinder and gentler" leadership at Mellon [see appendix 2].

I think people in the organization believed that. But the newspaper line about the change and the affability made me a little uncomfortable, because it was offensive to Cahouet. I wasn't interested in making him angry.

I don't know what the internal betting line had been between Kip and me; clearly it was down to one of us by the end. I'd like to think I was a popular choice. I think it was expected by most, except for the people in Boston or New York, who were more familiar with Kip and may have felt he would be more favorable to them.

On this Saturday night, after it had been in the paper that morning, a group of friends led by Tom Todd all met at somebody's house in the East End and marched about two blocks, yelling and singing, over to my house and knocked on the door. That was a high moment.

15

MY FAMILY

For Ann and me, these were busy years, with the bank, our involvement in the community, and the family. Chris had started at Shady Side Academy, which as it turned out really wasn't right for him. So he went to Kentucky Avenue School in Pittsburgh's East End, which was a school for kids who needed some degree of extra help and encouragement. He was there for several years.

Chris ended up going to Sewickley Academy. Even though it was geographically inconvenient, it was great for him, and there were five or six students around his grade from the East End, with a teacher who led the carpool. Sewickley Academy was academically very sound, but there was much more emphasis on the performing arts, though Sewickley also did well in sports. Chris got into both acting and singing. He actually starred in some of the musicals and really did well there, so it worked out great.

Patrick had been out in the world for some time by then. After college, he taught for a while in the Maryland and Virginia area, and then he went to the University of Virginia to get two master's degrees, one in political science and one in education. Then he got his PhD there as well. His thesis was the federalization of education policy, and he analyzed the process by which the No Child Left Behind legislation was passed. The irony was that it was being pushed by Republicans who were traditionally states' rights advocates, but this was a federal law mandating certain minimum standards. His thesis was a good combination of his political science and education master's degrees, and it was published in hard copy—quite an accomplishment.

Patrick, Ilana, and Chris at Patrick and Ilana's wedding

Patrick went to Brown on a postdoctoral fellowship for a year. Then he went to Colby College, in Maine—way up in the middle of nowhere—and taught there for a year. He then went to Drew University in Madison, New Jersey, where he's been ever since. He became chair of the political science department, and he teaches both political science and education policy. He has been recognized as one of the top teachers in the country in his areas.

Patrick is very independent. He wants to earn his achievements on his own. For example, he wanted to go back to Brown at some point; he really liked it a lot. I tried to intervene on his behalf. I had a friend write a letter, and one of the professors actually called him on it and wasn't very nice about it, which I don't think was fair. But Patrick was very embarrassed and said, "Dad, please don't try to help me unless I ask for it." And he won't ask for it, which is fine. That's his nature. I'd like to help, obviously, and I've helped them all financially. But in terms of getting a job and finding success, Patrick wanted to and has done it on his own.

Patrick has a sabbatical every few years, and he's been to Columbia twice. He also went to the Institute for Advanced Study at Princeton, where Einstein was a faculty member. Patrick is often quoted in the *New York Times* and listed as one of the great education policy scholars. Morristown, nearby, has been a great environment for his wife Ilana and their four daughters. Drew is a nice small institution. He's been able to publish a great deal and has been widely recognized. I'm very proud of him.

Ilana has retinitis pigmentosa, which by definition is a deteriorating disease. She is intelligent and very determined, and if you were with her in her own house you would hardly know she is legally blind. Ilana went to Cornell and then received a master's and PhD in clinical psychology from Yale. She and the Lidsky family are very committed to education. Their four daughters, Bailey, Carigan, Haven, and Payton, are all healthy and do very well in school. Bailey is at the University of Virginia, and Carigan is going to Yale.

After high school, Chris went to Lafayette for college. He did well there, studying political science. After he graduated from Lafayette, Chris went to Washington and got a job as a Bush political appointee to the Department of Labor. After a little more than a year (when Bush finished his term), Chris worked with a start-up company for several years. He then went to work with a contractor for the Department of Homeland Security, supporting the National Infrastructure Advisory Council, which was created after September 11, 2001.

Patrick and Chris

Reflecting the technology leadership of Mellon, I was one of two people from the financial services industry appointed by President George W. Bush to the National Infrastructure Advisory Council. Financial services was one of sixteen critical infrastructure sectors that if disrupted by terrorists or otherwise would cause serious harm

Patrick, Marty, and Chris in September, 2001 when Marty received the American Ireland Fund Leadership Award

120

Chris, Marty, and Patrick at a
Villanova vs. Virginia basketball game

to the nation. This council reported directly to the president. They wanted me to become chairman, but the government bureaucracy was just too much. They identified the problems pretty quickly, but I think there were seventeen different federal security agencies at the time, and they didn't coordinate, or even cooperate. If anything, they probably competed. That was one of our big problems in responding to 9/11. We had some good solutions, but there was no way we were going to be able to practically implement them, so I lost interest.

Ironically, Chris was providing staff support for this agency. Chris is a little different from Patrick. He is willing to accept my help. He

President George W. Bush and Marty

loves politics, but being a political appointee is difficult to sustain and makes it hard to establish a career. He also worked in the Department of Labor during the Trump administration. He was special assistant to the secretary and then policy adviser on the opioid crisis. With Trump losing the 2020 election, he again had to look for another job. He recently became the office manager for a for-profit addiction rehabilitation company.

Chris dated a girl from North Allegheny High School in suburban Pittsburgh for ten years, and then they got married. I'm very proud of Chris. He became an alcoholic and has gone through rehabilitation a couple of times. It's now been about five years that he has been sober, so he's doing great. Unfortunately, he and his wife got divorced. (They didn't have children together.) The irony is that he got help and got sober and came back, anxious to rebuild the marriage, but that's when she decided she didn't want to. This was a huge surprise and disappointment. Five years sober is a very big deal, but every day is a challenge. You're always a recovering alcoholic.

Chris married Kara Lauro in November of 2019, and in September of 2020 they had a daughter named Magnolia ("Maggie"). Kara is very easygoing, with a dry sense of humor. Maggie is a very good baby and has a nice disposition. And she's beautiful! They live in Washington, DC, in a townhouse Chris renovated. They are very happy.

Chris and Kara

16

TAKING THE HELM

GIVEN THAT KIP, STEVE, AND I WERE ALL FORMALLY APPOINTED IN JANUARY of 1998, we spent much of that year planning the future, so that when we officially took over on January 1, 1999, we could hit the ground running. When that day came, we reshuffled management and then on just the second or third day, we announced a name change from Mellon Bank Corporation to Mellon Financial Corporation. We were afraid that somebody else was going to beat us to it.

We wanted to send a signal that things were going to be different now—that Mellon was not a traditional bank, and this was going to lead to many changes. The important part of our strategy was to invest in the faster-growing businesses, such as asset management and asset servicing. At that time, part of what was holding our stock back was that two of the public companies with which we were often compared— State Street and Northern Trust—had no retail branches, and their stock prices were doing better than ours. Not having retail was seen as an advantage because retail was a slower-growing business.

We were considered a hybrid because we still had retail, so we decided on the name change and then recommended it to the board. The board was kind of surprised, as was Cahouet, but they agreed with the change once they understood. I remember running into Tom O'Brien, then CEO of PNC, at the Duquesne Club, and he said, "Oh, you son of a gun—we were thinking of changing our name to a financial company, but you beat us to it!" Much later, they did change to PNC Financial Services Group, Inc.

Prior to my taking over, I had asked Cahouet to sell the mortgage company, because the mortgage company was losing hundreds of millions of dollars. And he said, "Not on my watch." He didn't want to take the loss. That's a quote I'll never forget. We wanted to sell it, but we had to deal with the loss. We decided that the way to cover the loss was to sell the credit card business as well. I had been running it for about ten years, and we'd really turned it around so that it was going strong. But strategically, that was definitely a scale business. Chase and Citigroup together had about 60 percent of the market. We only had 5 percent, and we weren't likely to ever be able to grow it to the kind of scale where we could really compete. So strategically, it made sense to sell it, and because it was doing well, it was attractive and would garner a good price [see appendices 3,4,5].

The irony is that up until that time, I had been on the board of Mastercard USA, and they had just elected me chairman. Nonetheless, selling the credit card business was the right thing to do for Mellon. Ultimately, we sold both the mortgage servicing company and the credit card business, and the respective loss and gain offset financially.

I remember Drew asked me, "Are you going to offend Frank by selling the mortgage services business?" Cahouet had stayed on the board. I said, "Drew, this is the right thing to do." When he and the other board members heard the presentation, they were shocked that we'd lost that much money and they hadn't known about it. It wasn't that Cahouet had been hiding it; it was just lost in the numbers, and he hadn't put a spotlight on it. I said, "We just have to do it." After the presentation, everybody agreed. So we did it.

All of these moves really got us going, and the market liked that because it enabled us to grow faster.

At that point, in the retail market, PNC was very much a competitor, and they were probably growing faster. Overall, we were still bigger—and we were much bigger in asset management and asset servicing—but PNC was acquiring a lot of retail banks. We'd been trying to grow the retail business with potential acquisitions during Cahouet's tenure in Boston and Philadelphia, but we weren't able to complete those acquisitions. PNC had a good acquisition in New Jersey, and we never did get one in New Jersey.

I knew the CEO of PNC, Tom O'Brien, very well. He's a very affable, easygoing guy who had come from Mellon and had been in the Mellon management training program. At that time, PNC was going through a succession process, too, and Jim Rohr was the clear candidate. Rohr was always very competitive with Mellon and jealous of me only insofar as I was at Mellon. He grew up at PNC at a time when Mellon was larger.

I was on the board of the Carnegie Museum of Art—I wasn't chair at the time—and PNC was sponsoring an event there and had invited the board of directors. Rohr wrote me a note saying, "We've invited the board of directors, but I'd really appreciate it if you don't come." Of course, I sent a copy of the letter to everybody at the Carnegie Museums. I know Rohr very well, obviously. I remember one of my directors said, "You know, I have to tell you, if there was somebody I'd want to go out drinking with and be in the locker room with, I'd prefer Rohr." He was always good at telling jokes and a much better speaker than I am. "But," he said, "on strategy, I'm glad I'm with you." And I said, "Okay, I'll take that."

Bill Demchak wasn't brought in until after Rohr was CEO. The investment banks were selling a way of accounting for some bad loans. We had turned them down and said we didn't think the accounting was appropriate. But PNC did it. The regulators came in—and the government and the Justice Department—and entered into a deferred prosecution agreement with PNC. In essence, that means "You're guilty, but we'll put you on probation for a year, and if you're good boys and do some things to improve, then we'll let it lapse and it'll go away." That's when Demchak was brought in, and of course, later, he succeeded Rohr as CEO.

The other big thing that happened in our first year was planning for the year 2000—the so-called Y2K episode. That was one hell of an effort. First of all, it was a shock to everybody that the computers just couldn't adjust to the third decimal—recognizing that 000 comes after 99. We learned that the computers weren't programmed to deal with it, and we weren't sure what would happen.

We had started to realize that almost everything was dependent on computers. People thought everything was going to stop and the world was going to end. As a result, we invested a ton of money and time—again, we were a technology company—in preparing and making all the changes to our software and everything related to it. Every day, we tried to decide, "Did we think of this? Did we think of that?" Preparing for the time change to a new century was a major event and management focus in 1999.

I'll never forget that New Year's Eve. The group of friends we often traveled with was going off to the Galapagos Islands. We were sched-uled to go along, but I said, "Wow, I can't be off swimming with the turtles if the world's going to end." Obviously I didn't go.

On the evening of December 31, 1999, I stayed at our offices, and Chris and Ann came down and we had dinner at the Carlton restaurant, around seven p.m. After dinner I walked around our several buildings, checking everything. Of course at that time, the clocks had started to change, beginning in New

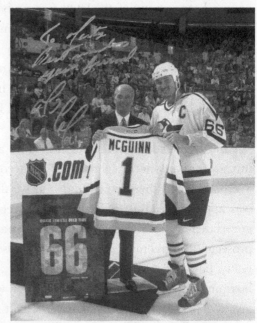

Marty and Mario Lemieux after Mellon purchased naming rights for Mellon Arena, home of the Pittsburgh Penguins

Zealand and rolling across the globe. It was both exciting and amusing. It was going well because everybody had prepared so thoroughly.

Finally, at two a.m., I went home. Nothing had really happened.

That was the end of our first year. We produced record earnings. At the end of 1999, we had $2.7 trillion in assets under management, administration, or custody, including $488 billion under management. We were the leading bank manager of mutual funds. We were off to a good start, and I felt pretty good.

17

CHANGING THE CULTURE

ONE OF THE FIRST THINGS WE DID IN THAT INITIAL YEAR WAS TO ANNOUNCE a program that we called "The Employer of Choice." Morale was really bad in the organization, and I wanted to let the employees know immediately that we intended to change this by investing more in them. (See Appendix 9)

In his first five years, Cahouet, appropriately, had to focus on restructuring the company by laying off employees and cutting expenses. The problem, in my view, is he never gave up doing that. It just turned out to be his nature. Even when the company was growing and doing well, he was still micromanaging, cutting expenses, and reducing staff levels, decreasing their salaries and forcing them to work extra hours, sometimes unnecessarily. He wasn't changing with the times or the situation, and that's why morale was so bad.

I truly believe that you get a lot more with sugar than you do with vinegar. You can only whip and fire people for so long and continue to expect good results. It's one thing in a turnaround situation, but quite another when you're trying to grow, when perhaps the urgency isn't quite as obvious. What we wanted to do was not just say, "We're going to change the culture"—we wanted to make it meaningful, to really become the employer of choice.

I traveled to all of our major offices around the world to conduct what I called a "listening tour." I met with employees to hear their views directly: what was working; what was not working; what we could do better. We used this input to decide on specific actions that would make Mellon the employer of choice.

There were many aspects to the Employer of Choice program. We looked at employee benefits to ensure they were robust. For example, we were one of the first employers to provide domestic partner benefits. And we made changes to the merit increase approval process and to salary increases for promotion. One of the big parts of the program—and I learned this from Dick Kovacevich at Norwest, and later at Wells Fargo—was that we gave every employee stock options. We called the program "Shared Success." This included everybody, all the way down to part-time workers, who got half of what the full-time people got.

This was a major program. I appointed Lisa Peters, who had been chief administrative officer in the legal department and chief risk management and compliance officer in retail banking, to manage the program. She's a very smart, hardworking woman who served as a sort of chief of staff for me along the way. I made her special counsel to the CEO. She was the one who was in charge of getting it done, and we did. (A few years later, I appointed Lisa as head of human resources.)

The overall idea was "You're an owner of the company. Think like an owner. We're going to succeed, and all will succeed together." It was a very simple message. The employees loved it.

Lisa Peters

There were restrictions and time periods before the shares vested. You didn't want them to vest all at once. You wanted long-term incentives—like a golden handcuff. You wanted someone to think, "I've got an investment in this company and I'm not going to give it up and leave." So it was something like, after one year, you were 25 percent vested. After two years, 50 percent vested, and so on. By the time we were able to roll it out, it was June of 1999. It took six months to get all the paperwork done. By June of 2001, some options had vested, and as our stock had been doing well, employees were seeing the benefits of owning Mellon stock.

After September 11, 2001, when the stock market tanked, unfortunately the options were "underwater," and they didn't come back for years. So while the employees got some benefit out of it, regrettably, it was not as much as I had hoped they would. However, it did work in terms of convincing the employees that we really did want to be the employer of choice, and that we were focusing on them.

At the same time, there was another undertaking that was very important. In many ways, I don't like the word 'culture' but in some ways it really is apropos. I was really trying to change the culture and the focus of the organization. Cahouet had always focused on the financials, or what I called the "internal" focus. I wanted to shift the focus to the outside—to our customers.

We started what we called a Customer Focus Initiative. We brought in some consultants and other helpers, and soon we were running projects all over the company, and all over the world, telling people what it meant to be focused on customers. The idea wasalways think about the customer. That was everybody's job, whether they were facing the customer on the front lines or in the back office, providing support to the people who were facing the customers. We trained the business managers and they trained their staffs. Specific action plans were developed, and results and ideas were shared. The senior management committee members had to provide monthly reports on the progress.

It was a big change, especially when you emphasized it. Everybody would say, "Hey, we're always focused on customers." But really, how much? Are you putting resources behind it? Are you walking the talk? To some degree it was different culturally for Pittsburgh, which, unlike many other cities, has never been much of a service-oriented city. In

Pittsburgh, people had traditionally been in the steel business and other primary industries where the customers often came to you.

I wanted to make the focus external, focusing on customers and on employees, because the theory was, if we took care of our employees, they would take care of our customers. And if we took care of our customers, we were going to grow and succeed.

Another thing we did was to have 360-degree peer reviews done by all senior officers. A psychologist then met privately with each senior officer to discuss the review results and help each one find ways to improve. A heavy emphasis was placed on finding ways we could work together as a team.

In the late fall of 1999, we convened our first-ever meeting in Florida of senior officers from around the world. People were meeting in person for the first time and learning more about other businesses, finding ways and sharing ideas for working better together. On the first night we welcomed the Mellon Stars. These were thirty low- to mid-level employees who were selected because they had done something outstanding to serve customers. This tied in with our Customer Focus Initiative and our commitment to being the employer of choice. All the senior officers stood and applauded as they entered the dining room. There wasn't a dry eye in the place. The next day they went with their guests to a nearby resort for a weeklong all-expenses-paid vacation. Then the senior officers started the first of three days of meetings and team-building exercises.

An important part of our effort to change the culture was to identify and reinforce our values. Employees throughout the company met to discuss what makes Mellon different from other companies, and what are the most important values that should drive our everyday actions. We also used surveys extensively to build inclusion and make sure the values rang true. At the conclusion of this process we decided that these shared values were integrity, teamwork, and excellence. We continuously emphasized that these were not abstract concepts but rather inherent values that guided us every day. That this was the way we do business. I believe bringing these values to the forefront helped employees to trust each other, nurtured collegiality, and facilitated teamwork.

An important initiative was LEAP (Lifting Earnings and Performance), a process led by consultants but run by senior officers to increase revenues and/or reduce expenses by $350 million on a sustainable basis. This was a program used by only a few other companies and was customized for Mellon. We recruited some of the best people in each business sector who spent all of their time for several months reviewing the operations of the entire company in an objective and dispassionate way. The goal was accomplished, and LEAP was a big success.

Not an initiative but an important part of my commitment to change the culture was a change in our management style. In all meetings everyone was expected to be constructive and honest. I traveled about 60 percent of my time to our offices around the world and met with all levels of employees, especially junior ones, in order to feel the pulse of the company (we called these meetings "coffee with Marty").

I also met with customers as often as possible, and did so with our sales managers, whom I also got to know. I wanted to hear from customers what we could do better. It was important for me to not just sit in my office but to be with our employees (30,000 at one point) and customers. Travel was critical for a company that aspired to be global and had its business based in so many locations. Asset management, asset servicing, and private wealth management were based in Boston; Dreyfus was based in New York; Treasury Services and retail and corporate banking (and support departments) were based in Pittsburgh; and European and other international businesses were based in London. In fact, we built a large office building in London to combine all of our employees there in one location, not only for efficiency but also to encourage collaboration.

Our executive management group met weekly by video conference and once a month in person, in Pittsburgh. In addition to Kip, Steve, and me, it comprised Dave Lamere, head of private wealth manage-

Princess Anne, who attended the opening of our international
headquarters office in London, and Marty

ment, based in Boston; Ron O'Hanley, head of asset management, based in Boston; and Steve Canter, head of Dreyfus, based in New York City. I believed this was a strong top management group, and the geographic diversity supported our goal to be more global. We also brought together at a meeting at the Pittsburgh headquarters, once every three months, about forty senior managers from around the world to reinforce the corporate culture and discuss common issues.

18

A BOLD MOVE:
SELLING THE RETAIL BANK

NOT LONG AFTER WE TOOK OVER, WE MADE A NUMBER OF SMALL ACQUISI-
tions of asset management companies—money managers, mutual fund
companies, and investment managers. For the next couple of years
those businesses did very well.

Then, in early 2001, carrying through with this notion that we were
a financial services company and not a traditional bank, we decided to
make a big change. We agreed to sell our retail bank branches.

From the beginning, we had tried to send a signal when we changed
the name from Mellon Bank Corporation to Mellon Financial Corporation. We weren't looking to sell the retail bank at that point, but we
were definitely thinking of emphasizing the higher-growth businesses.
Selling the retail branches seemed to be the logical strategic evolution
of this plan. I was the one driving this decision, as I'd run the retail
bank for about six years, but it was a team decision. We talked a lot
about it—Condron, Elliott, and I—and reached a consensus on the
thinking and planning.

The theory behind this decision and how we described it was as
follows: We were narrowing Mellon's strategic focus so that we could
be more of an asset manager and asset servicer, and be in other higher-
growth and higher-return businesses. Of course, we kept the wholesale
bank business for those corporations where we managed their pensions
and had custody of their assets. This meant we would be left with
corporate lending, cash management, all the asset managers, asset
servicing, and the private banking and trust business.

More and more of our retail customers were looking to mutual funds and investments, which is why we had bought Dreyfus. We'd had this tremendous bull market, which appeared to be a trend that was going to continue. Traditional deposits were becoming less valuable. Down the road, we found that more and more people were not using bank branches anymore. They were going online and using ATMs, debit cards, and credit cards. We realized that the retail branches were going to be less and less valuable in the future.

If we wanted to get the share price growth that State Street and Northern Trust were getting, it was the right move. State Street and Northern Trust were pure trust companies, with no retail branches. They were asset managers and asset servicers, too. Because their businesses were faster-growing and had higher returns, their stocks also received a higher price-to-earnings ratio. The traditional retail bank was an anchor in that regard, slowing us down.

In order to find a buyer for the branches, we selectively went to a couple of banks that we thought could afford it, as we had more than five hundred branches at that time.

There are in-market mergers and out-of-market mergers. The benefit of an in-market merger is you close a lot of branches, and cut costs, because there's a lot of overlap and a lot of synergy. There are efficiencies that can be gained, and that can be very compelling. The out-of-market mergers, which are also called market extension mergers, take you into adjacent or new markets. The attraction there is that you go into a new area, and you don't have to go in one branch at a time. You get a branch network and a business that's already established.

In that regard, PNC did well to get National City Bank in Cleveland. They got it for almost nothing, because it was broken. And they also got a major new market with the National City footprint.

We didn't go to PNC for the sale because there would have been antitrust concerns that would have made it impossible. Instead, we went to people we knew were trying to grow their retail business. Citizens

Bank was a retail bank; they didn't have trust or any of these other businesses. We only went to a few possible acquirers.

We had an idea of the price, and we said, "If you're willing to consider it and pay this price, we'll start negotiating." In terms of the price, you look at what other retail banks are being sold for. As with buying a house, there's also an emotional value and a strategic opportunity value. You don't want to miss it—if you do, it could hurt your competitive position. But if you overpay, it could also hurt you. It's like bidding on art at auctions. You have to ask, How much is it really worth? We believed we had a very successful retail franchise and that the sale should fetch a high price.

Meanwhile, we had to keep this decision confidential, which is almost impossible. I used to lecture the lawyers, "You know, everybody has a best friend. You might say you're only going to tell your best friend something, but then they have their best friend. And all of a sudden, you think something's confidential, but as a result of the domino effect, it's not."

We were trying to keep this a secret because if the news broke before we were ready to announce it, it would have all kinds of consequences for customers, employees, and competitors, and we would lose control of the process. Fortunately, we did a pretty good job of maintaining confidentiality.

We started the process in February or March of 2001. In late May, Chuck Corry, the president of US Steel—who was also on our board—came up to me at Laurel Valley Golf Club. He said, "I'd like to talk to you. I'm hearing some rumors that you're talking about selling the branches." I said, "Chuck, I really can't talk about it. You know, we look at a lot of things." I couldn't tell the board yet; there were too many people, and there was nothing specific to tell. Obviously they would have to approve it at some point, so it wasn't going to be as if they were not in control. But we just couldn't bring them something until we were ready to present it. We had to have something concrete for them to approve. I might have said something to the board during the

May board meeting; I can't remember. But if I did, I emphasized how preliminary it was and how confidential it had to remain.

We announced it publicly in a press release in early June, saying we had entered into an agreement, subject to board approval, to sell the retail bank to Citizens Bank, based in Providence, Rhode Island, which was a subsidiary of the Royal Bank of Scotland.

After we announced it, Cahouet (who was no longer on the board) called each one of the directors and told them to vote against it. He didn't tell me; I heard it from the other directors. All I could say to the directors was, "We think it's the right thing to do. We're going to present it to you, we'll answer all your questions, and then the board will vote on it." So that's what happened. The board did vote unanimously at the board meeting late in June to approve it.

The deal closed in December of 2001. Along with the retail branches, we also sold small business lending, which is mostly done through the branches. Small business includes restaurants and other businesses with 250 or fewer employees. They depend on the branches; that's where they do their banking. It's a nice business and it goes with the branch network, in that it's complementary and couldn't be divorced from the branches. We also sold middle market lending, which could have been divorced from the branches. Middle market serves businesses between $200 million and $500 million in revenue, roughly. Overall, it was a fairly big package, and we received almost $2 billion from the sale, which in those days was a lot of money.

This was a big change. Mellon had been in the retail business since the 1940s, and it was a big community brand. People in the community don't know our corporate bankers; retail is what's known on the street. So it was a bold move, to say the least.

One of the things we did with the sale was cut our dividend. This was very unpopular with a lot of people, particularly in the Pittsburgh area, who invested in Mellon stock and were like "coupon clippers." They counted on that dividend.

The reason we had to cut the dividend was because if you're in higher-growth, higher-return businesses, those businesses pay lower dividends so that you can invest more in the businesses. The dividend reduction made our payout similar to State Street and Northern Trust. But I want to tell you, the widows and orphans, they didn't think about that. They were used to getting a bigger dividend every quarter, and suddenly, they got less. This started when the deal closed.

Mellon had always increased the dividend—had been paying a dividend forever, in fact—so this was a very emotionally unpopular but necessary part of the deal, and part of the strategy to create more growth. It went with everything else. I remember some good friends of mine saying, "Oh my God, what did you do? You really made a terrible decision." I said, "What do you mean?" They said, "You cut the dividend." I responded, "We didn't just cut the dividend. We got rid of the slow-growth businesses and we're going to be adding more fast-growth businesses and get higher returns and stock prices over time."

Believe me, especially when it comes to money, emotions rule. The Frick and other museums had invested in Mellon, and they were really dependent on the dividend. This dependency, combined with the old Pittsburgh mentality of not liking things to change much, meant there was some resistance. Mellon was the gold standard—what do you mean by changing that?

Even though most of our shareholders were institutional, I'm sure that a high percentage of our individual investors were from Western Pennsylvania. You never want to say it, but the individual shareholders are not nearly as important as the institutional shareholders. The institutional investors, first of all, own a majority of the shares. Second, when they do things, they announce it and can have a much greater collateral impact. They write analyst reports and explain what they're doing, and it goes public.

We knew we'd take some lumps on the dividend, and we did, but not more than expected. I probably could have explained it better. The move was also unpopular in Pittsburgh because we had all these branches and employees, and they were, in effect, being sold; this meant all of the branch employees and all of the support staff—thousands of people. So it had a lot of emotional repercussions. We were cutting a lot of expenses and revenues, as well.

But we were getting paid $2 billion. The premium was about 17 percent, which was one of the highest in banking industry history for similar transactions. And, importantly, we insisted that the sales contract required Citizens Bank to retain all employees. We were betting that our stock price would now grow faster, which would more than offset the dividend reduction [see appendices 6, 7.]

19

TRYING TIMES

DURING THE FIRST TWO AND A HALF YEARS AFTER OUR TEAM HAD TAKEN over, we changed the culture and created the Employer of Choice program and the Customer Focus Initiative. Strategically, we sold the mortgage business, which had been losing hundreds of millions of dollars, and packaged it with the credit card business, which was never going to be significant. We made some strategic purchases and sold the retail business, bringing in about $2 billion.

The moves were designed to improve morale, make us more customer-oriented, and to best position the company for future—and faster—growth. We felt the pieces were in place for a very successful future, and our share price in the 40s reflected that.

Sometimes, however, despite your best efforts, events occur over which you have little or no control but which affect your fortunes nonetheless, and, in this case, the fortunes of the company. Sometimes luck, good or bad, plays a role.

The markets were an example of that. My predecessor Frank Cahouet was CEO during what had been until that point the biggest economic expansion in US history and one of the greatest bull markets of all time. From 1988 to 1998, the S&P 500 had a huge average annual increase of 16.5 percent. It was an unprecedented string of big up years.

My tenure started on an up note, with the S&P 500 rising 19.5 percent in 1999. But that was followed by declines in the next three years of 10.1 percent, 13.0 percent, and 23.4 percent. The years 2003 and

2004 were up years, followed by another down year in 2005. So during my seven years, the S&P 500 went up an average of only 1.6 percent a year—significantly below the historical average of about 10 percent a year, and one-tenth of the unparalleled increases during Cahouet's time.

Another example of something that perhaps can't be called bad luck, but couldn't have been foreseen—and certainly was disastrous—occurred in late April of 2001.

Our cash management business handled all kinds of payments, including Publisher's Clearinghouse, which used to have those ads where they'd present the big check, and all kinds of other payments. Mellon also processed individual federal income tax returns for most of the eastern United States. It was a huge business, and very profitable.

This was one of the reasons we had built a new client service center on Ross Street in Pittsburgh to handle that work. It was state-of-the-art, with all sorts of advanced machines and equipment there. This place was totally automated. The joke I used to tell was that the factory of the future would have one person and a dog. The dog would be there to make sure nobody touched the equipment, and the man would be there to feed the dog.

In this new facility, machines opened envelopes and took the checks out, and in the case of the IRS, which was our client, we gave the government instant credit, rather than waiting for the checks to clear. Money flow is very important in all of these businesses, and if you got credit for your money today, instead of waiting seven days, you'd have seven extra days of earnings. If you multiplied that by millions of dollars, that was big money.

The IRS came in and helped us design the layout and the equipment, so they had a lot of input. We had all kinds of backup plans and redundancies, in case the technology shut down, or if there was a power failure—anything you could think of. It was a factory, essentially, and it ran 24/7.

So one day hundreds of thousands of individual income tax returns came in. The April 29 deadline for processing the returns was looming, and the people on the night shift thought they were behind and would never finish processing that day's returns by the end of the shift. It turned out they weren't behind, even though they thought they were. The backup plan said to call for extra help, which was in place and available. But they didn't. Instead, they panicked, and they attempted to hide the tax returns out on a ramp. Later, the refuse collector came along and picked up the returns and sent them off to be shredded. So 77,000 returns were destroyed!

When I was called, it was a huge shock. My first reaction was, "You gotta be kidding me!" We had to first tell the government, and they weren't happy, to say the least. I went down to Washington, hat in hand, to see the head of the IRS tax filing business. It wasn't a good meeting. He was pissed. I tried to explain. "I don't want explanations," he said. "Don't give me excuses." I said, "I'm not making excuses. We accept responsibility, but I want you to know how it happened." He cut me off: "I don't care. You're terrible." And on and on. All those tax returns and refunds were now delayed, and everyone in the government was afraid they were going to be criticized.

We had to make a public announcement, and the US Attorney's Office got involved because we were talking about destruction of federal property. Soon, it got out of hand. We wanted to explain what happened and state that we would be responsible, but the government told us, "You cannot make any explanations." What about freedom of speech? No, no, not when you're dealing with the government, which has great discretion in prosecutorial decisions. It was a real catch-22: We wanted the true story to get out, but we didn't want to offend the government. So we just announced the fact of the destruction of the tax returns, but nothing to explain how it happened.

In the next few days, headlines like "Bank Destroys Tax Returns" were running all over the world. Everyone was thinking, "What a lousy bank they are." Can you imagine? And the prosecuting attorneys were saying, "Those terrible banks—are we sure they didn't do it purposely? I'm elected by the people, and I'm going to make sure there wasn't any malfeasance." Taking on a big bank can help the career of someone who aspires to be a politician. It was just one of the worst things I've ever been involved with in my life.

We said we would hold the government harmless, which we had to do, of course. We also said that for all the taxpayers involved, we would cover any additional costs. The government said the taxpayers wouldn't be penalized. So nobody was hurt in this thing except us, both financially and in terms of reputation. And we were hurt big-time in both. I'd call it a huge black eye, but it was worse than that. It was a disaster—even though it wasn't the fault of the management; it was just eight employees who panicked and went off the ranch. We had a brand-new, state-of-the-art building with all of these plans in place to handle the business and staff it, including all of the backup. To then have a freak incident—which was an avoidable series of events that ended in the shredding of tax returns—well, this was a terrible part of my tenure.

Obviously we fired the employees involved, and the eight who were specifically responsible were prosecuted by the government. In retrospect, the only thing that perhaps I should have done differently was to penalize or fire those in the chain of command who were supervising the employees who panicked. Cahouet probably would have fired half the company, and in retrospect, he may have been more correct than I. I guess it would have better demonstrated that there was accountability. I and several other senior officers had our bonuses reduced, but I didn't take the responsibility down through the chain of command because I really didn't think it was their fault. It was just such a quirky event. Can you imagine putting things aside and having someone come by and put them in the trash and shred them? What's the likelihood of this combination of events? It was just crazy.

The government didn't ultimately settle with us until after I had retired. We paid about $25 million in costs and fines, but it was a lot more expensive than that in terms of the damage done to our reputation.

When the terrorist attacks occurred on September 11, 2001, we had a lot of employees in New York City. Most of our offices were in the Met Life (formerly Pan Am) building on 42nd Street and Park Avenue, right over Grand Central Station. A lot of our people witnessed one of the planes literally fly by their windows. Since they were in one of the tall, iconic buildings in the city, they were understandably worried about how many more planes there might be. We also had Flight 93 crash close to Pittsburgh, so we had to close all of our offices. People were even calling from California, asking, "Can we close?"

My first reaction was, "Why close everything?" Then I realized it was purely emotional, and that sometimes, you just can't fight it. They weren't rational discussions, so you couldn't be rational. We basically closed everything and, like everybody else, tried to figure out what the hell was going on.

The markets fell 14 percent after the 9/11 attacks, continuing a downward trend that had begun when the speculative dot-com bubble had burst in late 2000. The decline in stocks was a grinding and continuing process that lasted for a couple of years and became one of the worst equity markets since the Great Depression.

This was a problem for us, because this was our business now—asset management and the complementary asset servicing, which involved all the back-office functions—the reports to investors about transactions, stock prices, and how their accounts were doing. It was a big business, but the market decline did two things.

First, it hurt our business. In most of our asset management business, we got paid by the value of the account, getting a percentage of that account value for each quarter and year. And so to the extent that this value declined, by definition we were paid less revenues and profits. The negative impact on our profits went on for several years.

And second, the market decline was also impacting our stock price.

The last big challenge of 2001 was that, after the closing of the sale of the retail branches, near the end of the year we had to try and figure out ways to minimize the taxes on the $2 billion gain. The only way to do so was to find another business and reinvest in it. It's like when you sell your house—if you reinvest within a year, you don't have to pay certain taxes. It's not precisely analogous, but similar.

We looked for another business to invest in—an asset manager or servicing company that would grow—but we just couldn't find the right one. We didn't want to make a bad acquisition; that would have been worse than no investment at all. There's a saying in business: Some of the best deals are the ones you don't do. I don't know that 9/11 really mattered, but maybe there might have been more opportunities had it not happened. In any case, not finding the right fit was a huge disappointment. We had this big bundle of cash, and of the $2 billion, a significant portion went to taxes, and we returned a lot of it to shareholders, in stock buybacks.

The next year, in 2002, we finally found what we thought was the right investment. The timing was not good, because we had missed the opportunity to minimize taxes, but we bought a human resources outsourcing business from PWC.

We thought it fit our strategy. It wasn't asset servicing, but a similar processing business. We were a technology company. We thought this fit the strategy because, for example, we already ran a large part of the human resources business for American Express. So with a lot of our large corporate customers, this would be another way of reinforcing our relationships with them. We were managing their pensions and lending them money; now we'd be managing their human resources and back-office processing, as well. We were already doing a lot of back-office processing—with shareholder servicing, handling payments of dividends and stock transfers, and the large cash management business.

So we bought the human resources outsourcing business, and I think we did a good job with our due diligence. It was a broken business, which we knew. We thought we could fix it, but the problem was, we never found the right managers. We ran three or four managers through there. This became a drag for us, and it hurt our earnings. We weren't getting the growth there that we'd hoped for, and the analysts thought it was hurting our stock price, too.

With the stagnant market during these years, consumers were slowing their investments in stocks. The irony was that bank deposits, which we had predicted would be less attractive, actually became more attractive over the short term of the next few years. Long-term, the strategy of selling retail was right, but the market downturn delayed the benefits. We were ahead of the trend, which turned out to be bad timing [see appendices 8, 9, 10].

20

CIVIC AND ECONOMIC
LEADERSHIP ROLES

DURING MY YEARS AS CEO, I REFUSED TO GO ON OTHER FOR-PROFIT boards, which frankly was a mistake. I didn't do it because I figured, number one, that my obligation to my day job was all-consuming. And, number two, I felt that in the community and the industry, it was important to play a leadership role. I thought that was important not just for me, but also for the company, given our reputation and position.

In 2002, I became chairman of the Allegheny Conference on Community Development, Western Pennsylvania's public/private civic leadership group. I had been on the executive committee, and when I was asked to take over the chairmanship, I agreed. I figured it was my turn, so to speak. I enjoyed it. I was on the board for seven years, and served as chair for the last three of those years. [see appendix 11]

On my watch, three major things happened.

The first was that we combined all the supporting organizations. There used to be the Allegheny Conference, the Pittsburgh Regional Alliance, the Chamber of Commerce, and the Pennsylvania Economy League. We thought there was too much inefficiency in raising money for these groups separately, as well as in operating them, so we made the Allegheny Conference the parent company—the umbrella company— and the other three, separate subsidiaries. They still existed and each had a head, but we only had one CEO.

Rick Stafford was the last head of the Allegheny Conference when it was a separate organization. Previously, the Conference had been very much a think tank, producing research papers and offering advice.

When we combined these various groups, we decided that we wanted to have someone in as the CEO who was not an economist, a professor, or a researcher. I chaired the search committee, and we ultimately hired Mike Langley for that role. He had a lot of energy and he was a real CEO, out there trying to get things done. Then, after my term, when Jim Rohr came in, he brought in Dennis Yablonsky from Harrisburg.

The second thing we did was form the Regional Investors Council. We went out and recruited all of these small and midsized companies to expand the Conference and get wider input, calling them "shareholders." (Previously, only large corporations and organizations were involved.) Each member of the Regional Investors Council had to contribute $1,000 each year, and we met a couple times a year. We kept them abreast of what was going on and sought their input. We also tried to make the board more diverse by bringing in Bill Strickland and the heads of the smaller colleges. This was the only way we were going to get diversity; we weren't going to get it soon enough from the large corporations and their CEOs.

The third and biggest thing we did was come up with plans and proposals to help Pittsburgh, and then lobby for those proposals in Harrisburg. The city was going bankrupt at the time, and we spent a lot of time trying to come up with solutions. What a lesson in practical politics!

One of our proposals was to get a non-resident wage tax for Pittsburgh, one of the few large cities that didn't have one at the time. If you go to New York or Philadelphia and you work in the city, you pay a non-resident wage tax. We knew that a large tax wouldn't fly because people coming into the city from outside were already paying a $10 occupational privilege tax. In many other cities, they'd be paying thousands of dollars, so we suggested raising the privilege tax to several hundred dollars.

There were only two ways to help the city: We had to cut expenses and raise revenues. It's not that complicated. Those were the only two levers we had. We had all kinds of ideas to cut expenses and to raise revenues, and this proposal was the main one. We thought, "Raising the occupational privilege tax from ten dollars to several hundred—nobody's even going to complain about such a small increase to help save the city." Piece of cake, right?

We went to Harrisburg, and it was the Republicans who said, "Well, that's a tax increase." Well, yes, but a relatively small one—and by the way, the city's going bankrupt. Pittsburgh needed money, and where were you going to get it? The politicians said, "Oh no, the next time I run, they'll just say that I raised taxes." We told them, "Well, you can explain it—you can say that you helped save the city."

No, they wouldn't do it. They hated Tom Murphy, who was Pittsburgh's mayor at the time. "Oh, we're not helping out Murphy," they said. And we replied, "This isn't Murphy—it's the city." Murphy had been in the legislature previously. He was kind of a nice guy, but somewhat impractical and naive.

Then Elsie Hillman, a prominent Republican and the wife of Pittsburgh billionaire Henry Hillman, wanted to get involved. She approached the former head of US Steel, David Roderick, and they formed a special commission. They basically came up with the same proposal we did. I didn't join the commission. We'd already put forth our ideas; we didn't need to do it again.

So the politicians finally worked something out. I think they took the privilege tax from $10 to $52 (a dollar a week!). And of course, the city is still a mess financially.

In my view Pittsburgh has a lot of momentum now because of things like the Pittsburgh Promise (which provides scholarships to students graduating from city high schools), shale gas, technology companies, the universities, and health care. There are a lot of positives. But underneath, we still have all the infrastructure problems, and we have the staggering pension problems, which are almost criminal. Those aren't going away. My view is you have to take the current momentum and, while you have it, try and solve some of those other problems.

The Allegheny Conference spent a lot of time on the city's problems, and I think we played a constructive role. But the final decisions had to be made by the politicians, and they never really solved the issues. They lacked the will to make tough decisions—like raising taxes. They all kick the can down the road and keep running for reelection. It was disappointing to see how the process really worked, and how the politicians were unwilling to rise above their own self-interests. I understand human nature and politics, but why not act in a way that would be good for the community and one's fellow citizens? The attitudes are just entrenched.

Being CEO of Mellon obviously was a major responsibility, and it was humbling in a lot of ways. Clearly the first responsibility of a CEO is to customers, shareholders, and employees, but there's at least a tradition, if not an obligation, to be involved in the community. This was especially true at Mellon, where it was sort of expected. I wanted to try and help make a difference.

Similarly, I wanted to help in our industry if I could.

One of the unusual aspects of our business was that a lot of our customers were other banks and financial institutions. We had custody of their pension assets. We did their back-office work because they weren't in that business. That's why the annual World Economic Conference at Davos, Switzerland, was such a big thing for me. I could go there and meet with more customers in four days than I could in two weeks of traveling around the world. It was an interesting part of our customer base that many people didn't think about.

In 2004, I became chairman of the Financial Services Roundtable, which is basically a trade association and lobbying group for the one hundred largest financial institutions in the United States. I led this group for a one-year term. It used to be that there were two groups—one for bankers, and one for insurance and investment bankers. We really were one financial services industry, so we decided we'd have more leverage if we could pool our resources. That's how we became one entity. I spent a lot of time lobbying for our industry in this role.

At the same time, I also served a three-year term on the Federal Reserve Advisory Board, representing the Federal Reserve Bank of Cleveland (which included Pittsburgh). The Federal Reserve Board in Washington, DC, is like the parent company, and there are twelve subsidiary banks. Each of these banks regulates the banks within their respective district, and that's where many of the bank regulators come from. Each district has one representative on the Federal Reserve Advisory Board. For a three-year term, I was the representative from the Cleveland district.

We had four meetings a year, and we had to prepare for them. The Fed would give us four or five questions. What are you seeing in the markets? Is loan demand increasing or decreasing? They would ask us about interest rates. They would also ask us to add questions, too, so we eventually came up with a total of about ten questions, which we'd answer. The twelve of us on the advisory board all got our economics departments, regulatory lawyers, and legislative affairs people to work on these questions, and we did a lot of research and work. Then we would meet in Washington. The first day, each district would get to comment on the various answers to the questions, and then we would make revisions and come up with consensus positions. The various districts sometimes would see things differently. Our job was to represent the country in a composite, aggregate way.

The next day, all twelve of us would go and meet with the Federal Reserve Board of Governors. Alan Greenspan was then the chair. He was like the Buddha. Everyone would be sitting there—even the other governors—and he would walk in. Only then could we start the meeting! One of the representatives from one of the districts would present a question and the response, and we would have a discussion about it. We advised the Fed on various issues from the perspective of what was going on in the field—from out in the hinterlands, the real world. So this experience was really interesting. I became the president of the Federal Reserve Advisory Board in my last year [see appendix 12].

To Marty —
Best wishes Alan

Alan Greenspan and Marty

The night before the meeting, we'd have a dinner, and the Comp-troller of the Currency or the head of the US Securities and Exchange Commission would come and speak to us. Or maybe Greenspan would come. With Greenspan, it was a little bit like he had a direct line to God. I have an autographed picture of him in my office. He's very inscrutable. He looks at you and you don't know what he's thinking—or whether his mind is someplace else. He didn't make much small talk, but when he spoke, he was the oracle—an amazing and interesting person to be with.

Greenspan is getting up there in years now, like Henry Kissinger. I met Kissinger once. I have a picture of us sitting next to each other at lunch at the Eisenhower Foundation. When I first came on the foundation board, he was on the board. As the new guy, I was seated next to him at lunch. He's in the same category as Greenspan. He didn't say much, and he didn't listen much, either.

I also served on the board of Carnegie Mellon University for seven years, which was fascinating especially in view of its growing stature.

These were experiences that were not part of being CEO of Mellon Bank but were a consequence of that position. They were integral in many ways because they weren't honorary positions. They were real positions, whether it was lobbying and representing our industry before Congress and regulators and trying to get changes in legislation (with some wins and losses), or working with the Federal Reserve, contributing to the understanding of the economic circumstances of the country and therefore the setting of economic policy, or helping to oversee one of the country's preeminent universities.

21

THE BEGINNING OF THE END

IN 2001 AND THE FOLLOWING FEW YEARS, WE EXPERIENCED THE CONFLUENCE of events I mentioned earlier: The IRS fiasco was a black mark. And after 9/11, there was a lousy stock market, the worst since the Depression. We had sold the retail bank, and because of the stock market collapse, bank deposits became a little more valuable. So while selling the retail bank was clearly the right decision long-term, in the shorter term, it was not the best timing.

In addition, we had invested in the human resources consulting business, which fit our strategic focus on back-office processing and served a lot of the same corporate customers. But in the meantime, IBM and EDS had gotten into the market, so the competitive environment had changed drastically. And, we had trouble getting the right managers in place, and we weren't executing as well as we should have—for which I have to take responsibility. In late 2004, we'd started to try to sell the human resources consulting business because it was a drag on earnings, and that sale closed in May of 2005.

Until that sale closed, from 2001 through 2005 there weren't a whole lot of positive things happening. There wasn't a single negative event that could have been foreseen or was entirely our fault; it was just a continuation of a period of market malaise. (We were proud that, among the four trust banks, Mellon stock performance during the period was the second best.) A lot of it was timing, but it was still a problem. That's the way of the world.

Cahouet had stayed on the board after he retired. It had been a tradition that when the chair retired, the chair would go off the board. It's pretty much standard everywhere, with few exceptions. For instance, if someone new comes in, they'll keep the chairman on for a year to help with the transition, but it typically only happens if there's a special circumstance. Cahouet didn't want to leave, period, and he was trying to hang on however he could. He had built an office for after he retired, with steps coming down to our floor below, and he told us he was going to come down each day and check on us—literally.

His staying on the board did have a kind of chilling effect. As I mentioned, even Drew Mathieson said, "You're going to sell these businesses? Isn't that a slap in the face to Frank?" And I said, "Well, no. It's not intended as that, but it's necessary because . . ." And after hearing my reasons, he said, "Well, okay, you've got to do it."

To give Cahouet credit, at the board meetings he usually went along with the things we presented, but after about a year and a half, it was just getting awkward for us. We would go in to make a presentation, saying, "We want to make these changes . . . ," but we couldn't really get into all the facts. It wasn't a question of blaming someone; it was simply that times had changed after Cahouet's twelve years as CEO, or that maybe in hindsight, the earlier decision wasn't the right one. We had to give the board the rationale for selling these businesses so they would approve it, which meant that ultimately, it became more and more awkward with Cahouet on the board.

It's a tough business moving people off the board. You can get rid of a board member, but it's risky. It's like the old saying: If you're going to shoot the king, you had better not miss. I had a problem with one director who was a vociferous voice against me—a lawyer from Los Angeles. Cahouet had brought him in because he had represented Dreyfus. He was a pompous ass. He pleaded with the other board members and told them how important it was to him, to stay on the board, so he stayed. He did leave the board eventually, and finally, Cahouet also departed.

Cahouet was upset with me for selling the retail bank and other perceived slights, and we weren't talking. I think it came up one time that he wanted to use the plane for personal reasons, and I said, "No, you really shouldn't do that." We were ignoring each other, at least. The directors knew he wanted to stay on so he could keep his influence, and the board recognized the problem. Finally the chair of the nominating committee, Jay Connolly (the president of Heinz, and a good guy), said to me, "Look, you don't need to do anything. We understand it's gotten a little tense and it's inappropriate. And we're going to say to him that it's time to retire." And he went to Cahouet and said, "It's really time to step aside." And so that's what happened.

The big thing was that Cahouet had called the directors to vote against the sale of the retail business. But then afterwards, with the change in the markets, he was saying, "See, I was right. And now you've got to get rid of McGuinn." This was his way of getting back at me. And I believe that's what started to happen.

Cahouet had a history in that regard. He had been at Security Pacific in Los Angeles, and then he went to Crocker Bank in San Francisco. He had a real reputation for being mean and, if somebody slighted him, for getting back at them.

At the same time, we began to get some criticism from a few analysts and investors. All they cared about was Mellon's stock price. One activist investor was Highfields Capital Management. They came in early 2005 and purchased 1.5 percent of the stock, which is a lot of stock. They were trying to put pressure on us. This kind of thing goes on all the time. Activist investors come in and try and make a quick buck and get out. They've got ideas on how to bump the stock, but that's what it usually is—a bump in the share price, not a long-term increase.

Highfields's proposed solution was to get rid of the asset servicing business so Mellon would just be a pure-play asset manager. Prior to that, I'd had discussions with Merrill Lynch about buying their asset management business, and the CEO had come out to talk with me. He was willing to sell asset management, but he wanted to keep a piece of it. In a way, that was a compliment to us—he wanted to keep a 30 percent ownership because he had confidence in us. Someone reported that it fell apart because there was an argument over who would run it. That wasn't true. They wanted to sell control of the asset management business because it wasn't their primary business; their main focus was brokerage and investment banking. Merrill would later sell it to another company.

I wasn't happy about the idea of Merrill keeping a piece of it, but the real stumbling block was that they wanted us to get out of the asset servicing business. I said no—they went together. We'll buy your asset management but we won't get rid of asset servicing. So it fell through. This never got beyond a discussion between the two of us—but it was a serious discussion.

The pressure was building to do something—specifically, to get rid of asset servicing. Highfields bought at $30 a share and they wanted it to go up to $40. So they started coming in and being very public about the idea that we should break up the company. They wanted us to sell off asset servicing and be a pure-play asset manager, and we said, "No, they're complementary businesses with a lot of the same customers. Asset servicing supports asset managers. We disagree."

I'm not sure Highfields was really convinced that selling the asset servicing business would be a better long-term strategy. A lot of these people—particularly Highfields—would be in and out of the stock in six months. They're investment guys who are in it for the quick buck. There's nothing wrong with it; that's what they do. They're not in for twenty years. Everybody knows it. It's just a different game.

By the end of 2005, Mellon stock was up 29 percent after we sold the human resources business in May. Highfields got out. I wrote them a letter and said, "You've owned the stock for six months, and it's up 29 percent—what's your complaint?" [see appendix 13]

But more pressure was building to do something, and that brought more attention to the fact that our stock had been languishing for a couple of years.

And then the California Public Employees' Retirement System (CalPERS) came in and started complaining about management and the fact that the stock price wasn't doing well. It turned out that their real complaint was about our anti-takeover provisions.

These provisions had been in place for fifteen years. As general counsel, I put them in place with Cahouet because we were trying to deter hostile takeovers. They're called "anti-takeover," but even in Pennsylvania law, they're actually called shareholder protections, and it's not just a euphemism. None of these protections prevent a take-over—the board can always vote for it—but what they do is allow the board to consider the offer and decide whether they can get a better offer or negotiate to get a higher price. So they truly are shareholder protection provisions. Nonetheless, a lot of shareholder activists don't like them, and they call them anti-takeover and bad corporate governance. They think it keeps the share price from getting a premium because it reduces the possibility of a takeover and the ensuing premium by dissuading suitors.

We went out to Sacramento to meet with CalPERS. They were such pompous, arrogant people. We were supposed to meet with the head of their investment division, but she didn't show up. We had this whole presentation to show all the facts, because we knew they hadn't done their homework. They just thought they could get a little publicity and show that they were trying to protect their pensioners and everyone else.

We made our presentation, after which they didn't do anything. It was like, "Don't tell me the facts. My mind's made up." But their questions get publicity, too. So we said we were willing to consider changing the anti-takeover provisions.

By the June 2005 board meeting in Miami, I had been CEO for six and a half years. At that board meeting, Robert Mehrabian, who was on the board's human resources committee, suggested it was time to start considering finding my successor. He said, "Well, you know, you're sixty-three. It takes a year and a half to find a CEO. And by the time we find one, you'll be sixty-five." I said, "Well, I don't really think that's true. It takes six months." He said he was in the process of doing the same thing with his company (where he would stay on for another ten years!).

I didn't want to resist a corporate succession process, which was good corporate practice, so I said, "Well, I think we have some candidates from within. But I agree that we should look outside, too." We had what I thought were a couple of very viable candidates inside the company, but the board agreed that any search should be as broad as possible.

The board felt that we should hire a president and chief operating officer. They said that it would take at least a year to get him or her, and then that person would be groomed to succeed me—and that it would provide for a good transition. On that basis, it was very hard for me to argue against it. I wasn't aware of it then, but another agenda by several directors was beginning to play out.

At that point, after six and a half years of my being CEO, it was time to accelerate the planning. You always have succession plans. One is if the CEO gets killed by the proverbial bus; you always have a plan where someone could take over immediately in that situation. The second plan was that, in the normal course of events, I would serve until I was sixty-five. I was all in favor of succession planning. In fact, we were already doing it.

We began the process of talking with recruiting firms, and spoke with two of them. One said, "Well, you can't go to someone and say it's going to be a year and a half and maybe you'll be the CEO. If you can't guarantee it, we don't think that's the right approach. We think you should wait." Another firm said they'd do whatever the board wanted, and this is the firm they hired.

So the recruiting process began. As part of the process, I brought in a couple of people I knew in the business and had them interview with the directors. I ultimately agreed they weren't the right people for the job, but that's why you interview and do research.

At that point, board member Wes von Schack, who was chair of the human resources committee, had been saying, "Why don't we sell the company?" for at least a year. He would raise this point during our annual off-site strategic retreat meetings, where we spent three days focusing on long-term strategy. At the June 2005 meeting, he raised this question again, at the same time the human resources committee was suggesting we needed to start a search for a president and COO who would succeed me.

I made a trip to New York City to meet with von Schack, one-on-one.

I said, "Wes, this is not productive. It's distracting to people. People wonder if you have some other agenda, or if there's something you know that they don't." As I told him at the meetings, it really wasn't a viable strategy to sell the company. That's giving up—throwing in the towel and saying, "The future of the company with our present strategy is not good. We'll make more money for shareholders by selling it and getting out of the business." I said, "We can always do that. I don't think it's the best course of action. But before you get to that conclusion, you have to go through all the other possible strategies and have a very thought-through, rational conclusion that we'll sell out."

He seemed to accept this, but while I was there—it was just the two of us at the University Club—he said to me, "Well, you know Cahouet had a lot of really good candidates to succeed him, including you. But you don't have any good candidates to succeed you." I didn't think of it at the time, but Cahouet had stayed on longer—he was sixty-six or sixty-seven. I was sixty-three. I should have said, "Come to me when I'm a little older and I'll have more candidates." I didn't say that because I wasn't quick enough, but it was absolutely an explicit criticism of me.

I told him to give me a little more time. In fact, I did have good candidates. My top candidate was Ron O'Hanley, who's now CEO of State Street. He was a vice chairman of Mellon and head of our asset management business, and there were others, including Steve Elliott, the senior vice chairman.

Von Schack had been CEO of Duquesne Light but had left Pittsburgh to become head of another company. The same was true of Mehrabian; he had been president of Carnegie Mellon University before he went to California to become CEO of Teledyne. Von Schack had actually been a good friend of mine. He lived out in Quogue in the summer. We were roughly the same age. I knew him from around town, and we got together socially out on Long Island. I think he was a big help in having me selected as CEO. But somewhere along the way, we ceased being friends. I believe that Cahouet and Mehrabian got to him and turned him.

After the two recruiters came in, made their presentations at a meeting, and then left, Wes started to say, "Well, maybe we should delay this. Maybe they're right—that you can't go out and hire a president and wait a year and a half to see if they'll become CEO without a guarantee. And how are you going to give a guarantee to someone who's brand-new?"

Immediately, Mehrabian stood up and said, "Oh no, that's fine— this can work." It was almost as if he was saying, "Hey, Wes, you're off script. Let me get you back on course."

After he said it could work, everyone else said okay, and they kept to the plan.

In the second, third, and fourth quarters of 2005, we beat Wall Street expectations, and had excellent earnings. In November of 2005, we had the annual meeting of senior management from all over the world, which was a big success because we had so much momentum and everyone was feeling good about our progress. We'd gotten rid of the albatross, the human resources business, in May. The stock was up 29 percent from May/June until the end of January. Things were going great. Really great. We were either number one or number two among the four trust banks in stock performance. We had built Mellon during my tenure to make it an industry leader in our businesses: We had $4.7 trillion in assets under management, administration, or custody, including $781 billion in assets under management). And in 2005, we were *Fortune* magazine's Most Admired Company in our category [see appendix 14].

At that point, we had made some big sales, but I really wanted to make a big acquisition. The purpose of a company over time is to grow. Acquisitions and mergers are an important way companies grow. It's all part of the process of an active, hopefully growing corporation.

So in the fall of 2005, one of the things I was doing was talking with Blackrock and Larry Fink, because they were largely an asset management company. They had an interesting part of their business process—an analytic tool for managing risk. It was a little different, but it would have been a good fit with our processing business. And Fink was intrigued by the idea of merging. He would have become the CEO, and I would have stayed around as chairman for a year or so. We had quite a few meetings with Blackrock and with investment bankers in the fall of 2005.

Blackrock was located in New York, and I told Fink that Pittsburgh would have to be the co-headquarters, and he'd have to spend a day a week, or at least a significant amount of time, in Pittsburgh. We were good friends. I admired him, and thought it would be great to combine companies. This wasn't a charade by any means. Blackrock is now the largest asset management company in the world. And in my eyes, we would become a better company together. He was a proven, successful leader who could satisfy our succession needs.

I brought it to our board and met with them, but they were a little skeptical. Why would he want to do that? I think for some of them, it was against their secret agenda.

22

FORCED OUT

WITHOUT MY KNOWLEDGE, ALTHOUGH I HAD SOME SUSPICION, THERE WAS a cabal on the board, and Cahouet was driving it. It was composed of Cahouet, von Schack, and Ruth Bruch, the CIO of Lucent, all of whom were also on the board of Teledyne, led by Mehrabian. I believe their aim was to get me out and to sell Mellon to the Bank of New York.

In November of 2005, I got a call from Rodgin Cohen, the lawyer from Sullivan & Cromwell who was a close friend and adviser, and who frequently represented Mellon. He was very attuned to the industry and was the dean of all bank lawyers.

Rodge said to me, "I'm hearing in the marketplace that the recruiters are telling the people they're interviewing that they want someone to come in and be CEO immediately." And I said, "That's not what the board has said." He said, "Well, I'm just letting you know."

So I called von Schack. What I should have done is call the recruiters, but I called my directors instead. Von Schack said, "I'll call you back." He called back with Mehrabian on the phone and I told them what I was hearing. "Oh no," they said. "That's definitely not true. Absolutely not."

Why would they deny that this is what they were doing? Because I could have started to lobby the board and could have done a lot to fight it. Instead, I accepted their word.

At that point, the human resources committee was made up of several people, including John Surma, the CEO of US Steel; Mark Nordenberg, the chancellor of the University of Pittsburgh; Mehrabian;

Ruth Bruch; and Ted Kelly, who was CEO of Liberty Mutual Insurance from Boston. I don't think Surma and Nordenberg were pushing it. The human resources committee was driving the search process. The rest of the directors may not have known what was going on, but why they went along with this charade, especially later, is still beyond me. I've spoken with a couple of them since then, and one of them said, "Well, I thought we had to defer to the human resources committee." I told him that all of the directors shared the same fiduciary obligation.

That fall of 2005, articles started appearing in the *Pittsburgh Tribune-Review*, the city's secondary, conservative newspaper owned by Richard Mellon Scaife. Starting in November 2005, the *Tribune-Review* was writing these articles every week, with headlines like "McGuinn Should Go." They said I was going to sell the bank. They said I lived in New York. As I said earlier, we did have analysts saying we should restructure the company, but the bad press on me personally from the *Tribune-Review* just muddied the waters [see appendix 15].

Literally once a week Scaife was publishing these articles. (I'd be going down to the Duquesne Club and someone would ask, "What's going on?" People knew Dick Scaife was odd, but his articles were part of an apparent campaign to stir things up, and I think that was their purpose. Scaife had gone after Jim Rohr at PNC another time, and Rohr and his board just waited him out until he finally went away.

At that time, our board meetings were becoming fractious. Some people were saying we should speed up the succession process. Some said we should not. We should do this. We should do that. Candidates were coming in, and one of them was Bob Kelly, who ultimately became CEO. He was one of the candidates that I had recommended, and although I liked him, I said, "You talked about getting someone with operating experience. This guy's been the chief financial officer. He doesn't have any operating experience. What are we talking about here? Let's be honest with ourselves."

I got another call from Rodge Cohen saying that several board members were pushing this agenda of speeding up the hiring process.

At that point, alarms started to go off for me. They should have been exploding by now, but I was still trying to run the bank and believed what the board was officially telling me. You can call it naiveté or stupidity, at least in retrospect. In fact, Ira Gumberg, a director who was held in high regard by other directors, had told me to focus on being chief executive of Mellon and he would take care of managing the directors.

So after the call from Rodge, I did something that was used against me as a big mistake, and maybe it was, but I didn't think so at the time. I went to the chair of the nominating and governance committee, a fellow named Jim Orr, who was sort of acting as the lead director, and I said, "I think we should replace von Schack as head of the human resources committee." This in itself isn't that bad, because the CEO usually does make such recommendations. Someone had alerted von Schack in advance. He went and got a lawyer—to this day I don't know who it was. And they came back and said that what I was recommending was illegal, which it clearly was not. It may have been bad politics, but it wasn't illegal.

So Jim Orr had me meet with von Schack in my office the next day. Orr said, "Hey, look, the board's all upset. We don't think we should go ahead with replacing him. You two make up." We agreed to put it aside. I said, "Wes, I hope you're being honest with me." And he said he was. This was at the time of the January 2006 board meeting.

After the board meeting, later in January, I went off to Davos, which I'd been doing every year since I was CEO. This was my seventh year. For me, it was all work, and it was good work. The conference was held at a ski resort—but I don't ski—and it's filled with business meetings. I got there on a Wednesday, and that Friday night, I was attending a dinner hosted by one of our biggest clients. I got a telephone call and a message saying to call the office immediately.

I excused myself and called. Orr and von Schack were on the phone. They said that the board had voted unanimously to hire Bob

Kelly, and at his insistence, they had made him CEO immediately. They said I had to be out in two weeks.

Holy cow! I was shocked. I had heard what they'd said and knew it was a fact, but I couldn't comprehend it. At that point, I felt I'd been betrayed—stabbed in the back. How could the other directors go along with it? I was hurt, but that doesn't seem strong enough. I was also angry. I felt it was grossly unfair.

I went back and finished dinner.

I called Kelly (whom I knew) the next day and congratulated him. I said I'd do anything I could to help him, to make the transition a smooth one. We agreed to have dinner in a couple of days.

I flew back the next day and pulled together the key team—Steve Elliott, Carl Krasik, Lisa Peters—and told them we had to make an announcement.

My team was disappointed and felt sorry for me and wanted to help with the transition. But the other thing you could see happening right away was "The king is dead—long live the king." Although this is natural, it was a little disappointing. My own secretary had my stuff packed within days and was trying to position herself to become the secretary for the new CEO.

Another irony is that one of the reasons I could be replaced so quickly was that the company was doing well and we had a good management team in place, enabling them to bring someone in from the outside.

Kelly had been at Wachovia in Charlotte. The plan, and what they had earlier agreed to, was to hire a president and COO. At the last minute, two board members told the board that Kelly wouldn't take the job unless he became CEO right away, so the board agreed to change its plan. What the board members didn't know was that they were not being told the truth.

When I went out to dinner with Kelly, he told me up front, "I just want you to know, I did not ask to be CEO. I was told to say that." Rodge Cohen supported this statement later. I don't think the rest of the directors knew that. I think a couple of board members were manipulating the process, and this was the final part of their planned coup, guided by Cahouet [see appendix 16].

23

POSTMORTEM

I WAS SHELL-SHOCKED DURING MY LAST TWO WEEKS AT MELLON, WHICH I spent cleaning out my office and wrapping things up. The day it was announced that I was leaving, the stock actually went down a point or two, which is minor, but still made me feel good. It may not have even been related, but I took some pleasure in that.

One thing they had actually said to me during the phone call was, "We'll honor your contract." I had a contract, which was good. It wasn't something I would have thought of, but Cahouet had had a contract, so Condron, Elliott, and I each had one, as well. My contract did not end until a year and a half later. They made it sound magnanimous, which wasn't the case at all. It was a contract. I wasn't being fired for cause. They said they'd honor it. Well, big deal. I didn't have to worry about money or anything else. Everything was guaranteed. Plus, I had a good retirement package. Financially, I was treated very well and would never complain about that.

Beyond that, though, I truly felt that I'd been stabbed in the back. And it really hurt. At the time, it was very emotional. Mellon was doing very well, including the stock price. In fact, Mellon's total return to shareholders from January 1, 1999, when I became CEO, until January 27, 2006, the day before my departure was announced, was 23.7 percent. This compares to the increase in the S&P 500 of 16.4 percent. And there was a lot of momentum. Here I was, a guy who'd been at the bank for twenty-five years, and they told me to get out in two weeks! The chairman and CEO? Was there no dignity or fairness?

Even if some of the directors had wanted to be mean and do what they did, why did the other directors go along? That's the part I still can't fathom to this day. One of the directors apparently said, "Well, look, there's been all this disruption and commotion raised by some shareholders , all this noise—and we've got someone who's good, and we have to move on in a year or a year and a half anyway, so why don't we just move on now?"

What really added to the hurt was the idea that outsiders and even employees might think there was something wrong with the bank. Had there been some fraud committed? Was I a bad person who'd done something illegal or immoral? My reputation was damaged, to say the least. My reputation in the industry had been very strong, and when I was fired, people probably thought, "There must be more that we don't know. Obviously, it's bad. If it were good, he wouldn't have been fired."

In retrospect, should I have been better prepared for what happened? Should I have managed the board better? The answer is "yes." I wasn't paying enough attention to the board, and, as I mentioned, one of the reasons was that Ira Gumberg was telling me to focus on running the bank. He would take care of the directors.

The ultimate board meeting where they decided to fire me was at the urging of four directors in late January 2006.

This effort was driven by Cahouet. He wanted to get rid of me partly for revenge—and I think the others went along—but I think in the larger scheme of things, they wanted to get rid of me so they could sell the bank. Mellon was just beginning to gain momentum when the board initiated the search process in June 2005. One director had been raising the idea of selling the bank in our strategic planning meetings since 2004. He had been starting to write me down in some of the appraisals, saying the bank wasn't doing as well as it should. Another was challenging me on things. They were becoming antagonistic and coming up with excuses for acting the way they did.

At the time, I was thinking that things had been tough, but now they were getting better. After the sale of the human resources business in June of 2005, our profits were strong and our stock price had gone up significantly.

It was not obvious to me until later, but what was really driving this was that Cahouet saw an opportunity. I think he held a grudge against me because I had sold the retail bank, and he perceived that I had pushed him off the board. Cahouet enlisted a new ally, Dick Scaife, to join the others in an effort to move me out. I never made the connection between Cahouet and Scaife in 2005 because I thought they were enemies. But I guess they found a common enemy in me, which brought them together.

I have no way of proving this, but I think the origins of this effort started a few years earlier, in connection with my wife, Ann.

Ann and I were very involved and visible in the Pittsburgh community, always in the newspaper's society column and getting awards because of my involvement in the bank. Ann was on the symphony board, among others. I do think our involvement in the community, both separately and together, was very positive for a bank that was very visible—especially when we had a retail bank. It was almost like branding or marketing. In that sense, and socially, I would say Ann was very helpful to me in getting my job. And on the job, she continued to be helpful. She is a gregarious and innately intelligent person.

In June of 2002, Pittsburgh mayor Tom Murphy and Allegheny County executive Jim Roddey asked Ann to chair the opening event for the Pittsburgh Convention Center. Before the September 2003 event, The *Pittsburgh Post-Gazette* and others were running articles saying the economy was terrible and the event should be postponed or canceled. Why should public money be spent on it?

The event was held and the media was not allowed to attend, so naturally there were negative stories to come. The newspaper articles continued into the following year, asking for an accounting of the $500,000 in public money that was spent on the gala.

I didn't realize it at the time, but the biggest thing that was to become a problem was that the event was going to recognize certain founding families in Pittsburgh, such as the Mellons, the Heinzes, the Hillmans, and others. A representative of each of these families was invited to come and receive an award at the opening event on behalf of the family.

For the Mellons, Prosser Mellon was chosen. Dick Scaife apparently was furious. I'm convinced that this is how he and Cahouet got together. They had hated each other, but now they had a common enemy—me.

So Cahouet was going to get me for selling the retail bank, and Scaife was going to get me for being the husband of Ann McGuinn, who he thought had publicly disgraced him by not recognizing his stature in the community and place in his family.

How they initially got together, I don't know, but something catalyzed it and now they had a common cause. I know they met that fall of 2005 several times. Someone told me, "Oh, Cahouet was coming up each Friday to meet with Scaife." And that's when these diatribes against me began in The *Tribune-Review.*

Ultimately, it was a confluence of many events. Analysts were saying the stock price should be doing better and that we should break up the company, and that maybe this wasn't the right management to do it because they were going to be defensive. CalPERS was saying, "Break up the company and get rid of some of the shareholder protections." And then the *Tribune-Review* was coming out with weekly attacks.

I think a few directors on the board had a separate agenda, so ultimately, it wasn't a question of whether our strategy was right or wrong. It was a question of what Cahouet told them: "You've got to get rid of McGuinn." When they started the search in June 2005, they were committed. Even though the quarter before and the following two were record quarters, and our stock price was going up, they didn't back off and say, "Maybe we were wrong—look at the facts."

I left on February 6, 2006, and when the first-quarter earnings came out in April for the period ending March 31, they were at a record high. When I ran into Jerry Cohon, who was then the president of

Carnegie Mellon University and a Mellon board member, he purposely came up to me and said, "Marty, I know these are your earnings."

Of course they were. Kelly couldn't do anything in his first six or eight weeks, and they had to take a $20 million hit because they had to extrapolate and account for all of my retirement benefits and what they had to pay me over my lifetime. This was no "golden parachute:" these payments were required under my contract. Even with that hit, they had record earnings.

Almost all of the directors called me at some point, and I had lunch with some of them. Some have apologized to me and tried to explain or rationalize their decision to replace me, saying things like, "Well, we weren't really in favor it. We didn't push it, but it was kind of decided by the directors on the human resources committee, and we just felt it was better for the sake of calming down the company." I would start making arguments to refute this, but it was water over the dam. I still wonder how they could be that unfeeling—that unfair. I still see many of them today, but I've stopped talking to them about it. What am I going to do?

The other thing is remembering that the community got a lot of its information from the *Tribune-Review*. One of the things that's always bothered me is that people think if they're reading it in the newspaper, it must be true. Scaife's paper was saying that I didn't live in Pittsburgh, that I lived in New York.

The irony is, I'm still in Pittsburgh. I did have a co-op apartment in New York, which I used on business for Mellon because I used to go to New York every week or two. I'd stay in my own apartment and save the company money. It was only four blocks from the Met Life building, so I could walk to our office there. At one time, I thought I'd retire to New York, but that was before I realized how nice it is in Florida. I still have a residence in Pittsburgh, where I have many friends and remain active in the community.

24

STEPPING BACK

AFTER I WAS FORCED OUT AT MELLON, THE FIRST THING I SAID TO MYSELF was, "I've got to step back." I didn't want to just go out and look for another job. I didn't want to look for boards to join or anything else. I wanted to take a few months off, which I basically did.

We had a group that we traveled with a lot, and Ann and I decided to take a trip. It was organized by Jean Anne Hattler, who was in charge of the travel program at Duquesne University. Her late husband Brack Hattler had become one of my best friends. He was not only a great heart-lung transplant surgeon but also a great philosopher. He would give me books and we'd talk about stuff. He was such a smart, thoughtful, understated, low-ego person. This group was going on a safari to Africa, and I called up and said, "I know it's only a couple weeks from now, but could we come along?" So we did.

It was an eighteen-day trip to Africa with a lot of good friends. We started in South Africa, went down to Cape Town, which is just a fabulous place, and then we went to the wine country and the Cape of Good Hope. We went on a safari at Kruger National Park, which was great, and then we went off from the group for three or four days to Singita Lodge, which at the time was rated the top resort company in the world. It was really pretty comfortable. This was not camping out under the stars. We were in these beautiful huts with great food and wines, and then you went out during the days and at night, too.

I expected to see animals in Africa, obviously, but what surprised me were the stars. Even in those days, one of our friends had an app on his phone that showed the stars. We'd go out at night, and with there being no ambient light, the sky was just so clear. It was a whole new hemisphere and set of stars.

Then we spent seven days in Namibia—I think three might have been enough. It's a lot of hilly desert, where you can actually do a lot of climbing, but there's just not as much to see and do. Then we came across southern Africa to Victoria Falls. It was a fascinating trip.

The traveling helped with my transition. I was really trying to forget about what had happened, or at least not think about it all the time. For a long while it was very hard for me to forget the shock and betrayal, the bitterness and disappointment. I couldn't stop thinking, "This can't be true" and "Why?" Part of my intention during this time was to distract myself by having something to do that was enjoyable, that would help me move on. Being busy and doing things with friends helped.

When I got back, it was the end of March 2006. The summer began in late May. It only took me three or four months to realize that I didn't want to just fall off a cliff and do nothing. I thought, "How can I find something to do that I enjoy?"

I was looking forward to no longer going 120 miles an hour. But I didn't want to just park. I was looking forward to going 60 miles an hour. My advice to people when they retire, hopefully more voluntarily than I did, is that they make it some kind of gradual transition rather than a sudden dead stop.

I realized I didn't want a full-time job, but thought I would enjoy going on some boards and maybe even working with an investment bank. I thought I'd better start doing some networking before people forgot about me. And I did. I called and met with lots of people. I had one offer of a job with an investment bank, and I got very far down the path, and then they said, "We have this office for you." And I said, "Whoa, wait a second. I don't want an office." I realized they were expecting me to do a lot more than I really wanted to do.

I'd been chairman of the Financial Services Roundtable, so I knew all the CEOs of those companies. The head of Chubb called me up and asked if I'd consider going on their board. I'd been offered several other boards that I had turned down for different reasons. But when Chubb called, I said, "Absolutely."

There are personal and practical things that affect those decisions. For instance, I didn't want to go to some place in Maine or some place in Louisiana for board meetings. I wanted to go to New York City or London. I also wanted to be on a board that had other directors I'd be interested in working with, ones I thought I could work with. I wanted to be involved in a business that had a good management team and had a bright future. All of those things were important to me, and Chubb fit the bill. It had a great brand name. I always thought the personal casualty business was a lousy business, but they had made it work.

I had previously been on the board of the General Reinsurance Corporation, so I knew a little about it. And I had a high regard for Chubb's CEO, John Finnegan. I met with their nominating committee, which interviewed me. It was interesting. It was chaired by a guy who was a professor at Harvard Business School and also on the board of State Street. I really liked him a lot. He was smart as could be. When there were difficult tasks at hand, he would take care of them because he was so diplomatic, and such a nice person. He said to me, "I have to ask you this question: We know you were forced out of your job. Do you want to tell us about that?"

It was a fair question. I was forced out. He wanted to know if there was something hidden here. Why would I be forced out at a moment's notice?

I told him the story—as much as I knew about it then. And he said, "Fine, we appreciate that," and they brought me on the Chubb board.

Then he said, "I have to tell you that at State Street, you were at the top of our succession list." I guess that had been the case for the previous couple of years, before I was forced out. This was another irony, and of course it made me feel good.

Among the four trust banks, we were all known to one another, but this was especially true at State Street. Very early in my tenure at Mellon,

I had gone to State Street and suggested a merger between the two of us. We got pretty far along in the process, and I was going to be the CEO of the merged company. We were down to naming people who were going to be on the combined leadership team. Their board, which was highly parochial, pulled the rug out from under their CEO and forced him out, bringing somebody else in instead of doing a merger with Mellon.

With so-called palace intrigues, there's usually an explanation that can be understood. But in my case, I think some people must have been wondering. Nobody came up to me and said, "What did you do?" I was getting close to retirement anyway, so I think a lot of them just figured, "Well, he got a successor who wanted to take over, so he did." There are all kinds of variations of this kind of corporate politics ; I'm not the only one who's been hurt or stabbed in the back.

Afterward, I got tons of letters, and people mostly treated me very nicely. Most people had bought the story that I was living in New York. They wanted to let me know, "Oh, we're going to miss you." One of the reasons I wanted to continue to be more visible in Pittsburgh with my community work was so that people would know it was a lie that I was living in New York.

It's been fifteen years now since my departure from Mellon—a long time. And it's interesting. I thought there would be times in my con- tinuing nonprofit work when, if I disagreed with somebody, they would say, "Well, what the hell do you know? You were fired." I thought I'd get more of that. I frankly haven't, which has been a pleasant surprise. Whether I was advocating for something or asking for money on behalf of an organization, I was concerned that someone might say, "Well, you just don't have any credibility." That hasn't happened, which has made me feel good. It was a fear I had, especially because the whole thing was never explained.

The fact that I stayed around in Pittsburgh and that the bank was sold just months after I left Mellon.—along with the fact that I had fought the Bank of New York's hostile takeover attempt years earlier—I think all of this helped to overcome a lot of that concern.

25

THE SALE OF MELLON

THREE OR FOUR MONTHS AFTER THE MELLON BOARD REMOVED ME IN January of 2006, it was in negotiations to sell the company to the Bank of New York. The sale was announced on December 4, 2006 (it took all of that time to negotiate the details).

Steve Elliott called me the day before the announcement, as a courtesy. The boards had approved it and signed the documents. The name was going to be Bank of New York Mellon. They'd use the name BNY Mellon as a way of doing business. The headquarters would be in New York, and Bob Kelly would be the CEO.

I was surprised but not shocked, as Bank of New York had been pursuing Mellon literally for decades.

Bob Kelly came in February from Wachovia in Charlotte, where he had been chief financial officer. While he'd never been a CEO, nor an operating guy, running businesses, he was very talented. To his credit, he'd been named CFO of the year at least twice. Wachovia had done a lot of mergers and acquisitions, and he had managed those activities.

So-called social issues are the big things in mergers, and usually the biggest social issue is who the CEO is going to be. Others include the location of the headquarters and the name of the company. Almost always, those are the things that are determinative. However, the board has to approve everything; they have to be very careful with their fiduciary duties, making sure they're not letting the social issues outweigh the financial matters that will benefit the shareholders.

Usually, the CEOs initiate the discussions. Very rarely would the board recommend or initiate any kind of merger; that's considered a management prerogative.

I assume the merger negotiations were initiated by the Bank of New York. With my being gone, they had a new opportunity. And Tom Renyi, who was the CEO of BNY, was approaching sixty-five, so it was a classic time for him to do a merger.

I surmise that Renyi called Kelly in March or April. When this started, Kelly hadn't yet moved into the house he'd bought in the Pittsburgh suburb of Sewickley. Renyi probably said, "We really should talk. We line up against each other well. The economies of scale are important. I'm going to retire—you can be CEO."

At the surface level, there was an obvious fit. They were two of the four trust companies. We had sold our retail bank back in 2001, and they had sold theirs in 2005, so they were kind of following our strategy, if you will. I'm guessing that the initial discussions between Kelly and Renyi went on for at least a month. After a month of such discussions, including the social issues, the two CEOs were probably saying, "This looks interesting. It looks like it's a good thing to do. Let's start getting our directors involved."

Everything had to be put into a proxy for a shareholder vote; I remember reading it. The board had designated, I'm sure at Kelly's request, that von Schack would be the lead director, and the active director in the negotiations. We hadn't previously had a formal lead director. We had one director who was the chair of the nominating and governance committee who kind of acted as the lead director.

In truth, I wasn't convinced that we needed a lead director. The lead director is involved in various corporate governance issues. A related question was whether you separate the chairman from the CEO. Part of the theory was that the CEO could focus on management and not worry about managing the board. But the CEO reported to the board, and in my opinion, you can't separate those two things. The CEO has to work with the board as closely as possible. I believe the titles of CEO and chairman of the board should go together, and that's still the way it's routinely done. The exception to that could be when you bring in someone new and the old chairman will stay on for a year to help with the transition, or if you have a troubled company and they're restructuring, and you want to bring in someone and have a separate chairman.

What became kind of a compromise was having a lead director, so the CEO could still be the chairman, but one of the directors would be designated first among equals. This person would be the primary liaison to the CEO and chairman, and would chair the executive sessions when management was not present. The lead director would be the primary conduit between the board and the chairman and CEO. Today, a combined chairman and CEO is still the most common arrangement, and there's a lead director at most companies.

They decided they needed a formal lead director, and von Schack was either chosen by the board because he had led the human resources committee, or he was chosen by Kelly, who may have felt beholden to him. It was decided that this was going to be a "merger of equals," which is almost always a euphemism; in fact, very rarely are the two companies equal. The reason you do it is so one side doesn't have to pay the other a premium. In most acquisitions there's a premium paid. That's one of the reasons the acquiree agrees to be acquired. Not only do they think that, by selling, they'll be better off by not implementing their own strategy, but they're also getting a pop in the stock.

They hardly ever use the phrase, but legally the phrase is a "change of control." So before the deal, Mellon shareholders obviously controlled Mellon. With the deal, there was a change of control. That means there were more directors from Bank of New York, more shareholders from Bank of New York, and more senior managers from Bank of New York.

BNY paid a very small premium; it was worth almost nothing. But Kelly got the CEO role, which was an argument for saying it's more equal, even though he'd been with Mellon for just a short time.

You can call it a merger of equals in your press release, but legally, in this case, it was a change of control. And that change of control triggered a lot of accelerations of stock benefits to various people in Mellon management. Usually stock options vest at certain trigger points, either time periods or performance periods. And it's the same with restricted stock. That's the whole purpose; these are incentives. If you have a stock option at $10 and it won't vest until it's worth $20, then you work hard and double the stock so you'll get a bonus in stock. But all of these things got accelerated because there was a change of control. That protects the management.

But Kelly and the board made all Mellon managers waive their rights in order to stay. I think that every one of them, except for one or two, waived those rights. The idea was, "You shouldn't benefit from this—it wasn't intended for that. So if you want to stay with the company, waive it." And that's not illogical at all.

I was retired, so nobody would have asked me to waive my rights; I wouldn't have, in any case. So the change in control accelerated and vested all of my restricted stock, which was a benefit to me.

When the deal was announced, the share price popped. In most deals, the share price will immediately go up to what the offer price is. But it wasn't that much higher; it was about $43 a share.

If a company is independent, it has what's called an "acquisition premium" built into its stock. That's because if you do sell, you typically get a premium. If you haven't sold, the premium's still there. So by selling, Mellon lost that.

It's been fifteen years now, and the stock price has done very little. In the same time period, Northern Trust is up by about 73 percent, State Street is actually down slightly, and PNC, Mellon's former Pittsburgh rival, is up 159 percent.

I was disappointed by the sale. I was interviewed by the *Pittsburgh Post-Gazette* at the time, and I said Mellon didn't have to be sold. I thought Mellon's strategy and position were strong and Mellon could do better on its own. After that article, Mellon had a lawyer call me, and he said, "If you ever say anything again, we'll take away your office and see if we can take away your retirement benefits, too."

I think many people were surprised by the sale and the fact that it was for little or no premium. But I think people on Wall Street saw the fit. These were two logical competitors who could be stronger together. Now there would be three trust banks, and BNY Mellon would be the biggest. So there was a lot of logic behind it. But the cultures of the two organizations were drastically different, and making the "merger" succeed would be difficult.

After being asked about moving the headquarters out of Pittsburgh, Cahouet was quoted as saying, "Oh well, New York is the capital of the world. So it's a logical place." That wasn't really the issue, though. The issue was whether Pittsburgh should lose a Fortune 500 company headquarters—not whether New York would be the logical place for it to relocate.

Why didn't the board fight harder to keep it in Pittsburgh? It's a little like why didn't some of them fight harder to keep me in the job? Maybe some didn't want to jeopardize their board seat. In the merged company, the number of directors from Mellon would be reduced. The compensation for a director was $200,000 to $250,000 a year, half in cash and half in stock.

The merger took a while to close because it needed regulatory and shareholder approval. But after about six months—by July 1, 2007—the deal was done and implemented, and the merged company was off and running.

26

AFTERMATH

It's amazing how many people—including the man on the street—said to me afterwards, "Why'd you sell Mellon?" That's something that really upset me. All I could say was, "I didn't." You're not going to get into a prolonged defense of the situation on the sidewalk. There was a lot of misunderstanding, for sure, because it happened so fast after I left. By the time they started negotiating, it had been only three or four months since my departure, which is very fast.

I was upset, first of all, that Mellon was being sold to anybody, but I was particularly troubled that it was to Bank of New York. We knew them very well from having voluntarily tried to do a deal with them previously. We knew they hadn't invested in their businesses, especially in their technology. We knew they had a different culture—they were more of a top-down organization and didn't have the employee and customer orientations that we had built. I thought their lack of investment and their culture were problems.

I also thought we had a good strategy and were better off on our own. Our strategy was working—particularly in the last seven months of my term, after we got rid of the human resources business and markets were starting to recover. If the reverse had been true, it would have been harder to argue.

I wouldn't have done the Bank of New York deal because I didn't think it was as good a fit as it appeared to be; however, I would have done a State Street deal and I would have done a Blackrock deal. We had already purchased a bunch of smaller asset management companies. I thought we had to be more global in order to diversify, and for greater sources of revenue.

One of the biggest acquisitions we had done but which hadn't closed when I left was in Scotland—Walter Scott. Kelly called me and said, "They've called me—tell me why you think it's a good idea." And I did, and he went ahead with it. And of course he got credit for the acquisition. So we were up to about 25 percent of our revenues coming from outside the country.

Smaller acquisitions were easier to do because there was no question about who was acquiring whom. They're easier to integrate because you're incorporating a smaller business into a bigger one. You don't have the same social issues. It's a more reasonable way of growing, albeit a little slower. Instead of going for the big gobble all at once, you have to do several smaller bites. In some ways, acquisitions are hard to do, so if you're going to attempt it, why not do a big one? Ultimately, it really depends on the specific circumstances.

I would have done other deals if they had made sense. But I definitely would have resisted losing Mellon as the surviving company, and therefore Pittsburgh as the surviving headquarters.

Now, having said that, if the deal had been compelling, and good for shareholders and other stakeholders alike, once everything had been negotiated, then I would not have resisted that kind of deal (for instance, if we had gotten a 20 percent or larger premium—something like that).

When I was on the Chubb board, we didn't think anybody was big enough to acquire us. Ace came along and offered a 30 percent premium. Guess what? We sold the company. It was compelling, and it was overwhelmingly good for shareholders.

When somebody comes to you, even with a great offer, you have to be careful. They can say 30 percent, but if it's an all-stock deal, their stock could tank, so it may not really be 30 percent. You have to do your due diligence. But if the acquirer meets that burden and they are willing to do a lot to protect the community—with a community fund, for example, and protections for employees—then it can be a good thing all around.

At Chubb our stock price was at $100 and they offered us $130, so the question was, "How long is it going to take us to get to $130?" And if you say, "Never," that makes it easy. I don't think anyone would say "Never." But if you said, 'Maybe it's ten to fifteen years," well, then too much can happen in that many years. You could have a depression or a world war. If you don't have the strategy to get there and they have the money to buy you, I think you've got to sell. I think most boards would readily agree to sell in that situation. After a price is agreed upon, then you can negotiate protections for the community and for employees.

When we sold the retail bank, we had protections for the employees, including no firing. These were all branches we'd been running, and we thought we had run them pretty well.

With any deal, I would have tried to protect Pittsburgh, because Mellon Bank was founded in Pittsburgh more than one hundred years ago. It was a major part of the community. In some states, including Pennsylvania, the corporate laws were amended in the early 1980s when interstate banking was introduced and mergers and acquisitions became more common. The amendments say that, while corporations are run for the benefit of the shareholders, as part of their fiduciary obligation directors can nevertheless take into account employees, communities, and other facets in making corporate decisions.

In terms of the community, if it's a sale, as it really was with Bank of New York, clearly you're going to lose the headquarters, but you're also going to lose a lot more. If you're positioning it as a merger of equals, which they did, Pittsburgh gets a little more. The only way we would have kept Pittsburgh as headquarters would have been if Mellon had been the acquirer—or if it had truly been a merger of equals.

One of the things that is very common in mergers or acquisitions is for the acquirer to give certain benefits to the acquiree—particularly the community, because it's losing its headquarters. This helps get the approval of the selling directors and the shareholders, and it's an important incentive. These benefits are to help get the deal approved and get you through the early years, after which they're often gone.

Bank of New York did that. They set up a community fund of about $200 million to support charitable groups—a very positive thing for the Pittsburgh community—because Mellon had been a major community supporter for years. From the acquirer's point of view, that $200 million is just a cost of doing the deal.

Bank of New York also said they'd try to keep as many people as possible in Pittsburgh, and they have in terms of the number of people, but not in terms of the level of employee. To this day, BNY Mellon still has about 7,000 employees in Pittsburgh. So the numbers are there, but there are very few senior officers still in Pittsburgh. Some were around for the first two or three years, after which they either retired or went to New York. Some middle officers and junior officers remain in Pittsburgh.

Having the senior officers living in the city is a big benefit of hosting the corporate headquarters, because the senior officers themselves are involved in the fabric of the community as leaders who support the community. It's not just the corporate support; it's the individual support. And so now, Pittsburgh has obviously lost some of the corporate support and the individual support from the senior officers.

Another thing that was lost was Mellon's culture, which I think was important. It really had changed through our tenure with theEmployer of Choice initiative, which included giving employees stock options—the whole package. We stressed our values of integrity, teamwork, and excellence, and increased our focus on customers. I think people believed in it for the most part, and it was a big contrast with the culture at Bank of New York. While they were happy when they worked in this new culture, they were unhappy to lose it with the Bank of New York transaction.

I still had an office at the old Mellon headquarters in Pittsburgh, which is how I heard directly from people about the difference in the cultures. At Mellon, we had an open culture. I wanted people to be open and honest and respectful, and it was very important for them to be forthcoming in meetings. I would hear that at Bank of New York, they would have meetings where nothing was decided, and after the meeting a few people would make the decisions.

One of the things that made me feel very good was that Mellon was well positioned going into the difficult 2008 period of the Great Recession. Even though the sale of retail was untimely in the short term, it turned out to be a very good thing that we had sold our mortgage business and our retail business. Another thing our management team had done was to reduce our corporate lending. One of the things about trust banks is that they have a relatively smaller balance sheet than, say, J. P. Morgan or Citibank, which make a lot of loans. We were into asset management, so we didn't need much capital at all. We had to lend to Alcoa and Ford and General Motors, because we were managing their pension funds and they insisted.

We would use the argument—which was true—that since our balance sheet was smaller, from a risk management point of view, if we took a hit if a loan went bad or a company went bankrupt, that would hurt us relatively more than a lender who had a big balance sheet and more capital.

Our strategy also led us to get out of the real estate lending business, which is by definition a cyclical business. So we had really reduced our balance sheet in terms of corporate loans, which a lot of employees were very unhappy with, because corporate banking was part of our tradition, as was real estate lending. Some of these things were controversial in the company because they affected people's jobs. A case in point: all the retail banking jobs. They had been Mellon bankers for twenty-five to thirty years, and all of a sudden they were Citizens bankers, even though they had the same or similar jobs.

But one of the very good consequences of this was that when the Great Recession came in 2008, Mellon was much better positioned than the Bank of New York. We didn't have the real estate loans. We didn't have the mortgage loans. We didn't have a lot of the big corporate loans, which really hurt many banks during that period.

Bank of New York had had some regulatory problems and was under special regulatory supervision. The regulatory climate was awful in those days, and they were under some kind of special order because they had got caught money-laundering with Russia. I don't think they did it intentionally, but they were associated with it by the regulators.

At the same time, when the Troubled Asset Relief Program (TARP) was happening, when Hank Paulson was secretary of the treasury, a couple of the banks were in big trouble. Paulson called in the top twenty-five banks and said, "Several of you have asked for special funds. We want everybody to take the money, because we don't want public recognition of some banks being stronger—or weaker—than others." There was a certain logic to that. I know that BNY Mellon and others were literally forced to take the money.

Kelly got the bank through that time, but his tenure was rocky and fairly brief, and the board ultimately forced him to leave.

When he came from Wachovia, he really had no connection to Mellon or to Pittsburgh, and when he quickly got the opportunity to be CEO of a combined bank twice the size of Mellon, he obviously found it compelling.

After Kelly was at BNY Mellon just a couple of years, Bank of America was in trouble and was looking for a new CEO. Kelly was among the people they approached. Kelly went and negotiated with them, and supposedly he said, "Well, if you will move the headquarters to New York, and if you will give me this salary, I will take the job." Bank of America was in Charlotte at the time.

Bank of America apparently said, "We can't pay that much money, and we're not going to move the headquarters." So Kelly supposedly said, "Okay, I'm not going to take it." He then went to von Schack, who had become the lead director (and who stayed on until just recently). Kelly said, "I want to tell you, in case you hear it from somebody other than me, that Bank of America approached me and that, while I did talk to them, I turned it down."

Then, later in the year, the talks with Bank of America resumed. Kelly told his board that he was leaving, but the talks fell through at the last minute, and he told the BNY Mellon board he decided to stay. Supposedly, von Schack and the board were very surprised that he would even consider taking another job after turning down the previous B of A job, and they told him that they had invested a lot in him and were counting on his loyalty.

In 2009, *Fortune* magazine did a big article on the B of A situation. Kelly's relationship with his board never recovered, and they fired him in August 2011. He was not a stupid guy, but some of his behavior seemed rash.

Ultimately, with regard to Mellon's decision to fire me, abandon our strategy, and sell, the facts speak for themselves. In terms of the stock price, State Street and Northern Trust stayed independent, and I think they've done a whole lot better. And certainly PNC had a different strategy, but they've also done much better. I think Mellon would have done much better on its own, too.

A most interesting fact: On January 27, 2006 (the day before I was terminated), Mellon's stock price was $36.11; ten years later, at the end of the first quarter of 2016, BNY Mellon's stock price was $36.83.

Today, I think that in the industry and in the community, people have seen where the stock price is; they see that the bank was sold, and that very few senior people are left in Pittsburgh. They've heard me say publicly that I wouldn't have sold Mellon. With all of this, I'd like to think my reputation has been resurrected to a certain extent.

But what's been most heartening is that, with my office being in the BNY Mellon building in downtown Pittsburgh, people still come up to me in the lobby or elevators and say, "Boy, I wish you were still here." I'm sure some are just being nice, but I think many of them are sincere. It's always made me feel good.

With BNY Mellon being in existence for about fifteen years, and having had several CEOs, I think there is now a single culture and strategy that has a better chance of success. I also believe the current CEO, Todd Gibbons, and the management team he has built are the right people to make that success a reality. I hope so.

27

BEYOND MELLON:
A LIFE OF CONTRIBUTING

AFTER MELLON, I SPENT A GOOD DEAL OF TIME SERVING ON THREE CORPO-
rate boards and also a number of nonprofits. Two of the corporate
boards—Celanese and iGATE—came about via Pittsburgh friends.

I thoroughly enjoyed the experience of being on the Chubb board.
It was a first-rate company with a great board and management team. I
served on this board from 2007 until 2015, when we got the offer to sell
with the 30 percent premium. We sold, so unfortunately, that was the
end of that. I had been on the audit committee and had been chairman
of the human resources committee. Even though I didn't like math as
a youngster, because of my experience I'm what's called a "financial
expert" by legal definition.

Then I got a call from Paul O'Neill, the former Alcoa CEO and
treasury secretary, who was a friend in Pittsburgh. He was an adviser
to Blackstone, which had purchased Celanese, a great old chemical
company. Blackstone had taken it private and moved the headquarters
from New Jersey to Dallas. They were going to take the company public
again, and needed some independent directors. Paul said, "Why don't
you look into this? I think you'll find it interesting."

I didn't know anything about chemicals, but they already had a
lot of people who knew chemicals, so I brought some diversity. I knew
about financial matters, human resources, audit, corporate governance,
and government affairs, so I hoped I could add value. I enjoyed my
work on the Celanese board until I was seventy-three—six years ago.
That was their retirement age.

The reason boards want retired corporate executives is that most active CEOs still on the job only go on one board (if their own boards allow them to), because they're so busy. So they like to get recently retired executives, who are hopefully still mentally acute, physically active, and so forth.

I liked the idea of being on three boards, so the third board I went on at the beginning of 2007 was iGATE, with Pittsburgher Sunil Wadhwani, who was the founder and CEO. It involved technology that I was familiar with from Mellon. I first chaired the human resources committee, and then I chaired the audit committee, so there was a common thread. I went to India at least once a year for board meetings, which I'd always done at Mellon anyway. Celanese also was very international. We had board meetings in China, in Barcelona, and in London. All three companies were fairly global, which I liked very much.

Most of our iGATE meetings were in New York City. When I went on the iGATE board, the stock was at $6, and I told Sunil I'd like to take my fee in stock. He thought that was a good idea, so he offered it to the other directors. Well, in 2017, we sold the company for $48 a share. So Sunil and his company made a ton of money—and the directors did well also. Sunil, to his credit, has a foundation in India and has developed mobile hospital units there.

So we sold iGATE and all my boards went away. With one, I had reached retirement age, and the other two we sold. They were all interesting experiences, and I was really glad I did them.

Being part of the Pittsburgh community has been an important part of my forty years here. Pittsburgh's very important to me. In Pittsburgh, I've been involved in very visible ways for quite a long period of time, and I think for those who questioned it, this has restored my standing in the community. For those who believed in it from the beginning, it's reinforced it.

One of the first things I did after leaving Mellon was get involved with Pittsburgh Public Schools, where Mark Roosevelt was then the superintendent. He was a very interesting guy, a little bit of a Don

Quixote. He was a Massachusetts legislator and had been a proponent of some major educational bills, so he had a lot of experience in politics and education. His problem in Pittsburgh at the end of his tenure was that he was just getting beaten down. He was going to meetings every night, and the board of education is a dysfunctional group, to say the least. Mark finally left and went on to Antioch College—from the frying pan into the fire. But he was very engaging, and I liked him a lot.

In April 2006, after I got back from Africa, I went to Mark and said, "I'd like to work with you and do what I can to help. But I don't want to just go and sit in meetings. I want to do something."

First he got me involved with the teachers and other community people, talking about ways we could change the schools. I went to one of these meetings and everyone broke off into sessions. I said, this isn't working for me. I wasn't interested in having philosophical discussions over topics like: "You can't teach until the schools are safe, so what can we do to make the schools safe?" You could talk about these things until you were blue in the face. The board of education and all the unions were just unwilling or unable to fix things, so it seemed like a waste of time.

Mark said he had another idea: He wanted to open a technology school much like the district's performing arts school. He had asked a group of about eight students at Carnegie Mellon University's business school to research this idea, and wanted to know if I would become their adviser. I agreed. I would go and meet with them once a week for a couple of hours. They were great students—all bright. They were doing research around the country, finding out what other technology schools were like.

My question was, "How are you going to start it?" We came up with a notion of doing a lottery to pick the enrollees at random rather than by merit exams, as was done in other cities, which resulted in major racial imbalances. Then we discussed the fact that if you're going to have diverse students, there was a good chance their levels of preparation may not be the same. So we actually came up with a program that started in the sixth grade, so that by the time they got to the high school level, all students would have had the math and science courses they'd need to succeed in the program.

I worked with them for six or seven months, and we finally got it approved by the board and by the city. One of these students was Sam Franklin, who graduated and went to work for Mark and became the project manager for building the school. It was a great story. And it happened. They got the unions to agree that faculty members wouldn't just be chosen by tenure, but that they'd actually go out and find the most qualified teachers they needed to be able to teach there.

I visited several times, and it was very satisfying; I was able to give them practical advice. Once it got presented and approved, there was nothing more for me to do, so I was out of it. But if you go down Fifth Avenue in the Oakland section of Pittsburgh, you'll see the old school they took over and renovated, which is now the Pittsburgh Science and Technology Academy.

Back in the 1980s, I had been on the West Penn Hospital board. I had resigned once Cahouet arrived, because I didn't have much extra time. In 1991, George Taber, who worked at the R. K. Mellon Foundation and was chairman of the Presbyterian Hospital board, contacted me and asked me if I'd join the Presbyterian board. I said yes.

At that point, it wasn't the University of Pittsburgh Medical Center (UPMC). It was Presbyterian, which everyone called Presby. And Presby had just combined in 1990 with Montefiore Hospital, which had been founded in 1908 as a Jewish hospital. So at that point, those were the only two hospitals in what would become the UPMC system. I recently retired from the UMPC board after spending twenty-seven years on the board, which I really enjoyed, because it was a time of special growth. They've acquired and acquired and grown and grown. It's been fascinating to watch and to be a part of.

The board meets once a month for two or three hours. There are committees and there was always homework for the board and committee meetings. I was usually on the committee of directors that would meet with the directors of the hospitals to be acquired. I would convince them to negotiate some of the social issues—such as the name, and how much money we would give to support their community commitment.

I chaired the community affairs committee, and also served on the executive committee and the human resources committee. In later years, I chaired the nominating and governance committee, and I'm still on the committee that was formed about ten years ago called "international and enterprises." There were originally only three of us and now there are five, and this committee oversees all of their international investments, which are significant. It's fascinating. They're building five hospitals in China; they've got four hospitals and a cancer center in Ireland; and they have one of the largest transplant centers in Europe, in Sicily. It's just amazing what they've done.

This committee also oversees "enterprises," which covers their commercial investments. For example, they had a fifty-fifty joint venture with General Electric to produce digital pathology reports; all of these reports were previously done by hand and were totally inefficient, not to mention often incorrect. We also invested in start-up companies where we were the clinical trial. This way we benefited from both the clinical trial and the financial investments. They have made hundreds of millions of dollars in these investments over the years.

Former UPMC CEO Jeff Romoff did a hell of a job, and has built a great hospital system. Beyond that, he focused on how to leverage this world-class, academic medical center in a no-growth or slow-growth region. His strategy was to take our intellectual capital, export it, invest it outside the region, and then bring the proceeds back to support clinical research and education in Pittsburgh. It has worked beautifully.

UPMC's contribution to this area is unbelievable. There are now forty hospitals with $23 billion in revenue. They have close to 100,000 employees. UPMC supports the University of Pittsburgh to the tune of several hundred million dollars a year, an outright grant to the medical school. After all, it is called the University of Pittsburgh Medical Center. The chancellor and the dean of the medical school sit on the board and come to our meetings.

Jeff is an intellectual and a visionary for strategic thinking about health care. Before he retired in August of 2021, I'm not sure there was anybody who was as good as he was. I think he only sleeps two hours a night. If I was in Europe, say, and e-mailed him at two a.m. Pittsburgh time, I'd get an e-mail back just minutes later. I worked with him for a long time, and he was pretty incredible. Jeff was succeeded by Leslie Davis, who had been in charge of all the hospitals and was an excellent choice.

In the early 2000s, the strategy for UPMC was to become an integrated delivery and finance system (IDFS). There were maybe one or two other hospital systems in the country at the time that qualified for this designation, which means you have hospitals, an academic medical center for both research and education, and an insurance company. The logic is pretty amazing, because if you're the insurer, you can hopefully make better decisions about what should be insured because you're also controlling the care. It actually works. In every case where you have this integrated system, it's been a hospital or delivery system that has expanded into insurance, never the reverse—until 2011.

At that time, Highmark, which is the Pittsburgh Blue Cross Blue Shield insurance company, was providing insurance and using UPMC hospitals. Every couple of years, Highmark and UPMC would negotiate reimbursement rates. In 2011, just before one of these negotiations, Highmark acquired the financially ailing Allegheny General Hospital in Pittsburgh. This is when Highmark moved into the delivery business, directly competing with UPMC hospitals.

Highmark refused to negotiate and provide what UPMC believed was a market rate for reimbursement. This led to UPMC saying, "We're not going to take Highmark Blue Cross Blue Shield insurance anymore. We'll open up the market." So UPMC opened up the market, and several big insurers, including UnitedHealthcare and Aetna, came into the market.

Highmark was furious, and blamed UPMC. For the community, it was very emotional; you had all of these people with Highmark Blue Cross Blue Shield insurance, and they were afraid they couldn't go to UPMC hospitals. UPMC hospitals enjoy a great reputation, but they also have specialty hospitals, like Magee-Womens Hospital of Pittsburgh, which are particularly desirable for patients.

There was an uproar in the community, and you had all kinds of people, including the former secretary of the treasury Paul O'Neill, taking sides. Government officials were being approached by people saying, "You've got to take care of me." People were saying health care should be government-run. I, for one, said, "No, we have a capitalist system. And competition—even in health care—is good."

Everybody had their own solution: "The government should take it over." "They shouldn't be able to make any profit." It was a chance for politicians to grandstand: "I'm fighting for the people against these big hospitals." The state attorney general got involved, and the dispute went on and on for years.

In the meantime, despite all that was said, Pittsburgh became one of the lowest-cost places in the country for health insurance. Now, instead of just having Blue Cross Blue Shield, there are other companies to choose from. Previously, Highmark Blue Cross Blue Shield had controlled 60 percent of the market, but as of three or four years ago, they only had 30 percent of the market. They gave up their monopoly in order to get into the delivery system and not pay fair reimbursement rates.

Romoff was a competitor, and he wanted to kill Highmark—literally—but that's one of the reasons he was so successful. Now Highmark is barely breaking even. This whole thing was a huge strategic mistake for Highmark. They had a virtual monopoly in insurance, and they were making tons of money. They paid their board outrageous fees; we used to joke about it, because we got paid nothing for being on the UPMC board. Instead of being this hugely profitable, focused insurance company, they had decided to expand their business, and they practically went broke.

During this whole period, there were arguments that UPMC didn't pay taxes, which was totally false. UPMC didn't pay taxes on the hospital revenues, but it did and does for the insurance revenues, and now the insurance revenue is more than 50 percent of UPMC's revenue. And UPMC pays tons of taxes on the real estate, not to mention payroll and other taxes. But it was very hard to get the facts out, between the media and the government people and Highmark, which were spinning a false tale. Part of that was UPMC's problem. The board was always saying to Romoff, "Jeff, you've got to do a better job of getting the story out. You have to do more lobbying."

But now, UPMC is strong, and it makes an overall profit—reinvesting that profit back into the community—of about $600 million a year. And UPMC is always investing for the future, as well. It's building three $500 million hospitals—a vision center, an innovation center, and a cancer center.

Jeff never wanted to retire. When we had the situation with Highmark, the feeling was, "Well, we can't let him go in the middle of this. There's too much going on." Then there was the Great Recession. And recently, the pandemic health-care crisis. There was always something. But in July of 2021, the board decided it was finally time for a transition to a new CEO. Jeff was in his mid-seventies, and there was a very capable group of senior managers in place.

Nick Beckwith has been chairman of the board for many years and is a good friend of mine. He did a good job of managing Jeff and putting in place many best practices for board governance. Nick deserves a lot of credit for UPMC's many successes.

The most interesting thing to me about being on that board for twenty-seven years has been seeing the growth and the evolution of UPMC and the changes in health care.

I was involved in the Pittsburgh Regional Health Initiative, which had been led by Paul O'Neill and Karen Feinstein of the Jewish Health-care Foundation. They started out trying to get all the hospitals committed to improving quality. Paul wanted zero tolerance in everything. When Paul went to Washington to the Treasury Department, I became chair, and I argued strongly and successfully that we should narrow the focus and start with two areas—prescription errors and infection rates.

According to statistics at the time, hospitals killed 100,000 people a year with infections they got in the hospital. That's big-time. You go to hospitals to be cured, and you come out and you die. There was something wrong there. And prescription errors were just silly. Everybody thought it was a joke that the doctors wrote in Latin in handwritten scribble that nobody could read. Well, guess what happened? There were all these prescription errors because nobody could read their writing.

The biggest problem was infection rates, because hospitals didn't report them on a consistent basis. The state also was trying to get consistency in reporting; everyone had an interest in improving the quality of care. It was hard going for a lot of reasons, and it's taken maybe longer than it should have, but there is a sense today in health care generally that, number one, we do have to keep better records. And number two, we need to report and measure and improve. So we had success with the Regional Health Initiative—maybe not enough, but there was progress, absolutely.

Another great thing was to see the evolution of UPMC with all the acquisitions and the progress that came through the economies of scale and investments we were able to make.

Technology was a great example. Everybody agreed that we had to keep better medical records, and that the way to keep them was not in handwritten form, and not just in one hospital, but computerized, and systemwide—especially when you had forty hospitals. When you go to the ophthalmologist, they ask you about your family history and what drugs you take. Then you go to your dermatologist and they ask the same questions. And you think, "Excuse me, you're part of UPMC, aren't you? Why don't you already have these records?" Well, the answer was simple. They didn't have the records because they didn't have the technology.

That's what's driven a lot of bank consolidation, too. Banks are heavily dependent on technology, and health-care organizations now realize that they are as well. But you need the money and efficiencies in order to make those investments in technologies. Instead of having forty hospitals trying to invent their own back offices and buy computers and software, you have one system doing it for all forty. Now, it's a behemoth, but it's amazingly well run. UPMC is what they call a three-legged stool. It's clinical care with the hospitals; it's education with the medical school and research; and it's insurance. And the technology really supports all three.

For me personally, the UPMC board was a chance to learn. I've always loved to learn. But in terms of a contribution, I had a lot of our technologists at Mellon help UPMC out from time to time. I knew a lot about acquisitions in terms of due diligence, implementation, and integration. And then in investments abroad, I had a lot of experience globally, so I actually think I was able to contribute in a way that was hopefully helpful. And that was very satisfying.

The Pittsburgh Promise, the program that provides postsecondary school scholarship money to Pittsburgh high school students who perform to a certain standard, has been another big part of my Pittsburgh experience. The Promise was an offshoot of UPMC, and specifically, Jeff Romoff. The Promise was really Jeff's idea at the beginning. Most people don't give him enough credit for it, but people in the know do. He originally said, "I really want a big idea to support—not just another project." He was the one who made the seminal decision that led to the creation of the Promise, when he decided UPMC would put up $100 million to support it. Without UPMC, it never would have happened.

That gift, however, has ironically had a double-edged effect. The organizers of the Promise had to raise $250 million. The $100 million from UPMC was supposed to be a matching grant, but too many people thought UPMC had covered the entire cost, and that misperception made fund-raising difficult.

I was asked to go on the Pittsburgh Promise board and I did, because I believed—and still believe—that it's the most important thing going on in Pittsburgh. It's keeping kids in high school, because they're going to be given a scholarship to go to trade school or college. It's keeping people living in Pittsburgh, because if you live over the city line, and you have kids, you don't get anything. And, importantly, it's creating a better-educated workforce for our community. We've changed the amounts people receive over time, to keep it viable. For a while, it was $10,000 a child—that's $40,000 if you have four children—just for living in the city.

I served on the Promise board for ten years, and eventually became vice chair. Franco Harris is the chair—the front man—and he's one of my favorite people in the world. Beyond being a football hero, he has

(L-R) Saleem Ghubril, Marty, and Franco Harris

done so much for our community. I was really acting as the primary financial adviser to Saleem Ghubril, the director. Saleem is terrific. He's very passionate, and he talks frequently to the kids, as does Franco, to interest them in the Promise and to encourage them to take advantage of it. Saleem is the true leader of the Promise.

I gave $1 million to Pittsburgh Promise, which at the time was the largest individual gift. Since then I've given more, and I've chaired the corporate fund-raising committee. The foundations have been great, and they're still very supportive, but in my opinion, the Pittsburgh corporate community has not done enough—with the exception of PNC and Mellon. The last time I looked, the corporate community had put in about $6 million, which as a percentage of $250 million is not very much. While raising $10 at a time from individuals helps, it doesn't get you very far.

I also helped the Promise in terms of working with UPMC. I went to Nick Beckwith first and then to Jeff Romoff, and I said, "There's a rumor in town that because the Promise hasn't been able to raise the matching levels, you're not going to come through." The $100 million pledge was to be paid over ten years, when it was matched by other gifts. They both said, "Fine, we won't wait. We will commit the whole thing, take the match off, and we'll commit it right now." UPMC's been great. The Promise has gone back to UPMC for more money, and UPMC has said no. I don't blame Jeff; he said it was time for the rest of the community to step up, and I agree.

At the beginning, the superintendent of schools was on the Promise board. The mayor was on it, too; that was when the "young kid," Luke Ravenstahl, was mayor. Luke stood behind whoever was making the announcement of the Promise, so his picture is in all the photos. When Mayor Bill Peduto got elected, he said, "That's Luke's thing." It wasn't Luke's thing. Luke was just there at the time and posed for pictures. I don't think Luke ever came to any of the board meetings.

I went with the head of the Heinz Endowments, Grant Oliphant, and called on Mayor Peduto. I'd known Peduto around town for years.

Bill had made that argument about Ravenstahl, and said, "I'm creating an after-school program." I said, "Bill there's not going to be anything after school if they're not in school. This thing really works, and it's important."

I think there are now about fifty of these Promise programs around the country. I told Peduto that this really enhanced Pittsburgh's reputation. I know that Google took that into consideration when they came here. I said to Peduto, "Even if you don't think you started it and it's not your thing, if this goes down—if it fails on your watch—it's going to be a huge black eye for Pittsburgh and for you." I thought that was going to be a persuasive argument, but it wasn't. We couldn't persuade him, so he never really got involved.

If you go back to R. K. Mellon and Governor David Lawrence, and even to the 1970s and '80s, and when I moved here in '81, Pittsburgh was the third-largest corporate headquarters city. Now I think it's number 25. Gulf went. Westinghouse went. But in those early days, when they were all here, there was a lot of truth to the notion that the corporate leaders got together at the Duquesne Club over lunch and got things done.

When we lost a lot of those companies, some of the big companies that were left—Mellon and PNC—were corporate banks, but their only branches were local, because that's all that was allowed back then. Well, now they're global, and they've got to give money all around. And so those two things—the fact that we've lost a lot of large corporations, and the fact that the remaining companies are more globally oriented—mean there's less money available in Pittsburgh. And that's why at the Pittsburgh Promise and the Allegheny Conference, we really tried to reach out to medium and smaller companies. Maybe it took ten of them to equal the impact of a Westinghouse. You had to work harder to get ten, but you had to do it because you didn't have Westinghouse anymore.

The reason I finally got off the Promise board about three years ago was that it was getting to the point where it seemed like I'd walk in one door and people would walk out the other, because they knew I was going to ask them for money. I'm not really comfortable asking people for money, but you've got to do it. You can't ask for just any cause, but I really believed in the Pittsburgh Promise, which made it a lot easier. I finally got off the Pittsburgh Promise board because I felt they needed new people and fresh blood to go out and find new sources of income.

Ann and I co-chaired the United Way campaign once, and I had to ask for a lot of money. This campaign takes place every year, so you're really trying to find new sources. There aren't as many of those in Pittsburgh. I co-chaired the Children's Institute campaign with Ann and Milt and Sheila Fine, and I gave $1 million to them, and I've also served on the Salvation Army board.

I've also been on the Carnegie Museums board since 1984. I came in 1981, and in 1984, Carnegie Museums decided to form what they called the Carnegie 100. I was about forty then, and somehow they came up with 100 names of people who weren't really involved in the community yet. I was one of them. The idea was to get a group of young people together to give advice. What do you like? What don't you like? What can we do to make it better? How about outreach for new members? So after that I was asked to go on the Carnegie Museum of Art board. At that point, the Carnegie only had the Museum of Art and the Museum of Natural History. I didn't know very much about art, but I was interested, and I was happy to do it because I wanted to learn.

Then after a couple of years I went on the Carnegie Museums Board—the parent company board—and those early years were busy and productive. In 1991, we started the Science Center, and then in 1994, the Andy Warhol Museum. It used to be that you served on the subsidiary board first and then you were asked to go on the "Big Board." They're no longer doing that, which I think is a mistake. Now they're getting other people on the big board who have little idea what's going on at the museums.

In 2007, after I retired, I became chair of the Museum of Art board, and I did that for eight years. The board meets six times a year. It's an advisory board; we had a finance committee, and many others. We were there to help them. What can we do to raise revenues or trim expenses? They want the experience of people who have done similar kinds of stuff.

Overall, I served for thirty years on the Museum of Art board. On the Carnegie Museums of Pittsburgh board, I was elected a life trustee, one of sixteen supposed successors to the original trustees appointed by Andrew Carnegie, who started the museum in 1895. I'm also a member of the Andrew Carnegie Society. I've given several million dollars to the museums over the years. Now I'm emeritus on both boards, but I still attend meetings.

28

PHILANTHROPY AND PERSONAL

IN THE EARLY 2000s, I CREATED THE McGUINN FAMILY FOUNDATION. I wanted to create a vehicle for charitable giving that would get my sons involved in philanthropic activity and continue beyond my lifetime. The family came together and we retained professionals to help us with details such as documentation, so it would be properly established. We spent a lot of time setting forth the purpose and mission and laying out the guidelines for choosing grantees and disbursing funds.

Our main goals were to support our communities (with the majority of support going to Pittsburgh, where the money came from) and to emphasize education and the arts. I strongly believe that education is the most important key to a fair and equitable society, and to offering opportunity for individual success. A critical part of the Foundation was to be sure we were not just writing checks, and that the impact of our grant was much more than the face value of the check. I contributed $2 million to start the Foundation. Ann, Patrick, Chris, and I were the initial directors. The directors meet once a year to consider and approve grants. Each director can propose a total of $25,000 a year for grants, with no grantee receiving less than $5,000.

The Foundation has achieved all of its goals and continues to function well. The grant process is very thoughtful, with the grants supporting innovative projects. Patrick and Chris have studied the needs of their communities in Morristown, New Jersey, and Washington, DC, and have decided wisely on what to support. They have become active in several charities through memberships on boards and otherwise. Some of my testamentary bequests will go to the Foundation, but the Foundation will "sunset" five years after my death. I have been fortunate to live a relatively long life, during which I have made significant contributions to support the charities I wanted to support. I have also made bequests to my family (beyond the trusts already functioning) to enable them to continue their personal charities after the Foundation terminates.

I spent seven years at Villanova for college and law school, so it has obviously had a major impact on my life—a very positive one, I believe. I have been a major supporter of Villanova. In early 2021, I committed $10 million to support the implementation of the university's strategic plan, including money for college and law school faculty research, and for supporting veterans. Father Peter M. Donohue, the president, is doing a spectacular job of leading the university, taking it to even higher levels as an outstanding academic institution. My recent gift brings my total giving to Villanova to almost $16 million. Other academic interests I support include the McGuinn Irish Scholarship, which brings four college students from Ireland each year to Villanova for a semester. Over forty students have benefitted from this program so far. Recently, a new dormitory on campus was named McGuinn Hall [see appendices 17, 18].

For many years I served on the board of consultors of Villanova Law School, including two years as chairman. I gave the commencement address at a Law School graduation and, in 2013, Pat O'Connor and I were awarded honorary degrees. Much of my support for Villanova has been designated for the Law School. I have funded the McGuinn Professorship for Business Law and made a large contribution to the new Law School building. I am glad the Law School is doing well, and the leadership provided by Dean Mark Alexander, together with a strong faculty, has been very positive.

Other organizations I provide substatial financial support to are museums beyond the Carnegie, the Pittsburgh Symphony Orchestra, the Pittsburgh Cultural Trust, and many other colleges and schools [see appendix 19]. I have contributed more than $1 million to the Catholic

Diocese of Pittsburgh, and have provided major support to the Marine Corps Scholarship Foundation. Their mission statement says it all: Educating the children of Marines.

I have been a very fortunate person. Good fortune, by definition, is not something anyone can control. I like to spend my personal time travelling, reading, and playing golf. While I travelled frequently and extensively for business, there was little time for personal sightseeing or even side trips. But most of my vacations were spent on family trips to places such as Italy, Ireland, France, Alaska, and to a dude ranch in Jackson Hole. My other travels included many places in Africa, Asia, Europe, South America, and, of course, the United States. Beforehand I would always read about the place to be visited, then while I was there learn as much as possible about the place and its people and culture, and then afterward, read more to get a fuller perspective.

When I was in grade school, my parents bought a multi-volume series (I think there were twenty volumes) of the "The Greatest Classics of the World." And over my later grade school and high school years I read all of them, which really began my interest in reading all types of books. While working, I would mainly use free time to read fiction, particularly Irish fiction, and thrillers or mysteries to provide an escape from the intense pressures of working. I then began to favor historical fiction and, since retiring, have enjoyed continuing to read fiction but also a great many biographies and autobiographies. I really read a great deal, particularly during the summers.

I've enjoyed playing golf since my late twenties. In fact, many of my travels have included trips to play golf in Ireland, Scotland, and New Zealand, among other places, including at golf courses throughout the United States. I am a long-time member of the United States Seniors' Golf Association, which holds tournaments at many of the best golf courses in the country. In Pittsburgh I play at the Fox Chapel Golf Club and Rolling Rock Club. I played for many years at Laurel Valley Golf Club but recently resigned since I don't spend very much time in Pittsburgh in the summer. In Long Island, where we have a summer house in Quogue, I play at National Golf Links, Westhampton Country Club, and the Quogue Field Club. In Florida where we have a condo in Palm Beach, I play at the Gulf Stream Golf Club. I enjoy golf because it's a way to walk outdoors and spend enjoyable time with friends.

After family, friends are a very important part of my life. My wife Susan and I are fortunate to live in several places now, so we have friends who are dispersed geographically. We spend lots of time with friends, especially in Pittsburgh, Quogue, and Palm Beach.

(L-R) Tina and Paul Powers, Fred and Kate Jahnig,
Frank and Rebecca Ryan, Tom and Marcia Borger

Marie and Pat O'Connor

Marty and Pat O'Connor

Marty, Jerry Shanley, Larry Rafferty and John Weisser

Nick Beckwith, Rick Brand, Marty, and Duff McCrady

29

REFLECTIONS

ANN AND I WERE MARRIED FOR ALMOST FORTY YEARS, AND WE HAD MANY good years together. Then, particularly after I retired, I remember her syaing, "Well, you may be retired, but I'm not." Certain words stick in your brain. I wanted to go to Florida, but she didn't want to go to Floria. I though she had changed, and I'm sure she thought I had changed; probably a bit of truth to both. It was clear to both of us that we were drifting apart. I remember one time we were at a club having dinner. We'd been arguing, and she said to me, "Give me half your money and I'm out of here."

Of course, life is complicated—and marriage, even more so. In 2014, I met Susan Jones Block, then president of the women'scommittee of the Carnegie Museum of Art. Our paths had crossed onthe periphery of Pittsburgh, but now we were meeting to discuss museum business. Our

Susan McGuinn

Marty and Susan

Susan and
daughter Caroline

Caroline, Susan, and Susan's mother Donna Jones

first meeting was one of the most thoughtful exchanges of ideas that I had experienced in recent years. A friendship blossomed and grew over two years, until we both found ourselves divorced and ready to take a chance on love. I was divorced in 2016 and she was divorced in 2017. Susan is a spectacular human being. She is smart and interesting. She has a wonderful sense of humor (which she has passed on to her daughter, Caroline), and she laughs a lot. It's nice that she's beautiful, too! We are very compatible and very happy.

Bailey   Carigan

Haven   Payton

Chris, Maggie, and Kara

My son Patrick and his wife Ilana have four daughters: Bailey is twenty-one and a senior at the University of Virginia, where she is a top student and very active. Carigan is eighteen and is starting at Yale.

Caroline Block, Susan's daughter and my stepdaughter

Haven (her name was inspired by the fact that Patrick and Ilana met in New Haven) is fifteen, and Payton, the youngest, is twelve. They're all bright and doing well. They're all good kids and have had the benefit of high-performing school programs in Morristown, which has a very good public school system.

My fifth granddaughter is Chris and Kara's daughter, Magnolia. Known as Maggie since birth, she just turned one in the fall of 2021.

Patrick is a good big brother to Chris, and he and Chris have a good relationship, which, of course, makes me happy.

My stepdaughter Caroline is fifteen. Caroline claims she is an introvert, but she has become much more outgoing, and is maturing beautifully. She just graduated from the Ellis School, where she was a class officer, was active in the performing arts, and earned top grades. She is now attending a boarding school in New England and is thriving. I love her as my own daughter.

In the summer, I see my sons and granddaughters a lot because they come out to our summer house for at least two one-week periods. At Christmas we get together in Manhattan for a theater show and lunch, and they sometimes come to Pittsburgh. We also do a lot of family trips. During the summer of 2019, we went out to Jackson Hole to a dude ranch. After Christmas in 2020, we were scheduled to go on an African safari, but we put it off because of the pandemic.

When each of my granddaughters reaches thirteen, I take them on a trip anywhere in the world they choose (except for Asia or Africa; nor-

Haven, Payton, Bailey, Marty, Carigan

Carigan, Bailey, Chris, Haven, Patrick, Payton, Marty

mally we have to do it during a school break, so we only have a week). The theory is that, number one, it'll be a memorable trip for them when they attain teenage status. And number two, it's a chance for my wife and me to spend a week with them alone, without their parents.

We also did a Disney cruise from Vancouver to Alaska with the whole family and Chris, and that worked out well. Susan and I took Caroline and her granny, Donna Jones, on a Baltic cruise when Caroline turned thirteen, also in the summer of 2019. I try to do things with the family that are special.

I've always enjoyed traveling, all over the world. I'm on the Temple University Rome board, which meets twice a year. My best friend, Pat O'Connor, was chair of Temple University, and they've had a satellite in Rome for fifty years. At the end of September each year, they have a meeting in Rome, and we spend five days visiting the school and advising and giving money. After Rome, we travel elsewhere in Italy.

Susan and I spent our honeymoon in Venice. We went to Positano another year. I make four or five trips abroad every year. I love London and Paris—I've been to those cities more than thirty times. Even if you go for four days, it's great. I became an Irish citizen in 2002 (which I could do because my grandparents were born in Ireland), and travel to Ireland once a year.

When the pandemic hit, at first I thought I'd really miss traveling, but I realized I really missed the interactions with friends and family more.

In addition to my love of travel, I also love to read, and I enjoy playing golf. I enjoy spending time with family and friends. I look forward to enjoying all of these things for years to come. I'm fortunate to have a house in the Hamptons, a condo in Florida, and a townhouse in Pittsburgh. I've been in Pittsburgh for forty years now. To me, it's a big city and a small town at the same time, with the benefits of both, including the cultural aspects and the sports. It's very manageable. I like being involved in the community—obviously a bit less so now. And we have lots of friends there.

At my next birthday, I will turn eighty. My attitude about birthdays is that I've had so many of them, they're not a big deal anymore—but I want them to keep coming.

Passing fifty, I was more sensitive to my family history of coronary weakness and cancer. There's not a whole lot you can do about cancer; it's more genetic, I'm afraid. But there's a lot you can do to strengthen your heart and improve your overall health. There's no guarantee, but at least you can improve the odds. So after fifty, I realized I had to be more disciplined in terms of exercise and healthy eating. Until then, I'd pretty much followed the usual American diet and didn't exercise regularly.

In Pittsburgh, the Duquesne Club has a fitness center that opens at 5:30 a.m. I started getting up at 4:30 or 4:45 a.m., arriving at the club around 5:20 a.m. I'd be ready to work out by 5:30, and I did this at least three times a week. That was easy, because nothing conflicted with it, so it became a good routine. I would get to the office before 7:00 a.m., so I'd still be there early. I kept that schedule until I retired. Even today, I continue to believe that it's imperative to eat a healthy diet and have plenty of exercise.

As I look back over my life, I've always been driven to succeed. I wasn't going to count on my father to give me money, or a job. I wasn't going to depend on a classmate to introduce me to the right network. I had to go out and do it myself. It was almost intuitive. It wasn't a philosophical or intellectual decision—it was just a matter of competing.

At Villanova Law School, I felt the top of our class was competitive with any law school, but because it was a relatively new law school, its reputation was limited. As a result, we had a chip on our shoulders. We had to prove ourselves, and the way to prove yourself is through performance. Generally, performing well comes from working harder—or smarter—than someone else. This really drove us as a group; we were going to prove that we were as good as anybody else. And in fact, that's what happened.

It was similar at Sullivan & Cromwell. I was the first Villanova law student hired there, and I wanted to prove that I was the equal of others at the firm. So I came into the office earlier each day and worked harder.

I remember Tom Usher, the former head of US Steel, was giving a speech one time, and he asked me whether I thought people were natural-born leaders. At the time, I said no. I said it was something that was cultivated, like most everything else. There may be certain qualities or characteristics in a person that make it easier for him or her to be a leader, but I don't think you're born with that ability from day one. To be a real leader, it takes work. It takes effort. It takes a lot of help, and a lot of experience. It's an interesting question. But I don't think it's as much a philosophical question as it is an experiential question. You study individual people you think are effective leaders and analyze them and how they got to that stage, and then you emulate them.

Years ago, when I was at Mellon, I was talking with one of my friends who didn't work at Mellon but had grown up with me. I said, "I think I'm in the running to be CEO of Mellon." And he said, "Why do you think you can be CEO?" And I said, "Well, one of the reasons is when I look around at the competition, I think I'm at least as good as they are."

I never worked with the goal of earning X amount of dollars. I didn't have that Wall Street mentality, where you measure your success by the size of your income. The questions for me were: Are you doing something satisfying? Are you making a difference? Yes, I wanted to be fairly compensated, of course, but if you got the right job, worked hard, and did well, I figured the money would just come, which it did.

I'm a truly fortunate guy. It may be trite, but the harder you work, the luckier you are. It is amazing how, over time, you start to look back and realize how lucky you were. But then you remember that you worked hard, and earned most of your luck.

I worked all the time, from the moment I started delivering newspapers when I was in the third grade. I wanted money—not to pile it up and compare it to what others made, but to go buy candy or clothes, or to be able to go on a date. We weren't poor. We were middle class, and my parents were saving money. But I learned that if you wanted something, you had to go get it yourself. You had to go out and earn it. That's just what you've got to do—so you go do it. This builds over time into a more successful approach to life.

Writing this autobiography has been a journey down memory lane. Remembering many times and events was a pleasure. Remembering some others was not as pleasurable but cathartic. I think this is true for most people as they review their lives. In looking back on my life, there are lots of things I would do differently, especially with the benefit of hindsight. But there are many more things that turned out well. So, all in all, I have been a very fortunate person [see appendicex 20].

ACKNOWLEDGMENTS

I FIRST WANT TO ACKNOWLEDGE THE ASSISTANCE OF DOUG HEUCK, WITH-out whom this autobiography would not have become a reality. Doug is the former business editor of the *Pittsburgh Post-Gazette,* the founder and primary owner of *Pittsburgh Quarterly* magazine, and a friend. We began our combined efforts in November of 2020. Doug conducted more than fifteen hours of interviews with me so that when the first draft was transcribed, it consisted of my words. We then began the mutual editing process. Doug has also advised on how to publish this book and on all the various aspects of making the book a reality. His journalistic experience, intellect, and positive attitude have been invaluable.

Roy Engelbrecht is a photographer extraordinaire who with his creative and considerable skill made the photographs and documents clearer and more usable, and was he a pleasure to work with.

James "Jed" Lyons, the publisher of the Rowman & Littlefield Publishing Group, Inc., is a friend, and was also instrumental in encouraging me to write this autobiography. He is a seasoned and successful publisher, and I am so glad he was willing to publish this book and be personally involved in the editing process.

Rick Rinehart, Executive Editor of Lyons Press, and Melissa Hayes, freelance copy editor, provided professional support and many helpful edits. Rick was particularly helpful in shepherding the book through the publishing process.

I want to thank Mary Radziminski, who has been my personal assistant for more than fifteen years, for all of her help in typing many drafts and finding source materials.

My former colleagues, Steve Elliott, Lisa Peters, John Buckley, Michael Bleier, and Jim Gockley, have also been extremely helpful. I asked them to review the chapters covering my tenure at Mellon Bank, and each gladly reviewed those pages in order to make my descriptions as complete and accurate as possible. John Buckley was particularly helpful in advising me on the presentation and construction of this book.

Last, but not least, I want to acknowledge the important role of my wife, Susan, who has encouraged and supported me generally, advised me on many aspects of the book, and has proofread many sections of the book and suggested improvements.

To my friends—I hope you find this account to be interesting. And to my family, I hope you find my recounting of my life's experiences to be helpful as you navigate your own journey.

APPENDICES

APPENDIX 1

Pittsburgh Post-Gazette

ONE OF AMERICA'S GREAT NEWSPAPERS

SATURDAY, JANUARY 17, 1998

VOL. 71, NO. 170 1/17/98

The new CEO has been running Mellon's retail banking operation since 1993.

Mellon Bank's chairman to be Martin McGuinn

By Patricia Sabatini
Post-Gazette Staff Writer

Mellon Bank Corp. late yesterday ended rampant speculation about who would succeed longtime Chairman and Chief Executive Officer Frank Cahouet. It named 17-year veteran Martin G. McGuinn as the heir to the top spot of the venerable financial institution.

McGuinn, 55, a vice chairman who has been running Mellon's retail banking operation since 1993, was among several insiders considered leading contenders for the job. The other contenders were also elevated to new posts yesterday.

Mellon said McGuinn would become chairman and chief executive of Mellon Bank effective April 1. It said Cahouet, 65, would remain head of the holding company — Mellon Bank Corp. — overseeing strategic planning and corporate governance until his scheduled retirement at the end of the year. At that point, McGuinn will assume the added role of head of the holding company.

McGuinn's appointment comes amid widespread speculation that Mellon, like other banks its size, is vulnerable to a takeover. Indeed, just last month, Mellon nearly struck a deal to merge with the much larger Bank of New York. The deal fell through, primarily because of Mellon's insistence on maintaining a strong management role in the combined operation, sources have said.

Neither Cahouet nor McGuinn would talk about the merger speculation yesterday.

Martin G. McGuinn

After the announcement, the affable McGuinn said he was "very excited and honored by the board's confidence and Frank's confidence."

"I'm not sure it's really sunk in," he said in a brief telephone interview. "We have a great team here. I really have the chance to continue all the good things that have happened."

SEE **MELLON,** PAGE A-8

APPENDIX 2

BUSINESS

E
SECTION

PITTSBURGH POST-GAZETTE ■ SUNDAY, JANUARY 25, 1998

Newly named Mellon Bank Chairman and CEO Martin McGuinn can survey the Pittsburgh region from his corner office in One Mellon Bank Center whenever he wishes.

Bob Donaldson/Post-Gazette

A kinder, gentler
chairman

Marty McGuinn's varied experience and communication skills have Mellon Bank employees pleased at his appointment

By Patricia Sabatini
Post-Gazette Staff Writer

Those who know Mellon Bank Corp. Chairman Frank Cahouet and his newly anointed successor, company insider Martin McGuinn, say the two men are alike in many ways. Both are hardworking, intelligent, determined and, of course, successful.

When it comes to their management styles, though, the contrast is striking.

One former senior manager at Mellon described the difference by recalling a big promotion he had been offered and then turned down.

"I called Marty and said, thanks, I'm flattered, but no," the manager said. "You could say that, just flat out like that to Marty. He was gracious and very understanding.

"But if I would have had to call Frank and say the same thing, well, I'm not sure I would have," he said. So intimidating was Cahouet that he might have taken a job he didn't want just so he didn't have to face him.

Cahouet, the demanding, hard-charging and sometimes gruff force at Mellon over the last decade, who engineered the rescue of the venerable Pittsburgh institution, announced nine days ago he would be handing over the reins to the 55-year-old McGuinn upon his scheduled retirement at the end of the year.

The selection of the affable head of Mellon's retail banking operations is being met with cheers, especially inside the bank, where some see it as a signal that the don't-makewaves atmosphere under Cahouet is about to be replaced by a new era of camaraderie and cooperation.

Everyone, it seems, likes McGuinn.

"He's one of the friendliest, most personable people I know," one 13-year Mellon veteran said.

McGuinn prides himself in being a "team player" and a people person. Don't even try to call him Mr. McGuinn. "It's Marty," he encourages employees and acquaintances alike.

He also answers his own phone, makes his own calls, and answers his own e-mail.

"To me that's no big deal," he said last week in an interview at his office on the 47th floor of One Mellon Bank Center, Downtown. "That's just part of communication" and of being "accessible."

"I think Marty will communicate with em-

Mellon

ployees more openly, and morale at the bank should get a boost," said James Schutz, a former Mellon vice president and now a banking analyst on Wall Street.

At the same time, McGuinn's accommodating style has led some observers to wonder privately about his leadership abilities.

But others, like Jeffrey Romoff, president of the University of Pittsburgh Medical Center where McGuinn serves on the board, said that speculation was unfair.

"He asks the difficult questions Ian UPMC's board], but in a non-confrontational way," Romoff said. "Being a gentleman without being weak is an essential part of his personality."

McGuinn officially steps in as head of the corporation at the end of the year, but will take

on increasing responsibilities in the meantime as chairman and chief executive officer of banking operations, effective April 1.

Christopher "Kip" Condron, the 50-year-old head of Mellon's giant Dreyfus mutual fund business and other investment-management operations, will succeed Cahouet as president, and become chief operating officer.

McGuinn said last week he believes the time is right at Mellon for a management style more akin to his own.

"Frank came to Mellon Bank in the midst of a crisis," he said. "My role today is a lot different. We're building on a lot of success."

As the bank continues to grow, he said, "getting people to work together is extremely important.

"Being a team player means you reach out to people," said McGuinn, a Philadelphia native and 17-year Mellon veteran.

A lawyer by training, McGuinn said he formed his attitudes about "teamwork and achieving goals" during his service as a captain and military judge in the U.S. Marine Corps during the Vietnam War. He described himself as "fair but demanding."

He said he has proven his leadership skills by producing results under Cahouet.

Indeed, under McGuinn's stewardship, the profitability of Mellon's retail operations has soared. Since he took over the unit in 1993, its return on equity has grown from 13 percent to more than 25 percent a year.

The feat was accomplished through a restructuring that included closing 30 percent of Mellon's traditional branches and replacing many, but not all, with lower-cost supermarket offices.

"He did a terrific job," said banking analyst Schutz of ABN Amro Chicago Corp. "Expens-

SEE **MELLON**, PAGE E-4

222

APPENDIX 3

THURSDAY, APRIL 23, 1998

*The Bank of New York's offer of $23 billion was rejected,
so it has gone public with a bid to buy a Pittsburgh institution.*

Mellon spurns takeover attempt

Unwanted offer creates concern for bank's fate

By Patricia Sabatini
Post-Gazette Staff Writer

After repeatedly failing to reach an agreement to merge with Mellon Bank Corp. on friendly terms, Bank of New York Co. Inc. yesterday decided to force the issue by going public with an unsolicited offer to buy the venerable Pittsburgh institution for roughly $23 billion in stock.

Mellon quickly rejected the bid, with Chairman Frank Cahouet issuing a terse statement declaring, "We are not for sale."

But the offer, equal to roughly $87 for each Mellon share, clearly put Mellon "in play" and stirred concern about the possible loss of one of the city's corporate stalwarts. The Mellon family founded not only the bank, but also financed the creation of Gulf Oil, Alcoa, Koppers and other giants that made Pittsburgh an industrial mecca.

Yesterday's activity fueled a betting game among investors and analysts over the ultimate fate of the 129-year-old Pittsburgh institution. Mellon family interests still own a large chunk of the bank, but the exact size of their holdings is not known.

Mellon may now find itself caught up in a whirlwind that could see it receive higher offers from other suitors, pressure from institutional shareholders to accept the offer, or even attempt a takeover bid of its own.

Observers also held out the possibility Mellon would successfully

SEE **MELLON**, PAGE A-14

☐ A takeover can hit where it hurts most: lost jobs. **Page A-13.**
☐ State law can help protect Mellon from a takeover. **Page A-13.**
☐ Mellon fights back, with lawsuit claiming Bank of New York used confidential info. **Page A-15.**
☐ Local employees say they're hardly surprised. **Page A-15.**

Tale of the tape

Bank of New York's bid to take over Mellon Bank pits two institutions that are fairly evenly matched in many ways. All numbers at right are as of the end of 1997, unless otherwise indicated.

	Mellon	The Bank of New York
Employees	27,000	16,494
Assets	$47.414 billion (as of 3/31)	$59.961 billion
Net Interest Income	$1.467 billion	$1.855 billion
Non-Interest Income	$2.257 billion	$1.564 billion
Total net income	$771 million	$1.104 billion

Detailing the deal

Highlights of Bank of New York's hostile takeover bid for Mellon Bank.

Cahouet of Mellon

- Bank of New York proposes to pay 1.4 of its shares for each Mellon share, for a 25 percent premium over Mellon's Tuesday price.
- Total value of the deal is $23 billion, the largest unsolicited bank takeover offer to date.
- Takeover bid comes four months after previous Bank of New York/Mellon merger talks broke down.
- Mellon Bank of New York, with corporate headquarters in Pittsburgh, would

- generate more than 60 percent of its revenue from fees.
- New bank would have more than $100 billion in assets.
- Bank of New York expects merger would produce roughly $700 million in annual cost savings.
- Approximately 6,000 to 7,000 jobs would be cut from a combined work force of 44,000 through attrition, retirements, a hiring freeze and layoffs, according to Bank of New York.

Renyi of Bank of N.Y.

Source: Bloomberg News, Post-Gazette

APPENDIX 4

Wall Street Journal
Friday Feb. 12, 1999
Page B-4

CORPORATE FOCUS

Mellon Bank Continues to Fight Battle for Independence

It Kept Bank of New York at Bay, but Skeptical Shareholders Still Circle

By MATT MURRAY
Staff Reporter of THE WALL STREET JOURNAL

Last year, Mellon Bank Corp. got squeezed by an unwanted suitor. This year, it is still feeling the pressure from shareholders.

Martin G. McGuinn, who took over as chairman of Pittsburgh-based Mellon on Jan. 1, has moved quickly, shaking up senior management and planning the sale of several underperforming units to shore up shareholder support and boost performance amid continuing takeover talk. Mellon, perennially mentioned as a desirable takeover target, has been feeling some heat since it unilaterally rejected a $22.1 billion takeover offer from Bank of New York Co., which threw in the towel in May.

Martin McGuinn

Shareholders openly wondered whether Mellon could do better alone than with Bank of New York, especially after profit and revenue growth slowed a bit amid the economic tumult of mid-1998. In the words of Rob Sharps, the bank analyst at Mellon's second-largest institutional shareholder, T. Rowe Price Associates Inc., "They've got a lot to prove. It'll be quite some time before people stop comparing their stock to the value of the Bank of New York stock they turned down." T. Rowe Price owns about 6.5 million Mellon shares.

Using a simple, admittedly imprecise formula, a number of analysts estimate that the stock value of the combined institutions today would be in the range of $90 a share. That's well above Mellon, which rose $1.5625 to $68.75 in composite trading on the Big Board yesterday. As inexact as that figure is, however, it adds to the pressure on Mr. McGuinn, especially since many analysts believe Bank of New York could spring again. "He's got his marching orders to make the franchise worth $90 a share in a very short time," says Eric Rothman, an analyst at Stephens Inc. in Little Rock, Ark.

Bank of New York won't comment.

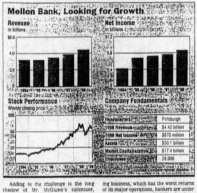

Mellon Bank: Looking for Growth

Adding to the challenge is the long shadow of Mr. McGuinn's successor, Frank V. Cahouet. Though Mr. Cahouet, an often abrasive manager, wasn't always well-liked personally on Wall Street, he was viewed widely as a commanding figure who saved Mellon from the brink of failure and reshaped it as a highly profitable asset manager and mutual-fund provider. Next to him, Mr. McGuinn looked like a less charismatic manager with big shoes to fill.

Man Under a Microscope

But so far, the new chairman has acted like a man under the microscope. Two weeks after taking over, he placed on the block three low-returning businesses—the credit-card portfolio, mortgage operations and automated-teller machine processing—to focus on higher-returning businesses such as asset management. Mellon is trying to free up capital to invest in higher-returning businesses. "The biggest job we have is keeping the revenue growing," Mr. McGuinn says. "That's what will drive our shares."

Meanwhile, in Mellon's corporate-banking business, which has the worst returns of its major operations, bankers are under orders to assess the profitability of each relationship. Corporate clients are getting pushed to consider Mellon's cash-management and other operations, which are far more profitable than classic corporate banking. Those that bite might win more favorable terms on a wider array of products. Those that balk might find Mellon asking them to take their corporate-banking business elsewhere.

"The broad sense I'm getting is they are less wed to the notion they have to emphasize traditional banking to be as successful," says Judah Kraushaar, a bank analyst at Merrill Lynch & Co. "Once, you had to be a big corporate bank. Here there's a little healthier skepticism."

Deploying New Capital

Mr. McGuinn also says he plans to deploy the freed-up capital—analysts expect the unit sales alone to generate as much as $600 million—to mollify shareholders. The company plans to begin buying back stock as soon as this summer. It hopes to continue making niche acquisitions that bol-

ster its profitable, fee-generating businesses such as mutual funds. And Mr. McGuinn says he plans to invest money in marketing, product development and salary incentives at some of the bank's existing businesses such as Dreyfus Corp., the mutual-fund company that Mellon, sometimes accused of being tightfisted, acquired in 1994.

"Clearly, investing in our businesses is one of the highest priorities," Mr. McGuinn says in a clear departure from his predecessor. "We see opportunities, for example, outside the United States in asset-management and trust and custody. Our higher-growth businesses like that demand continuous investment."

That talk is having an effect. "We like what we see," says Kevin Holt, bank analyst at Strong Capital Management in Milwaukee, which owns about 450,000 shares and was highly critical of the company's rejection of Bank of New York. "Focusing on some of the not-so-strong parts of the bank, i.e. the commercial bank, is positive. He's sending a strong message."

Mr. McGuinn sent another strong message during his first week on the job, when he ousted a longtime vice chairman and former rival, David R. Lovejoy. The move stunned many insiders because Mr. Lovejoy had been a close ally of Mr. Cahouet. Outside the firm, many saw the action as a sign that Mr. McGuinn wanted to assert an image as tough as his predecessor—possibly to alert Bank of New York and others that he is no pushover. "Marty's actions are those of someone who intends to run his company as an independent entity," says Michael Mayo, an analyst at Credit Suisse First Boston. "Nothing that Marty's done has given any indication that Mellon wants to join up with someone else."

Mr. McGuinn says he won't comment on personnel matters. But in general, he wants to position Mellon to go "to the next level, to be able to continue our growth and make sure shareholders will see tremendous appreciation in our investment. As a corollary to that, it means we continue to control our own destiny, and the team can show it's being very active and be very decisive in trying to do what's right."

Shareholders seem to like what they have seen so far, but Mr. McGuinn's term is still young. "They're doing the right types of things," says T. Rowe Price's Mr. Sharps, "but the jury's still out."

APPENDIX 5

THE WALL STREET JOURNAL.

© 1999 Dow Jones & Company, Inc. All Rights Reserved.

VOL. CIII NO. 2 CE/SH   ★ ★ ★   TUESDAY, JANUARY 5, 1999   INTERNET ADDRESS: http://wsj.com

What's News—

Business and Finance
• • •

Two senior Mellon Bank executives
are leaving, in a sign that the bank's
new CEO already is moving to shake
up the company's top management.
(Article on Page A3)

New Mellon CEO Shuffles Management

By MATT MURRAY
Staff Reporter of THE WALL STREET JOURNAL

Mellon Bank Corp.'s new chairman a
chief executive officer already is shaki
up senior management at the nation's 21
biggest bank, and two high-ranking exec
tives are departing.

According to an internal memo by Ma
tin G. McGuinn, who took over the reins
the Pittsburgh institution on Friday follo
ing the retirement of longtime Chairm
Frank V. Cahouet, one of the two departi
executives is Vice Chairman David
Lovejoy, who oversaw corporate develo
ment and held a series of senior posts ov
the years. The 50-year-old Mr. Lovejoy w
a longtime protege of Mr. Cahouet and
key player at Mellon.

Several Mellon insiders said Mr. Lov
joy, once considered a possible success
for Mr. Cahouet, didn't see a substanti
role for himself at the bank under M
McGuinn. The internal memo said M
Lovejoy is "seeking other opportuniti
outside Mellon." Mr. Lovejoy's office r
ferred calls to a company spokesman.

In addition, another vice chairma
Jamie B. Stewart Jr., 54, head of some co
porate banking and cash manageme
soon will announce that he is joining a
other company, according to the intern
memo. His office referred calls to a con
pany spokesman. His duties are expected
fall to Vice Chairman Jeffery L. Lening
No announcement was made regarding
new director of corporate development.

Mellon spokesman Steve Dishart co
firmed the moves, adding: "With the ne
management taking over and assumir
their responsibilities, it's typical for reo
ganization to follow. The changes repr
sent a natural progression), the manag
ment-succession plan that was put in plac
last year."

Indeed, analysts said the moves were a
clear sign Mr. McGuinn is moving to put his
stamp on the company. In succeeding Mr.
Cahouet, who headed Mellon for 11 years,
Mr. McGuinn faces substantial challenges,
not the least of which is filling the personality gap left by his stern, hard-charging predecessor. The bank's growth slowed notably in the latter half of 1998, at a time
when merger mania has exposed Mellon to
the possibility of a takeover. It angered
some shareholders by spurning overtures
last spring from Bank of New York Co.

Analysts said Mr. McGuinn already
seems to be developing more of a team approach to managing than Mr. Cahouet,
who ran Mellon as almost a one-man show.
The new regime is aligning responsibilities
under three senior executives. While Mr.
McGuinn is overseeing most corporate
banking activities, the new president,
Christopher M. "Kip" Condron, has oversight of consumer businesses, and Senior
Vice Chairman Steven G. Elliott is responsible for middle-market banking, technology and processing customers.

"If you look at how the three of them have
evolved through the organization, Marty
doesn't have a lot of experience in Kip's end
of the business," said analyst Lawrence W.
Cohn of Ryan, Beck & Co. "From the stand-
point of, 'Do they work as a team?' I don't
think they have any choice in the matter."

Insiders said the departures also represent the natural fallout from a longtime
succession race. At one time, Mellon had
as many as nine vice chairmen vying for
Mr. Cahouet's seat. Now it has only six, including newly promoted Allan P. Woods,
the company's chief technology officer,
whose new title was included in Mr.
McGuinn's memo.

Mr. McGuinn also said in his memo that
D. Michael Roark, head of human resources, is taking early retirement. Mellon
also promoted Stephen E. Canter, chief investment officer at Mellon's Dreyfus Corp.
mutual-fund unit, to the title of president of
that unit, succeeding Mr. Condron. Although Mr. Condron remains chairman
and CEO of the unit, Mr. Canter will have
day-to-day management responsibilities.

APPENDIX 6

BUSINESS

PITTSBURGH POST-GAZETTE ■ SUNDAY, NOVEMBER 11, 2001

MELLON VOWS SALE OF BRANCHES WILL MAKE IT STRONGER, BUT WINNING OVER INVESTORS REMAINS A CHALLENGE.

Completing the makeover

By Patricia Sabatini
Post-Gazette Staff Writer

With the blockbuster sale of its branch operations set to close in a few weeks, Mellon Financial Corp. has largely severed its ties with its more than century-old roots in the traditional banking business of taking deposits and making loans.

What will life be like for the venerable Pittsburgh institution once the deal's done?

Mellon has said that jettisoning the sluggish retail part will make it much stronger, leaving it with a bevy of faster-growing, fee-spinning businesses that Wall Street has embraced in recent years, such as money management, mutual funds, trust and custody services, corporate cash management and other processing operations.

Analysts generally agree.

But with the current stock market woes and ailing economy eating into money management fees and other revenue, Mellon could be headed for a bumpy ride, at least in the short term.

Its stock, along with shares of many other financial services firms, has taken a hit this year. Although Mel-

Steve Mellon/Post-Gazette

Mellon CEO Marty McGuinn has become as entrenched in Pittsburgh as his venerable bank's history, serving as chairman of the Historical Society of Western Pennsylvania (he is pictured above with a photo of Wiley Avenue in its heyday) as well as a trustee of Carnegie Mellon University, the Carnegie Museums of Pittsburgh and the United Way of Allegheny County. McGuinn vows that Mellon Bank will continue to be a local presence.

McGuinn's deals

Here's a rundown of Mellon Financial Corp.'s major acquisitions and divestitures since Chairman and Chief Executive Officer Marty McGuinn took over in January 1999.
(Unless otherwise noted, transaction prices weren't disclosed.)

Acquisitions

BUSINESS	LOCATION	YEAR
The Trust Company of Washington	Seattle	2000
Remaining 50% interest in ChaseMellon Shareholder Services	Ridgefield Park, N.J.	2000
Standish, Ayer & Wood	Boston	2001
Van Deventer & Hoch	San Francisco	2001
iQuantic Inc.	San Francisco	2001
Harbor Technology	Oakland, Calif.	2001
Eagle Investment Systems	Newton, Mass.	Pending

Divestitures

BUSINESS	BUYER	YEAR
Credit cards	Citigroup	1999
Commercial mortgage servicing	General Motors	1999
Network (ATM) services	U.S. Bancorp (Minneapolis)	1999
Residential mortgage servicing	Chase Manhattan	1999
Equipment leasing	GE Capital	2001
Asset-based lending	ABN Amr	2001
Branch banking ($2 billion deal is slated to close early December)	Citizens Financial	2001

Source: Mellon Financial Corp.

lon's shares have crept up in recent weeks, they're still down roughly 25 percent on the year and about 13 percent since mid-July, when the $2 billion sale of Mellon's consumer and small business banking business to Rhode Island-based Citizens Financial Group was announced.

"It's not the greatest time for an asset management firm," pointed out veteran banking consultant Arnold Danielson of Danielson Associates in Rockville, Md.

"I still think (the sale) is the right move. But it might be difficult to show the kind of post-sale returns they would have liked to."

Perhaps more troubling to Pittsburghers is the oft-stated view that by shedding its slow-growth banking business, Mellon has made itself a much more attractive takeover target.

"Without the slow-growth baggage, Mellon's a real plum, is how one former top executive at the company put it.

If Mellon disappoints Wall Street by failing to produce the higher growth rates promised once the retail bank is gone, it could end up being prime takeover bait for a host of well-heeled, giant-sized financial services firms with the resources to pounce.

"If they pull it off, they could be an extremely high-growth value company," the former Mellon executive said.

"But if they stub their toe, and suffer real earnings problems and the stock price keeps falling, they look like a nice bite-sized, tasty hors d'oeuvre to a Citigroup or (Germany's) Deutsche Bank or any major financial institution."

Investors probably will give Mellon several years to deliver, the executive said.

If it doesn't perform by then, the company probably "will be somebody's lunch."

Mellon Chairman and Chief Executive Officer Marty McGuinn doesn't disagree with that assessment, but said he's confident Mellon will "execute successfully."

"Mellon has always been an attractive franchise because of our growth rates, and that is why our P/E (the stock's price divided by earnings per share) has been higher than more traditional banks," the 59-year-old CEO said last week from his executive suite on the 47th floor of One Mellon Center, Downtown.

Post-Gazette archives

Retired Judge Thomas Mellon, above, and his sons, Andrew W. and Richard B., founded T. Mellon & Sons' Bank in Pittsburgh in 1869.

Steve Mellon/Post-Gazette

In 1987, Frank V. Cahouet was appointed chairman and chief executive officer of Mellon. He named a new management team to revitalize Mellon Bank Corporation and took the company's first steps away from traditional banking business.

APPENDIX 7

WEDNESDAY, JUNE 21, 2000

AMERICAN BANKER.

THE FINANCIAL SERVICES DAILY

Volume CLXV No. 119   www.americanbanker.com

Focus Sharpened, Mellon Shifts Sights to Possible Acquisitions

CEO McGuinn covets asset managers but won't do a bank deal

BY TANIA PADGETT

Since launching a major reorganization of Mellon Financial Corp. last year, Martin G. McGuinn has strived to convince the outside world that his company is changing.

Mr. McGuinn, 57, who took the helm of the $47.3 billion-asset Pittsburgh banking company in January 1999, has been shedding businesses — mortgages, credit cards, and processing units — while building Mellon's high-growth operations, including asset management. He also reorganized the company's top management to emphasize these changes.

Not all the divestitures came easily to Mr. McGuinn, who once ran Mellon's credit card and mortgage businesses. "The decision on cards was especially tough, because they had completed a great turnaround," Mr. McGuinn said in a recent interview.

Now the focus is shifting, and Mr. McGuinn is looking for ways to build on Mellon's new base. However, he has ruled out the course attempted by his predecessor, Frank V. Cahouet, whose efforts to buy CoreStates Financial Corp. of Philadelphia and BankBoston Corp. ended unsuccessfully.

Emphasizing that he will not attempt a bank-to-bank combination, Mr. McGuinn said he intends to go after asset management firms, particularly international ones.

"My priority would be acquisitions abroad," Mr. McGuinn said. "And the reason is we just see higher growth rates abroad. So much is going on in Europe in terms of people planning for retirement, the privatization of social security. It's like the United States was 10 years or so ago. The United States is clearly the biggest market, and there is plenty of growth left, but the growth rate is so much higher in Europe."

In 1998 the company acquired Newton Asset Management of London, which has been, according to Mr. McGuinn, "a grand slam home run" as far as performance. It also bought Founders Asset Management of Denver in 1998.

Mellon also has numerous overseas relationships, including a global custody alliance with the Dutch bank ABN Amro Bank NV; an investment management venture with Banco Brascan, a Brazilian investment bank; an investment management alliance with Bank of Tokyo-Mitsubishi; and an alliance with Bancorp SA, a diversified financial institution in Santiago, Chile.

Mellon also has strategic alliances with Hamon Investment Group Pte Ltd., a Hong Kong asset management firm, and with UOB Asset Management Ltd. in Singapore.

The businesses Mellon has divested in the past year were generally selected because they were too "scale dependent" and required investment that Mellon "did not care to make," Mr. McGuinn said at the time. It was better to sell the business and use the proceeds to invest in higher growth and higher return businesses, he said.

The units that were not sold were divided into two sections: The "Managed for Growth" division, which included wealth management, global investment management, and global investment services, and the "Managed for Return" division, which included regional consumer banking, specialized commercial banking, and large corporate banking.

The growth sectors' revenue made up 61% of Mellon's total core sector revenue in the first quarter, compared with 58% in the first quarter of 1999. The growth sectors also contributed 41% of Mellon's 26.06% return on equity during the first quarter, up from 32% in the first quarter of 1999 when the Mellon's return on equity was 25.41%.

Mr. McGuinn acknowledged that Mellon's retail banking is not growing as quickly as its asset management, trust and custody divisions. However, he has no plans to sell those units off, as its competitor State Street Corp. of Boston did last year. State Street's move, that won favor from the stock market.

Keeping the retail portion of the business helps keep Mellon's business unit diversified, Mr. McGuinn said.

And while its "revenue growth may only be 5% or 6%, the earnings per share growth is 12% or 14%, which is very strong," Mr. McGuinn said. The earnings per share-growth is so high, he said, because the company is keeping expenses as flat as possible.

He added that the specialized commercial banking and large commercial banking units help "feed into" Mellon's other businesses.

"We want to become the overall financial service provider for our customers," he said. "Last year we used to pay people to make loans. Now our team is going out there and trying to understand the needs of large corporations, and providing pension expertise, trust or custody expertise, or leasing expertise. We can provide all of those services to our customers and make a better return for the shareholder in the process."

Mellon has more than $2.8 trillion of assets under management, administration, or custody, including more than $500 billion under management.

Investors are still taking a wait-and-see approach about the company's new strategy. That has frustrated Mr. McGuinn and other members of Mellon's senior management. The market's biggest question is: "Are you really changing?"

Mr. McGuinn has been taking his message of change on the road, visiting New York this week to meet with Wall Street analysts. Mellon's first-quarter return on equity of 26.06% made it the fourth-most profitable bank among of the largest 50 U.S. banks, according to Keefe, Bruyette & Woods Inc.

Mellon's return on equity compares favorably with other companies that specialize in custody, trust, and other services for institutional and individual investors. Bank of New York ranked second on the top 50 list, but State Street and Northern Trust Corp. of Chicago ranked ninth and 13th, respectively.

But Mellon's stock, which trades around 33½, has not budged much since Mr. McGuinn took over last year. Mellon's price/earnings ratio of 16.6% is far lower than its competitors — 36.8% for Northern Trust; 27.4% for State Street; and 28% for Bank of New York — according to Keefe, Bruyette & Woods.

However, analysts believe that the company will deliver a considerable upside. Most have "buy" ratings on the company.

"Mellon has not been doing this as long as some of its peers," said Denis Laplante, an analyst at Fox-Pitt Kelton. "But their stock price will eventually catch up." ∎

Leaner Mellon Prepares to Build Business

Fresh start: Martin G. McGuinn is working to show investors that the changes at Mellon are not cosmetic.

APPENDIX 8

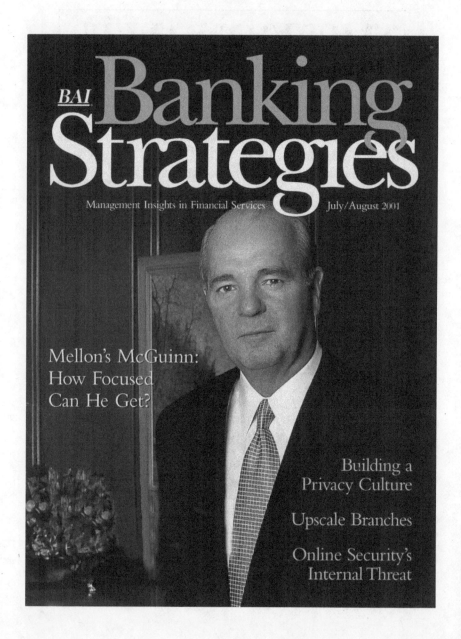

APPENDIX 9

APPENDIX 9

MARTY McGUINN, REVOLUTIONARY

TALL, LEAN AND QUIET, Martin G. McGuinn, CEO of Mellon Financial Corp., doesn't look the part of a revolutionary. Yet, he has torn his 132-year-old banking company asunder, suddenly selling off its retail and middle-market operations for $2.1 billion. These activities have accounted for almost a quarter of Mellon's revenue and net income. The buyer was New England-based Citizens Financial, owned by the Royal Bank of Scotland. Some may say revolutionary is too strong a word for McGuinn. For years, Mellon has been moving toward less reliance on lending and interest rate spreads and depending more on fee income. But stripping away a quarter of Mellon's business all at once? The 58-year-old McGuinn's gutsy move is designed to reduce risk and shed slow-growing businesses in favor of those which have a more robust outlook. In the following interview with *U.S. Banker* Editor-in-Chief Robert A. Bennett, McGuinn lays out his strategy.

COVER STORY

APPENDIX 10

ness

NASDAQ: 1,319.19 -40.09 | PG/BLOOMBERG: 149.16 -3.14 | S&I

Mellon's McGuinn to lea

By Dan Fitzpatrick
Post-Gazette Staff Writer

Martin McGuinn, chairman and chief executive officer of Mellon Financial Corp., is expected to be named this week chairman of the venerable Allegheny Conference on Community Development, succeeding Kirkpatrick & Lockhart lawyer Chuck Queenan Jr.

McGuinn, 60, would officially take over Queenan's position in January.

A former Marine Corps captain and Philadelphia native who assumed the top job at Mellon in 1998, McGuinn is one of three vice chairmen at the conference, along with PNC Financial Services Group's James Rohr and U.S. Steel's Thomas Usher. The CEO-driven conference, which gained national attention by helping to clean Pittsburgh's skies and redevelop the Golden Triangle after World War II, typically picks a chair from its list of vice chairs. In the 1990s, the chairmanship belonged to Queenan, Allegheny Technologies' Dick

Martin McGuinn, new chairman of the Allegheny Conference on Community Development

Simmons, PNC's Tom O'Brien and PPG Industries' Vince Sarni.

McGuinn will be named as the new chairman Thursday night, at the Allegheny Conference's annual Oakland get-together, inside the Carnegie Music Hall. McGuinn does not expect to attend the annual meeting, but instead plans to tape a message that will be broadcast that evening. The event typically draws hundreds of local people from the worlds of politics, business, economic development and philanthropy. The Allegheny Conference uses the forum to set a regional economic develop-

THE PRIVATE SECTOR

Either aid steel firms in this country or watch them fall. **PAGE E-3**

SECTION
E

TUESDAY, NOV. 12, 2002

P 500: 876.19 **-18.55** | RUSSELL 2000: 369.14 **-9.86**

Questions about delivery or service? Call **1-800-228-NEWS (6397).**

d Allegheny Conference

ment agenda for the coming year.

Ken Zapinski, a vice president at the Allegheny Conference, said McGuinn was unavailable for comment yesterday, but Zapinski also declined to confirm McGuinn's appointment. The Allegheny Conference, he said, "is not saying anything about who the chairman is or is not" until Thursday.

Simmons, when asked about McGuinn yesterday, said: "The great thing about having a banker in place, like Mellon Financial, is the fact that they have a deep and abiding interest in Western Pennsylvania. This is where a lot of their business is. [McGuinn] is a smart guy. He thinks about the issues that Western Pennsylvania faces. In his own quiet way, he is a very strong person.

"I'm delighted, if you are telling me he is the chairman."

Queenan, the first non-chief executive officer to chair the conference, has held the post since 1999. "We were lucky he was willing to step up and take over," Simmons said. Among the goals Queenan made

when he took over as chairman was to make Western Pennsylvania a more attractive place for young, skilled workers. Thursday night, conference officials are expected to unveil a multipronged strategy that takes on that subject, basing it on the work of a task force led by Chatham College President Esther Barazzone.

For the last year, Barazzone's group has been talking to youth-oriented organizations such as Pittsburgh Urban Magnet Project, Pittsburgh's Next, the Ground Zero Action Network and Onyx Alliance, asking them for input and ideas.

The group's preliminary recommendations, which may or may not be included in Thursday night's discussions, include the convening of a CEO roundtable to address the lack of diversity in Pittsburgh; the establishment of a way to collect the views of young people through surveys and data; and the creation of a "regional youth project" that would involve people from the worlds of media, politics, business, education and culture.

APPENDIX 12

Marty McGuinn

Mellon's McGuinn tapped for Fed post

By Patricia Sabatini
Pittsburgh Post-Gazette

Mellon Financial Corp. Chief Executive Officer Marty McGuinn has been elected president of the Federal Reserve System's Federal Advisory Council, which informs the Fed's board of governors in Washington, D.C., on general business conditions and issues related to the financial services industry.

The council is made up of representatives from the banking industry in each of the 12 Federal Reserve districts. McGuinn, 62, represents the fourth district, which includes Western Pennsylvania, Ohio, eastern Kentucky and the northern panhandle of West Virginia.

He has been a member of the council since 2003. Members customarily serve for three years.

The Federal Reserve, which sets U.S. monetary policy, uses advisory councils to get input and feedback from the public. Besides the Federal Advisory Council, there is a Thrift Advisory Council and a Consumer Advisory Council.

Patricia Sabatini can be reached at psabatini@post-gazette.com or 412-263-3066.

APPENDIX 13

 Mellon

Mellon Financial Corporation

Martin G. McGuinn
Chairman and Chief Executive Officer

December 29, 2005

Mr. Richard Grubman
Managing Director
Highfields Capital Management LP
200 Clarendon Street
Boston, MA 02116

Dear Richard:

It appears that our recent communications have crossed. I responded to your letter of December 9th on December 21st, the day after discussing your letter with our Board at its regularly scheduled meeting. Before I address the key points of your letter dated December 22nd, I note that I became CEO of Mellon Financial Corporation on January 1, 1999, not January 1, 1998.

As your letter makes clear, your principal objection to our business strategy is that you believe that Mellon could improve its valuation if it separated its asset management and asset servicing businesses. Although we respect your record as investors, as managers of the company we respectfully disagree, and I will describe some of the reasons in this letter why Mellon's current structure provides value to our clients as well as our shareholders.

Over the past seven years, this management team has not (to use your words) hunkered down, waited for others to act, maintained the status quo or wished for the right market environment. We have transformed Mellon's business model away from its roots of regional and corporate banking to being a leader in asset management and payments and asset services. In 1998, approximately 40% of our revenue and pre-tax profits were derived from asset management and asset servicing. In the third quarter of 2005 the relative contribution of these two businesses was over 80%. Virtually all of the growth over these years in Assets under Management and Assets under Custody and Administration has been organic. Similar to our close trust bank peers that also provide asset management and asset servicing to varying degrees, there is a dominance of one business over the other and for Mellon asset management represents approximately three quarters of this mix. We do not see, however, any significant difference in the long-term valuations associated with asset management or asset servicing. Indeed, over a number of periods during the past decade the market multiple for processors has been higher than that for asset managers.

One Mellon Center • Pittsburgh, PA 15258-0001
(412) 234-4966 Office • (412) 234-7525 Fax • mcguinn.mg@mellon.com

APPENDIX 13

Mr. Richard Grubman
December 29, 2005
Page Two

We are committed to the asset management and asset servicing businesses and our clients understand this commitment. Our single largest source of referrals for our institutional asset management business is from our asset servicing clients. We have over 400 corporate and institutional clients that purchase both asset management and asset servicing products from Mellon, generating approximately $1 billion in annual revenue split evenly between these two businesses. In addition, our successful family office business in Private Wealth Management is serviced through our asset servicing platform. We believe that all of the trust banks have recognized the highly complementary relationship of asset management and asset servicing.

Clearly there have been companies that have enjoyed greater appreciation in their share price, but few have undergone the same transformation in their business mix as Mellon has these last several years, and even fewer are truly reliant on just asset management or just processing. The market has recognized the changes in our business mix as our relative market multiple (forward P/E relative to the S&P 500) has increased from approximately 70% in 1999 to over 100% today.

Our strategy today is very clear in the marketplace – capitalize on growth opportunities in Asset Management and Asset Servicing, maintain our leading positions in Payments Services and manage our capital aggressively for high returns

Over the past two years we have met our expectations for the performance of Asset Management and Asset Servicing. Our success is based on the strength of our products together with the talent of our employees. In the case of asset management you note the importance of retaining and attracting top talent. Each of the businesses is managed to deliver the best product mix to its clients. Our institutional model is designed to generate alpha for our clients. We operate with a multi-manager approach that varies based on the investment style. Each investment boutique is compensated based on their respective performance. In Asset Servicing, we have a breadth of excellent products and outstanding service quality, which are being recognized by a high percentage of wins in the marketplace. Over the past two years, we have enjoyed pre-tax earnings growth in excess of 16% per annum for both asset management and asset servicing.

The profitability of our asset management businesses is competitive with similar peers. When measuring the margin of any business it is important to compare businesses based on their client and asset mix.

We have looked and continue to look at acquisition opportunities for Mellon to create significant additional shareholder value. But we do not believe that such a transaction necessitates a restructuring of the Corporation or that our current structure prevents or discourages such a transaction. As we have told you (in two separate meetings) we are open to any such transaction and "corporate ego" has not served nor will it serve as an impediment to the process. However, it is paramount that any transaction represents the best interests of all our constituents.

APPENDIX 13

Mr. Richard Grubman
December 29, 2005
Page Three

We believe that an active dialogue with the marketplace is important. Over the course of 2005 our management team has held almost 300 meetings with shareholders in our principal business locations, in their offices or through various Financial Services Conferences. During the course of these meeting, a few shareholders have proposed the idea of splitting our businesses, but upon understanding how our growth businesses operate, almost all see the value in the current structure.

The feedback we have had from most of our largest shareholders is that we are building a very successful franchise. We certainly had feedback from a number of shareholders that were concerned about our investment in the Human Resources business. While this fit our fee-based focus on the retirement imperative, the changing characteristics of the business and our position as a smaller player resulted in our decision to exit this business this past spring. Since we announced the final closing of the transaction on May 26th, our share price has increased 23% (outperforming our closest peers as well as the broader markets).

We appreciate the input from any of our shareholders (long term institutional holders, individuals and hedge funds) and as management we must balance the short term and long term opportunities for creating shareholder value. Highfields became a shareholder of Mellon in August of 2005. Since the beginning of August, Mellon's share price has increased by 14%, outperforming the S&P 500 (2%) and the BKX (5%).

Our management team maintains an open-door policy with shareholders, and we welcome a continuing dialogue with Highfields Capital.

Sincerely yours,

Marty

APPENDIX 14

Mellon Financial Corp. Scores First Place Overall in its Category in Fortune Magazine's Annual 'Most Admired Companies in America' Survey

Tuesday February 22, 11:13 am ET

PITTSBURGH, Feb. 22 /PRNewswire-FirstCall/ -- Mellon Financial Corporation (NYSE: MEL - News) has ranked first overall in its category of U.S. financial institutions in Fortune Magazine's 22nd annual survey of America's Most Admired Companies. Mellon was also rated first in "quality of products and services," "employee talent" and "social responsibility" within its category, and its overall score also rose.

Fortune's annual list is the definitive report on corporate reputations. To produce the list, Fortune's researchers took the 10 largest companies (by revenues) in 65 industries, including large subsidiaries of foreign companies, and asked 10,000 executives, directors and securities analysts to rate the companies in their own industries based on eight criteria: Innovation, Financial Soundness, Employee Talent, Use of Corporate Assets, Long-Term Investment, Social Responsibility, Quality of Management and Quality of Products/Services.

"This important recognition from America's most prestigious survey of corporate reputations affirms that Mellon Financial Corporation's goal of becoming the best performing financial services company is well within reach," said Martin G. McGuinn, Mellon chairman and chief executive officer. "We have worked hard to achieve measurable results in the eyes of our clients, employees, communities and shareholders."

Following Mellon in its category are, from highest to lowest score: Bank of New York, Fifth Third Bancorp, State Street Corp., BB&T Corp., SouthTrust Corp., Comerica, Regions Financial, KeyCorp and PNC. Complete rankings for each industry segment appear in the March 7 issue of Fortune Magazine.

Mellon Financial Corporation is a global financial services company. Headquartered in Pittsburgh, Mellon is one of the world's leading providers of financial services for institutions, corporations and high net worth individuals, providing institutional asset management, mutual funds, private wealth management, asset servicing, human resources and investor solutions and treasury services. Mellon has more than $4.0 trillion in assets under management, administration or custody, including $707 billion under management. Its asset management companies include The Dreyfus Corporation and U.K.-based Newton Investment Management Limited. News and other information about Mellon is available at http://www.mellon.com .

Source: Mellon Financial Corporation

3/1/2005

238

Pittsburgh**LIVE**.com

PITTSBURGH
TRIBUNE-REVIEW
Editorial

An editorial: Mellon is rotting on the vine; McGuinn must go

Tools

Email this article
Subscribe to this paper
Larger / Smaller Text

Sunday, January 15, 2006

The wholesale gutting of a Pittsburgh institution could be at hand. It must be stopped.

Bolstered by talk of a restructuring or takeover, Mellon Financial Corp.'s stock last week hit a 52-week high. The financial giant, founded four years after the end of the Civil War and a Pittsburgh icon, is at a crossroads reached after its divestiture of retail banking a few years ago.

What Mellon does now can be done anywhere. And at that crossroads lies the fate of 6,000 local jobs and the survival of Mellon as a Pittsburgh institution of national import.

Mellon *is* an underperformer and it *is* in play. It remains to be seen how forces inside the company and in the marketplace at large may decide its fate. But there are scenarios.

Will the board of directors take definitive action -- *now* -- to ensure that a large segment of this beleaguered region's economic foundation is preserved?

Will Mellon be sold, to leave town forever, or broken into pieces scattered to the four winds over three rivers?

Or will Mellon muddle along and, by the death of a thousand cuts, lose its vitality as has the city it calls home?

There are credible hints that Mellon Chairman and CEO Martin McGuinn, stung by high-profile shareholder criticism and seeking to

http://www.pittsburghlive.com/x/tribune-review/opinion/archive/print_413276.html   1/15/2006

APPENDIX 15

save his professional reputation, may be prepared to sacrifice Mellon.

We commend to your attention the names of nine members of Mellon's 15-member board. Some are local; others once were. Lest they look forward to a personal black eye, we call on them to grow a spine and do their civic duty in aiding a city that can afford to lose nothing more.

These high achievers must see to it that Mellon's management changes direction and, most specifically, that the stubborn and arrogant Mr. McGuinn is removed -- long before the September 2007 deadline for retirement he set for himself:

- Jared L. Cohon, president of Carnegie Mellon University

- Ira J. Gumberg, president, CEO and director of J.J. Gumberg Co.

- Robert Mehrabian, formerly president of Carnegie Mellon University; chairman, president and CEO of Teledyne Technologies Inc.

- Seward Prosser Mellon, president and CEO of the Richard K. Mellon and Sons investment firm; president and trustee of the Richard King Mellon Foundation

- Mark A. Nordenberg, chancellor of the University of Pittsburgh

- David S. Shapira, chairman and CEO of Giant Eagle Inc.

- William E. Strickland Jr., president and CEO of Manchester Bidwell Corp.

- John P. Surma Jr., chairman-elect, president and CEO of United States Steel Corp.

- Wesley W. von Schack, formerly chairman, president and CEO of DQE; chairman, president and CEO of Energy East Corp.

To their credit, Messrs. Mehrabian and von Schack have been seeking quick action to replace McGuinn. It's time for the others to get their act together.

Make no mistake: McGuinn, spending lots of time in New York these

APPENDIX 15

days -- and making about $800,000 *a month* in salary, bonus and stock options -- will not hesitate to split the company and take his decision, *pro forma,* to a board of directors far too compliant.

It is crunch time, gentlemen. If McGuinn will not go gently into that good night, then the board must show him to the door.

And before that door hits him in the behind, it must diligently begin working to save Mellon, if not Pittsburgh itself.

The Mellon board is scheduled to meet Tuesday. What is it going to be, gentlemen? *What is it going to be?*

APPENDIX 16

CONFIDENTIAL

January 30, 2006

To: Directors of Mellon Financial Corporation

At 8:45pm last Friday night as I was going with a group in to dinner with an important client in Davos, I received a message to call the office immediately. When I did I was connected to Jim Orr and Wes von Schack. They told me that the Board had decided unanimously that Bob Kelly would be both Chairman and CEO effective February 13. Bob had insisted. The Board would honor my contract. Goodbye. (I was shocked since in every conversation with the Board and individual directors we talked about a transition, a dignified process, etc.)

On Saturday, I called Bob and congratulated him, and stated my desire to work with him and make the announcement and do all else as effectively as possible. I also offered to help him however I could. He was gracious.

Now I want to step back and add some context. This management team began to narrow Mellon's strategic focus in 1999 and made some significant divestitures and a large number of smaller acquisitions since then, all of which were unanimously supported by the Board. But the last several years have been difficult in many ways. We sold the retail and related businesses in July 2001. After that September 11, we faced the worst equity markets since the depression. Even worse for Mellon, there followed a period of historically low interest rates (for example, Dreyfus had an outflow of about 26 billion dollars of money market funds in just one year.). Traditional banks were helped by this environment and had inflows of deposits and record levels of lending (including mortgages and refinancings). Mellon investment performance was also not as good as it should have been and major changes for improvement were made (and have been
reflected in recent investment performance). We actually had good earnings during this period but we didn't grow. The Human Resources business fit our strategy because it was built on what Mellon has done for more than a hundred years and the acquisition of Unify gave us capabilities for outsourcing. But continued investment demands were great and the weak environment slowed new business - - and IBM, EDS and others became more active competitors. The investment in this business, which would have been good for the long term, had a negative impact on short-term earnings. But keep this period to now in perspective: our share price did way better than Bank of New York, and even GE and IBM, and better than Northern Trust, and during this period we invested for our future, particularly using the proceeds from the very successful investment in Shinsei.

So, where are we? Since the sale of the Human Resources business our share price is up 29% through last Friday. The stock was up 10% in 2005. The fourth quarter results were the third quarter in a row of beating market expectations. And we have an operating plan for 2006 with 10% pre-tax income growth. Asset management and asset servicing currently comprise 83% of income, with strong growth rates, and we are dealing with PS&IS to eliminate the drag. (Indeed, there were several on the Board who argued strongly that we should keep Investor Services when we proposed to sell it). I am disappointed we were not able to acquire the Citigroup asset management business in 2004 (Legg Mason has received great credit for trading its brokerage business in order to purchase that business) or the Merrill Lynch asset management business or BlackRock - -

1

APPENDIX 16

any of which would have put Mellon in an outstanding position and virtually completed our strategic transformation.

So, what about looking ahead? Mellon is extremely well positioned and the momentum is strong. Asset management and asset servicing have grown in the high double digits the last two years, the strategy of increasing revenues from outside the United States is going well and aligning our products and services and distribution with the retirement opportunity is exciting. Investor Services is struggling but improving slightly and Global Cash Management is working on a possible joint venture to combine it's service quality which is the highest in the industry with the huge balance sheet of a partner to provide credit so that one half of a much bigger pie, which is growing, would be an important improvement. The environment going forward should favor Mellon and the Trust Bank group (which all have been effected by the difficult environment of the last several years). Equity markets, even at historical levels of 7 or 8% growth, interest rates approaching a higher level of stability (after measured increases over the last two years) contribute) to more favorable environment for Mellon. Our pipeline for new business is strong and the optimism at our most recent Senior Officers Conference and Senior Management Committee meetings was palpable in recognition of this momentum.

Interestingly, prospects for traditional banks in my opinion are not as good. It is a scale business and so banks must be national and over a longer time even global (or have one or a few strong niches). As a result of better equity markets and higher interest rates, deposits are now going to asset managers, and credit quality (both consumer and commercial) is heading into the next cycle of problems. The branch building boom will implode. And I also predict that others will by necessity modify their strategies. For example, I think Bank of New York will sell its retail and other businesses to be more like Mellon.

So, Mellon is well positioned. I'm sad to leave but proud of the accomplishments of my management team and so many talented Mellon people. At our Senior Officer Conference in November we recognized that Mellon employees really are the difference and that our culture is special. Mellon is a very different company today than it was seven years ago and the future is bright - - for all our constituents. The last year has included some disappointments which have been distracting and disheartening, not just for me, but for many. The intense regulatory environment, the ownership of our stock by several hedge funds, and media speculation about Mellon acquiring or being acquired and the succession process have been annoying to say the least, although I think they have been managed. Indeed, the regulatory environment is being handled relatively well although it is painful. Mellon just a couple of years ago was rated one of the few banks in the country as outstanding, but recently with new examiners was rated as needing improvement, even though we were in fact much better. But the important point now is that our responses have "exceeded expectations" and action plans, being managed under the Regulatory Oversight Management Committee which I have personally chaired, are on track.

So the new CEO is coming at a good time. The strategy is being successfully implemented, there is momentum with regulators and customers and our stock price has increased significantly. Of course, there are many challenges remaining, but I believe they are identified and manageable. (And, of course, terrorist activity, oil-price shocks and other geopolitical and external events could certainly make the environment more difficult for everyone.) And maybe most importantly, Mellon is a most admired company, for its tone at the top, for its integrity, for its people, products and services, and for its avoidance of mutual fund and other industry scandals. I'm proud of my 25 years at Mellon and 7 years as CEO.

Finally, the recent self evaluation by the Board revealed serious differences in opinion among those on the Board and its Committees. As one director said "a few have held the others hostage." The litany of issues with me read to the Board by one director in December was one-sided and unfair, and filled with inaccuracies. I have been extremely disappointed by the actions of a few directors but heartened by the support, advice and encouragement of the majority. The fractionalization of the Board has not only hurt me deeply but also interfered with the need for everyone to be solely focused on moving Mellon forward. Consequently, when the new CEO is in place the Board needs to work together and get back to doing what's best for shareholders.

2

APPENDIX 16

Recognizing that Bob Kelly is the unanimous choice of the Board, including me, there is an opportunity to come together to support him and move Mellon forward to take advantage of its wonderful position and potential. I hope the Board will now act as a single, cohesive group. Of course there is lots to do, but in a sense that's the good news, and I am very optimistic about the prospects for Mellon.

Marty

cc: R.P. Kelly
       C. Krasik
       E. Beck Oresti

3

Invested in the Future of Villanova

Martin McGuinn, Esq., '64 CLAS, '67 JD provides support to fuel scholarly research and boost educational access for veterans

After an illustrious career in the financial services industry, **Martin McGuinn '64 CLAS, '67 JD** knows all about smart investments and the lasting impact they can have. The retired chairman and CEO of Mellon Financial Corporation (now BNY Mellon) recently gave $10 million to Villanova to expand opportunities for faculty to conduct high-impact research and to open doors for veterans to pursue their degrees.

"Villanova is thriving now under the leadership of Father Peter, and my gift is intended to support him and the new Strategic Plan, which I am convinced will take Villanova—and the Law School—to new heights," McGuinn says.

University President **the Rev. Peter M. Donohue, OSA, PhD, '75 CLAS** has announced that a building in Villanova's new living-learning community, The Commons, will be named McGuinn Hall, in recognition of McGuinn's lifetime giving to the University—totaling $15.7 million.

It's an apt choice for an alumnus who found a home in Villanova's community as an undergraduate and Law student. "The seven years I spent at Villanova, including receiving a first-rate education and making friends for life, have had a major impact on me," McGuinn says.

APPENDIX 17

"Through his exceptional generosity, Marty has demonstrated a steadfast commitment to Villanova's mission and our vision that is reflected in the new Strategic Plan."

The Rev. Peter M. Donohue, OSA, PhD, '75 CLAS, Villanova President

As he rose through the ranks in the banking world, holding various leadership positions and helping to shape the global asset management and services industry, McGuinn's Villanova experience never left him.

A good businessman always looks at the return on investment. In this case, it's one McGuinn knows firsthand—and one that he's dedicated to passing along to future generations.

ACCELERATING ACADEMIC RESEARCH

A key initiative of the University's new 10-year Strategic Plan, *Rooted. Restless.*, calls for increased investment in high-potential research and scholarship. Across the University, McGuinn's gift will provide critical seed funding and support research and scholarly projects that positively impact society—and the world.

It also will provide funding to accelerate the University's most promising research projects through targeted faculty grants, as well as create a permanent funding source for high-level, impactful research projects. "The groundbreaking research and scholarship of Villanova's faculty has been a key factor in the University's continued national recognition," says Provost **Patrick G. Maggitti, PhD.** "These endowed funds will propel our research enterprise forward, creating even more opportunities for our teacher-scholars to innovate and create knowledge that positively impacts the world."

McGuinn has earmarked the majority of his gift to further support and advance the research efforts of faculty, particularly in the Charles Widger School of Law. In addition to being a proud alumnus of the Law School, McGuinn received an honorary Doctor of Laws degree in 2013 and served as chair of the Law School's Board of Consultors. He previously established the Martin McGuinn '64 '67 Endowed Scholarships at the Law School and endowed the Martin G. McGuinn Professorship of Business Law.

"We are so grateful for Marty's continued strong connection to Villanova—and especially to the Law School," says **Mark C. Alexander, JD,** the Arthur J. Kania Dean and professor of Law at the Charles Widger School of Law. "Our faculty's scholarship is at the cutting edge of law and policy, and his investment bolsters their reach and scope, ultimately influencing our community and world for the good."

A portion of McGuinn's gift will support Villanova Law faculty members, providing scholarship grant awards each year to help further

Real-Life Impact

The goal is for us to think, 'How can we help faculty solve the big problems or the unanswered questions within their discipline? How do we help faculty get the resources they need to take that next big step, or bring people together who might look at a problem in a different way?'

Mr. McGuinn's gift gives us a fantastic start to a key piece of the Strategic Plan—the Research Acceleration Fund. This will be a central bank of funds available for faculty to catalyze high-impact research initiatives and to provide seed funding for collaborative projects in all disciplines."

Amanda Grannas, PhD, vice provost for Research

Veterans bring incredible diversity to our campus because of the experiences that have shaped them as human beings, and they offer valuable perspectives in our classrooms and for other students. The boost to the Yellow Ribbon Program made possible by Mr. McGuinn's gift really creates access points to Villanova for our veterans and their families, which supports our Strategic Plan goal of opening pathways for underserved populations.

When you introduce more veterans to our college campus, they can contribute to and benefit from our strong alumni network, and this additional funding allows them to graduate with little to zero student loan debt. Those are real opportunities, and they are life-changing."

Michael Brown, director, Office of Veterans and Military Service Members

their research and promote awareness of their work. These grants will recognize Law School faculty whose scholarship has had a significant impact on the academy, the law, the legal profession and/or policy.

EXPANDING ACCESS FOR VETERANS

As part of its efforts to promote diversity, equity and inclusion and to embrace a broad range of perspectives and backgrounds, the University continues to focus on helping more veterans earn their degrees at Villanova.

A veteran himself, McGuinn served for three years as a captain in the US Marine Corps, including a tour of duty in Vietnam. He allocated a portion of his gift to grow Villanova's Office of Veterans and Military Service Members and the programming and resources the office provides to assist veterans, service members and their dependents. That includes increasing the number of veteran students at Villanova on an annual basis by expanding the Yellow Ribbon Program, which provides additional funding toward the cost of tuition and fees.

"Marty supports areas of the University that he feels passionately about, and, in doing so, he has helped elevate Villanova's stature and recognition," says Father Peter. "Through his exceptional generosity, Marty has demonstrated a steadfast commitment to Villanova's mission and our vision that is reflected in the new Strategic Plan."

APPENDIX 18

Villanova University Receives $10 Million Gift from Martin G. McGuinn, Esq., '64, '67 to Advance Faculty Research and Support Student Veterans

In recognition of McGuinn's lifetime giving, a new residence hall in The Commons on Lancaster Avenue will be named McGuinn Hall

VILLANOVA, Pa. – Villanova University President the Rev. Peter M. Donohue, OSA, PhD, today announced a $10 million gift from Martin G. McGuinn, Esq., '64 CLAS, '67 JD—retired chairman and CEO of Mellon Financial Corporation (now BNY Mellon)—to advance faculty research and to increase support for veterans attending Villanova. In recognition of McGuinn's lifetime giving, a building on campus in Villanova's new residences, known as The Commons, will be named McGuinn Hall.

"Through his exceptional generosity, Marty has demonstrated a steadfast commitment to Villanova's mission and our vision that is reflected in the new Strategic Plan," said Father Donohue. "Marty supports areas of the University that he feels passionately about, and, in doing so, he has helped elevate Villanova's stature and recognition. On behalf of the entire Villanova community, I would like to express my deep gratitude to Marty for his continued generosity and commitment to the University."

"The seven years I spent at Villanova, including receiving a first-rate education and making friends for life, have had a major impact on me," McGuinn said. "Villanova is thriving now under the leadership of Father Peter, and my gift is intended to support him and the new Strategic Plan, which I am convinced will take Villanova—and the Law School—to new heights."

Advancing Faculty Research

The University will receive $7 million from McGuinn to further support and advance the research efforts of its faculty. A key initiative of the University's new 10-year Strategic Plan, *Rooted. Restless.*, calls for increased investment in high-potential research and scholarship. McGuinn's gift will provide critical seed funding and support research and scholarly projects that positively impact society—and the world. It also will provide funding to accelerate the University's most promising research projects through targeted faculty grants, as well as create a permanent funding source for high-level, impactful research projects.

Included in this is $2 million that will support faculty members in the Charles Widger School of Law, providing scholarship grant awards each year to help further their research and promote awareness of their work. These grants will recognize Villanova Law faculty whose scholarship has had a significant impact on the academy, the law, the legal profession and/or policy.

"The groundbreaking research and scholarship of Villanova's faculty has been a key factor in the University's continued national recognition," said Patrick G. Maggitti, PhD, Villanova University provost. "These endowed funds will propel our research enterprise forward, creating even more opportunities for our teacher-scholars to innovate and create knowledge that positively impacts the world. We are extremely grateful that Mr. McGuinn has chosen to support Villanova's remarkable faculty in this way."

Supporting Student Veterans

As the University continues to focus on helping veterans earn their degrees, $3 million of McGuinn's gift will increase the number of veteran students at Villanova on an annual basis by expanding the Yellow Ribbon Program for tuition and fees. It will also be used to grow Villanova's Office of Veterans and Military Service Members and the programming and resources the office provides. For decades, the University has worked to obtain VA educational

APPENDIX 18

benefits for veterans and their dependents. Villanova has further deepened its commitment to veterans in numerous ways, including the formation in 2018 of a centralized Office of Veterans and Military Service Members—dedicated to assisting veterans, service members and their dependents.

"I'm thrilled that Marty has committed so generously to the University in these two critical areas," said Mike O'Neill, senior vice president for Advancement. "Marty continues to believe in—and support—the vision we have created to map Villanova's future. We are grateful to him for his ongoing commitment to this vision, which will ensure the University's continued forward momentum."

A formal dedication for McGuinn Hall is being planned for the fall.

About Martin G. McGuinn, Esq.: McGuinn retired in 2006 as chairman and chief executive officer of Mellon Financial Corporation (now known as BNY Mellon), after serving for seven-plus years at the helm of the global financial services company. During his 25 years with Mellon, he held a number of leadership positions. In 2002, he was appointed by President George W. Bush to the National Infrastructure Advisory Council, which makes recommendations regarding the security of the nation's economically critical infrastructures.

Prior to joining Mellon, McGuinn served for three years as a captain in the US Marine Corps. His tour of duty included service in Vietnam. He began his career as an associate with the Wall Street law firm Sullivan & Cromwell, before serving as managing counsel for The Singer Company.

McGuinn has been a member of numerous boards, including serving as advisory board president for the Federal Reserve Board and board chair for the Financial Services Roundtable and MasterCard International (US), Carnegie Museum of Art and the Senator John Heinz History Center. He has also served on the board of directors for the American Bankers Association, U.S.-Japan Business Council, Inc., UPMC Health Systems, Chubb Corporation and Celanese Corporation. At Villanova, he served as chair of the Law School's Board of Consultors.

With his most recent $10 million gift to Villanova, he has now given $15.7 million to the University during his lifetime. He endowed the Martin G. McGuinn Professorship of Business Law in the Villanova University Charles Widger School of Law. He previously pledged $1.25 million to establish the McGuinn Irish Scholars Program and $1.25 million to establish the Martin McGuinn '64 '67 Endowed Scholarships at the Law School.

McGuinn earned his Bachelor of Arts degree from Villanova and Juris Doctorate from the University's Charles Widger School of Law, where he served as editor-in-chief of Volume 12 of the *Villanova Law Review*. As an undergraduate, he was president of the student body, and in 2013 he received an honorary doctorate from the University.

McGuinn and his wife, Susan, reside in Palm Beach, Fla., Pittsburgh, Pa., and Quogue, N.Y.

APPENDIX 19

Appendix 20

Martin G. McGuinn, Jr, Awards

1985—Villanova University College of Liberal Arts Medal of Distinction

2000—*Pittsburgh Magazine* Co-Pittsburgher of the Year

2001—American Ireland Fund: for Distinguished Leadership

2002—Heinz History Maker Award in Business and Industry

2003—Veteran of the Year (Vietnam Veterans of Pittsburgh)

2003—Commencement Speaker, Villanova University Law School (Medal of Achievement)

2004—Ireland Chamber of Commerce in U.S. Achievement Award

2004—Villanova Law School Alumni Award of Excellence

2006—Ellis Island Medal of Honor

2013—Honorary Degree, Villanova University

2013—CMP Nobel Quartel Society (Lifetime Giving)

2018—Who's Who Marquis Lifetime Achievement Award